Jenn Louis's approach as an author is forthright, using a tone that I think is required under the auspices of a manifesto to be so convincing as to make even a non-believer start raising poultry. The basics, the pantry, the essentials so crucially laid out, like a prosecuting attorney making their case before a grand jury, culminating in the most powerful persuasion mechanism I know of, the recipes.

And how do I know? What makes me an expert? Fifty-nine years of chicken worship has to count for something. I am an unabashed chicken eater three times a week. I make soups and stews with chicken from dozens and dozens of cultures, and I have eaten the animal in a hundred more. And as any native New Yorker who happens to also be Jewish knows, chicken fat is this superhero's cologne of choice.

But, after all, the recipes are why you are holding this manifesto in your hands. You are either newly arrived at accepting Jenn's rightly placed reasoning that chicken soup is universally a bowl of perfection, or you came to this moment long ago, a member of our legion of chicken soup lovers. Regardless, we need guidance, and this global collection of recipes is a finely tuned collection of classics that will result in years and years of cooking and gustatory pleasure for you, your friends and family.

Organized geographically, my favorites are too numerous to mention but I would suggest cooking some Ethiopian Doro Wat, and then some chicken lemon soup from Greece, and then a classic braise of a meal in a bowl like Jenn's Fricot or Bott Boi, and explore all the nuance to be found in this specific but massive culinary category of awesome. Start perfecting your stock and broth techniques, experiment with coaxing the most flavor from your bones, fat and flesh. See all the ways you can increase the body of your stock, make it so rich your lips stick together when you sip it from a spoon. Celebrate our diversity and commonality by cooking your way through this whole book.

It will change your life.

Andrew Zimmern,
chef and author

Recipes From Around the World

The

CHICKEN

SOUP

Manifesto

JENN LOUIS

Hardie Grant

BOOKS

Contents

Recipes by Country

A pot of chicken soup is the ultimate gesture of love.

That notion really sunk in one autumn day when I was traveling home to Portland, Oregon, from a work trip in San Diego. I had woken up with a bad cold. Feeling miserable, I texted my sister, Stacy, about how I was not particularly excited to sit on a plane for the next several hours, especially while I was feeling so achy and ill. The flight felt longer than it was. I was uncomfortable and I lamented about that via text to Stacy, who also lives in Portland.

When I finally arrived, exhausted, at my home, there it was: a giant pot of chicken soup, made by Stacy, waiting on my porch. Grateful, I brought it inside, heated it up and immediately ate three bowls. Its familiar, rich, soulful flavor instantly took the edge off my discomfort. I finished (actually, demolished!) the rest of the huge pot within two days. Making that soup was one of the most loving things anyone has ever done for me.

I grew up in a Jewish home where chicken soup was a way of life. It was a cure-all – Jewish penicillin, after all – and noodle-filled or matzo ball versions were always fixtures on the table during every holiday. To me, chicken soup would become one of those sublime but essential foods. Whether rich, hearty and chunky, or light, fragrant and brothy, looking at the world through the lens of a simple bowl of chicken soup reveals volumes about a society and its people: the ingredients within their reach, the techniques that mark their style of cooking, and, often, a folkloric or family history, too.

4

I am a chef who is driven by the soul of food. I like some grit, earthiness and authenticity in my experience. I appreciate the specialness of simplicity and notice details in what is often taken for granted or unnoticed. I am also a chef who loves to travel, is crazy about cultural traditions and about how we all live similarly yet also so differently. I'm drawn by the ways that culture shapes a cuisine, how locality dictates ingredients, how ingredients combine for unique flavor profiles, and how food connects places and people.

Chicken is the animal protein that almost all cultures have in common. Chicken grows quickly, and in much of the world, the birds wander around the perimeter of the home and are raised domestically for food. Chicken is accessible, affordable and neutrally flavored, lending itself to countless flavor pairings. It is nutritious – low in fat and protein-rich. One of my favorite things about chicken: most parts of the carcass can be used, making it a highly sustainable meat choice.

By default, the cultures that enjoy chicken also enjoy chicken soup. Its history as a curative and restorative is well documented – it was already prescribed by the physician Maimonides back in the twelfth century. The dish continues to be thoroughly examined for its healing properties, most notably by the University of Nebraska, which published an extensive study in 1993. The restorative properties of the soup are a common thread across the world.

Based on region, chicken soups around the world vary in flavor profiles and ingredients, while sharing other qualities with kindred nations. The stewy Canja de Galinha (page 73), for example, the chicken soup of Brazil, arrived on the continent with the Portuguese language, all the way from Europe. Its starchy garnishes – rice, potato and sometimes bread – also translate across continents, while a poached egg and sausage make it a full bowl of sustenance. Molo from the Philippines (page 128) reflects the influence of Chinese cooking on the island nation; it features pork-stuffed wontons, the fermented flavor of fish sauce and the sweetness of prawns. Lemon and lime are common ingredients to brighten flavors in many countries, from the chowder-like Chupe de Pollo from Peru (page 90), a masterful blend of fiery chipotle peppers smoothed out with cream and brightened with a generous dose of freshly squeezed lime juice, to the light and sour lemon edge that characterizes Greece's Avgolemono (page 216).

Some countries have variations of the same chicken soup, just as ragu may vary from village to village in Italy. Garnishes rely on the region – potatoes in some places and rice in others; dumplings in some areas and noodles in others. Greens and other vegetables will appear in season. Chicken soup can be served light in the summer, or thickened with a roux or cream in the winter, with hearty additions such as beans or meat.

The Chicken Soup Manifesto is an account of the diversity of a commonality, much like my first book, *Pasta by Hand*, was for Italian dumplings. Each book lends craft to a dish that is often handed down solely by oral tradition, with recipes for noodles, dumplings and other garnishes that stand on their own.

Think about it: chicken soup is a culinary connection shared around the world. We express our cultures, feed our nations and convey our most treasured flavors through this delicious and humble soup. *The Chicken Soup Manifesto*, with its 131 recipes from around the globe, lovingly celebrates just that.

'We express our cultures, feed our nations and convey our most treasured flavors through this delicious and humble soup.'

The Basics

Chicken soup is a kitchen staple: make it for your family, or for guests –
no one will complain about a delicious hot bowl of chicken soup. A good recipe
and quality ingredients make an inexpensive and wholesome meal for many.
It takes just a little time to make from scratch, and the rewards are great.
Here is some useful advice before you jump in.

How to use this book

This book is a holiday: a trip around the world with stops only for chicken soup.
Soups are listed by continent and by country. Due to trade, travel and migration,
ingredients from countries other than the country they represent influence some
recipes. Other recipes use ingredients specific only to the country they hail from.
You can taste the influence of the spice route in soups from Turkey and Iran, and
the migration of people from Portugal to Brazil with slight differences in their similar
Canja de Galinha (pages 73 and 232). The recipes that follow are a collection from
traveling, research, family and friends. As you work your way through this book,
you will see how region affects recipes in the starch (rice, potatoes, noodles), types
of vegetables and flavorings (curry, lemon, chili). These are the variables around the
basics of the chicken soup.

Measurements

This book uses US cup measures, e.g. 1 cup = 240 ml (8 fl oz). In Australia, 1 cup =
250 ml (8½ fl oz) and in the UK, 1 cup = 285 ml (9½ fl oz), so Australian and British
cooks should be scant with their cup measurements. Tablespoons used in this book
are 15 ml (½ fl oz). If you are working with 20 ml (¾ fl oz) tablespoons, be scant with
your measurements. Teaspoons are 5 ml (¼ fl oz).

Cook with homemade chicken stock

I call chicken stock 'liquid gold', because the end result is worth the time, and
your home will smell amazing. There are many convenience broth/stock products
available, and they are fine, but none compare to the real deal: homemade chicken
stock. Make larger batches and freeze strained, cooled stock in reusable containers,
then you will have a supply whenever you need. Make sure to skim off the rendered
chicken fat (see pages 17 and 239) and store it for later. Check out the section on
Chicken Essentials (page 14) for a more complete guide on chicken cuts and how to
best use them.

Buy quality chicken

There are many types of chicken available. Try to buy fresh, free-range (cage-free)
when possible, and ideally vegetarian fed and free of hormones. Good-quality
chicken tastes better, cooks better and is nutritionally superior for your body.

Keep a simmer

When making stock or soup keep your broth from boiling. Keep at a slow to active simmer at all times, but never boil. Boiling will emulsify fat into the broth, giving an oily mouthfeel, and it will keep your chicken from reaching a lovely tenderness.

Gather ingredients before you start cooking

It is always handy to have your ingredients close by. In restaurants, we call this mise-ing (meez-ing) out the recipe (organizing our mise en place or ingredients) so that we can easily execute the recipe. Try this method; I think you will find it handy.

SOUP VS STEW

Soup and stew are siblings that each take after a different parent. They are similar, made up of the same general ingredients, but soup relies on more liquid and yields a brothier texture, while stew is a thicker consistency, often served with a starch (mashed potatoes, polenta, rice). Liberty has been taken in this book. Some stews have been included due to their iconic place in the chicken soup/stew lexicon.

Troubleshooting

Here are some of the most common issues that may come up when making chicken soup:

— Don't boil stock or broth: the fat will emulsify into the broth, giving the soup a greasy mouthfeel.

— Cooking noodles in soup can cause the broth to become cloudy from the extra starch. If a clearer broth is desired, cook noodles in a separate pot, then add to the soup.

— When planning to store the soup, add cooked noodles when reheating. If noodles are stored in the soup broth, they can absorb extra moisture, making the soup very thick. Rice can have this effect, too.

— Having trouble finding some ingredients? Look them up. You can substitute ingredients like bacon for pancetta or prosciutto. Have fun cooking, don't sweat the small stuff: this is just chicken soup!

— Always skim the foamy dark impurities that develop and float on top of a simmering pot of stock. The 'scum' is impurities from the chicken and skimming keeps the broth clear and gorgeous.

— Keep your simmer gentle or you will lose too much liquid needed for the soup and the meat will not be as tender as you would like.

— If there is less liquid in your pot than you would like, add additional water or stock to make up the difference. No big whoop.

Tools and equipment

No fancy equipment is needed to make chicken soup, just the basics: generally, just a heavy-bottomed pot, a chopping board, a wooden spoon and a knife. Here's the equipment I would suggest having on hand and why.

Storage containers
Use glass or plastic airtight tubs or other containers for storing chicken soup. Airtight tubs that stack are good for saving space.

Mason or canning jars
It is easy to store soup in jars and then take to work for lunch. You can reheat in the jar and eat right out of it. Jars are airtight and leak-proof. Also, save jars that you like from jarred foods; take the label off with hot water and a label remover.

Wooden spoons
Wooden spoons are my favorite for stirring pots of soup. They are gentler, softer and do not conduct heat.

Good knives
You really don't need much more than a 15–20 cm (6–8 in) French chef's knife, a serrated knife and a paring knife. Keep them sharp, store them in a block or on a magnet, and never, ever put them in the dishwasher.

Wooden chopping board
Always have a spray bottle of diluted bleach (1 tablespoon bleach to 950 ml/ 32½ fl oz/4 cups water) for cleaning. Wash the board down with soapy water first and then bleach it. Plastic chopping boards are fine, too. Just make sure your board is large enough so that you have the space to work comfortably.

Vegetable peeler

A 'Y' peeler (also called a Swiss peeler) is best for peeling woody stems and skins from carrots, potatoes and other vegetables.

Scale

It's true, we are just making chicken soup. I recommend scales for baking, but did write these recipes with weight in mind. Weighing ingredients on a digital scale will yield the best results in my recipes. I recommend investing in a good digital scale that can measure in grams, and following the gram measurements in this book.

Other tools called for in this book

— Blender that can finely purée and/or food processor
— Instant Pot and/or pressure cooker
— Microplane or other fine grater
— Immersion blender
— Stand mixer

CHOOSING THE PERFECT POT

A good pot is essential. Invest in a good pot that will last you for many years and ensure good, even cooking. Here are my top seven qualifications for a good pot:

— **Size:** A 4.7–5.7 liter (5–6 quart) pot is a good size for most of the recipes in this book.

— **Good construction:** This pot will last forever. Clean it after each use, scrub all food residue off the surface and dry it well.

— **Stainless steel:** Stainless steel will conduct heat well and, with a bit of scrubbing, look like new for years to come.

— **Heavy bottom:** A pot with a heavy bottom will ensure that your soup will not scorch and will cook evenly.

— **Cover:** A matching lid that fits the pot well will be helpful for some preparations and for keeping soup hot when it is done.

— **Not nonstick:** Choose a pot that does not have a nonstick interior. For soups, it is best to not put the heat and wear and tear on the coating of nonstick pans.

— **Good side handles:** Make sure you have two side handles that are well attached. It will make the job of moving the pot to and from the heat source easy and practical.

Pantry Necessities

Oils and fats

Rendered chicken fat

Rendered chicken fat, aka schmaltz, is gold. It is lovely to use when making roasted potatoes, chopped chicken liver and, of course, chicken soup. Don't think twice to use half butter and half rendered chicken fat to make a savory pie dough (pastry). It is easy to render chicken fat by skimming it from homemade stock (see pages 237 and 239). It is sometimes available from your local butcher. The flavor is delicious; however, if you are not used to using rendered chicken fat, it may have a richer flavor than you are accustomed to. Think brilliantly golden, crisp chicken skin and then liquefy it.

Extra-virgin olive oil

I often cook with extra-virgin olive oil and prefer those from California, Italy, Spain and Israel. The range of flavors is astounding – some are floral, some are pungent, some are spicy and there is a whole range of tastes in between. There are different varieties of refinement. Save your best, premium extra-virgin olive oil for finishing, and use lower-grade extra-virgin olive oil for cooking and salad dressings. I always like to have that one bottle that might cost a bit extra on hand for drizzling on fish, vegetables or greens.

Sesame oil

Toasted sesame oil is essential for many Asian dishes, whether a cooked dish or a salad dressing. I use it because of its great flavor and depth. Toasted sesame oil has a nuttier flavor, a deeper brown color and a lower smoke point than light sesame oil. You can use a blend of more neutrally flavored oil and a little toasted sesame oil for quick sautés, but it is too pungent for longer frying.

Neutral oils

Good neutral vegetable oils are my go-to oils for general sautéing or frying because of their high smoke point. I opt for un-hydrogenated grapeseed or sunflower oil for recipes that call for vegetable oil.

These oils are also useful for baking, dressings and marinades. I usually fry in vegetable oil, and sometimes in olive oil if I want the extra richness.

Salt

I use basically three types of salt: kosher, fine sea salt and flaky sea salt. Kosher salt is the backbone basic in my kitchen. It has a clean taste and heightens the flavor in foods. I like to use one that dissolves quickly, has a neutral flavor and is good for consistent flavoring.

Fine sea salt is more intensely salty than kosher salt, so make sure you taste as you go and season a little at a time until you get the feel for using it. There are so many good fine sea salts, so taste a variety to see what you like best.

Flaky sea salt is great as a finishing salt, for that last burst of flavor while adding a crunchy texture. Maldon sea salt is readily available online or in gourmet groceries, so it is my go-to salt for any recipes that call for flaky sea salt.

Spices

Keeping your pantry well outfitted with good-quality spices is a must for adding flavor to nearly anything you cook. I like to toast whole spices before grinding or, better yet, grind all the spices together and add to the vegetables when sautéing. This way you can toast the spices and save a step.

Stocks

A good homemade chicken stock is like liquid gold. Your house will smell great and the flavor of the stock is incomparable to that of store-bought. I like to make a double-strength stock (aka Rich Double Chicken Stock, page 237), which yields a deeper and richer flavor. For more information on Chicken Stock, see page 237.

Rice

Basmati rice
Basmati is a fragrant, nutty-tasting long-grain rice grown in the Himalayas and Pakistan and used in cooking from North Africa and the Middle East to India and some Asian countries. 'Bas' in Hindi language means 'aroma' and 'mati' means 'full of', hence the word Basmati – or 'full of aroma'. The key to making basmati rice that is light, tender and fluffy is to rinse the starch off the grains before cooking; otherwise, the cooked rice will have a gummy and sticky texture. Place the rice in a bowl with water, then swish it around to release any excess starch. The water will be cloudy at first, but after several rinses, it will become clear.

Jasmine rice
Named after the sweet-smelling jasmine flower, jasmine rice is a long-grain rice native to Thailand with a delicate floral and buttery scent. Most pack instructions call for 360–480 ml (12–16 fl oz/1½–2 cups) water for every 200 g (7 oz/1 cup) rice, depending on if you prefer rice cooked al dente or a more tender texture.

Broken jasmine rice
Broken jasmine rice is often used for rice porridge (jook), a breakfast dish in Thailand. They are grains of rice that have cracked and broken during processing, which are separated from the whole grains since they cook differently and have a slightly different texture when eaten. Broken kernels take up more water than whole kernels in cooking. The cooking water will also be cloudier and the texture more glutinous. Do not rinse this rice prior to cooking.

Potatoes

The potato is a tuber from the nightshade family. There are about 40,000 varieties worldwide, with about 200 grown in the US. All potato varieties fit into two main categories: starchy (russet, yukon gold) and waxy (red bliss, new potatoes or fingerlings). Starchy potatoes have low moisture and sugar levels, and high starch content. The high starch content makes them collapsible and makes them a good choice for baked, mashed, fried or roasted potatoes. Waxy potatoes are the opposite, with high moisture levels and low starch levels. They hold up well in casseroles, roast well and are a good choice for potato salad.

WHAT'S THE DIFFERENCE?

— Stock
A long-cooked liquid resulting from cooking mostly bones with some meat. (Sometimes, vegetables are added; I prefer a stock made out of bones and meat only. It is cleaner and more versatile.) My favorite recipe is on page 237. The end product is rich and nutritious. Bones and meat trim from stock are fully exhausted of their qualities when the stock is done and are discarded.

— Consommé
A clear liquid that results from clarifying stock. Consommé is a clear and clean stock typically used for clear soups or as a French preparation of gelatin for setting garnishes.

— Broth
A shorter cooked liquid that is clean and lighter than stock, made with bones and more meat than stock. The idea is to pull as much flavor as possible from the meat, but to still use the meat when it is cooked. Sometimes the meat is used in the broth for a soup, sometimes it is used for another preparation.

— Bouillon
Dehydrated stock that can be used as instant broth in simmering water. Typically, it contains dehydrated vegetables, meat, MSG, fat, salt and seasonings and is formed into a small cube. Refrigerated bouillon can also be purchased in the form of a paste.

— Brodo
The Italian word for broth.

— Bone broth
Another name for stock. This may be confusing since the name highlights bone (richer stock) and broth (lighter broth), but it is essentially the same thing.

Chicken Essentials

How to select, handle and store chicken

Quality chicken meat should be firm yet tender, retain a soft pink color and smell clean and fresh with no off-putting odor. Raw chicken skin should be taut and light in color, excess fat should be white to yellow in color. The color of uncooked chicken fat may vary as it is a result of chicken breed and diet.

A fresh chicken should be moist, but not pooling in liquid. Raw chicken meat showing excess moisture can be the result of a previously thawed chicken. Never freeze chicken that has previously been frozen. Once frozen chicken has thawed, cook it immediately.

Always handle raw chicken with clean hands and place on a clean surface. Soap and water are great sanitizing tools; keeping a squirt bottle filled with 1 tablespoon bleach per 950 ml (32½ fl oz/4 cups) water is handy for a spray sanitizing solution after washing a chopping board or work surface with soap and water.

Store fresh raw chicken refrigerated in an airtight container until ready to use. If the chicken is frozen, remove it from the freezer and allow to thaw overnight in the refrigerator before cooking. Never cook chicken from frozen. If you choose to freeze fresh chicken, do so when it is very fresh and make sure that its container is airtight.

Rancid chicken is simple to detect – it will smell terrible. Sometimes, raw chicken will have a barnyardy odor – that is not rotten. It is usually a sign of type of chicken, not rancidity. When meat is rotten, it will tell you loud and clear.

Stock 101 and basic cooking tips. And, how to decide what to use in each recipe.

Good stock is one of every chef's favorite ingredients. It will transform any meat braise, soup or broth into a complex and special dish. Good homemade stock is nutritious, satisfying and healing. It is filled with protein, collagen and satisfying warmth. Below are the definitions of specific broths. These days, language is casual and many are used interchangeably.

Stock is more viscous due to the collagen that seeps out of joints and bones during long-term cooking. (Collagen is the rich protein that helps build skin, bones and connective tissue.) Broth is thinner and is made with more actual meat (versus meat-stripped bones used for stock). Recipes in this book often call for stock, which will yield a richer soup with more depth. Using water, instead of stock, and chicken on the bone, will make a thinner and lighter soup. All recipes in this book can be made with stock or water, see section below (Using whole chicken vs parts) when choosing types of meat for altering soup recipes.

I hope a supply of good homemade chicken stock will now be a staple in your freezer as it is in mine.

SERVE SHREDDED OR IN PARTS

Depending on the recipe and style of soup, the chicken can be served shredded in the soup, in larger portions in the soup, on the side of the soup, or in another dish. More rustic soups will feature larger pieces of chicken (Colombian Sancocho, page 76), while more refined dishes (French Crème de Volaille, page 212) will include smaller bites of chicken. Some soups give the option, and others leave the meat out of the soup, stretching the meat for another purpose.

Using whole chicken vs parts

Whole chicken or quartered

There are many ways to make chicken soup. Using a whole chicken – or, much easier, a carcass cut into quarters – and water instead of stock will yield a clean, thin broth. This is, perhaps, the most traditional of many cultures' soups. Cooking a whole chicken, cut into quarters, in stock, will yield a richer soup. Using either method, cook the chicken at a very gentle simmer until the chicken pieces are done, about 7–10 minutes for breasts and 15–18 minutes for legs and thighs. This is estimated for a 1.35 kg (3 lb) chicken. Larger chickens will take more time. The meat should separate from the end of the leg bone when cooked, a thermometer should read 74°C (165°F) when inserted into the thickest part of the thigh or breast and the juices of the chicken should run clear.

Chicken breasts

Chicken breasts (white meat) are known to be very lean and are often overcooked. The secret is that chicken breasts are delicate and delicious when cooked gently. If using chicken breasts (on the bone or boneless), cook in a very gently simmering broth. There should be no evidence of a rapid simmer or boiling broth when cooking chicken breasts; simply maintain the soup at a slow simmer until the chicken breasts are cooked (when a thermometer reads 74°C (165°F) when inserted into the thickest part; the juices of the chicken should also run clear). When reheating soup, make sure to follow the slow simmer and do not overcook to maintain the moist, tender meat. Chicken tenders are white meat, so treat the same as breasts.

Chicken legs and thighs

Chicken leg and thigh meat (dark meat) is tender and juicy when properly cooked. The meat should be cooked (with the bone in or boneless) at a gentle simmer until the meat tenderizes and gently pulls apart. This process takes a bit more time than when cooking chicken breasts; dark meat has a tougher muscle structure. The meat should separate from the end of the leg bone when cooked and the juices of the chicken should run clear.

Skin vs skinless

The skin question is based on preference. Some cultures are very accustomed to the soft, fatty texture of chicken skin cooked in a braise or soup; some cultures are not. It is easy enough to remove the chicken skin post cooking, when shredding the meat. Chicken skin adds flavor to the broth and keeps the meat moist while cooking. The skin is very traditional to include when making soup or stock.

CHICKEN SOUP WITH A ROASTED CHICKEN

Sometimes an extra chicken was roasted, or a rotisserie chicken was picked up from the supermarket. Either way, this is an excellent opportunity to make chicken soup. Shred the meat off the bones, then place the bones in a container and place in the freezer. Use the bones for the next batch of stock. Proceed with any chicken soup recipe, using stock (page 237) instead of water, and place the shredded chicken in the soup after all the steps are completed. Be sure to use the amount of chicken specified in the recipe and reserve remaining chicken (if any) for another dish.

Tips for straining and skimming, shredding meat and removing skin

Two substances need to be skimmed when making stock or soup: scum and fat. Scum is the impurities that rise to the top and reveal themselves as foam. Simply take a spoon or ladle to the soup and skim any impurities from the soup. This will help create a clean flavor and appearance.

Fat is the clear yellowish puddles floating on the surface. Simply use a spoon or ladle to skim the fat off of the stock or soup and reserve to render with chicken fat (page 17) after the stock or soup is finished. Boiling soup, rather than gently simmering soup, will cause this fat to emulsify into the broth and render a greasy mouthfeel when eating the soup.

Shredding meat is simple; just make sure the meat is cool enough to handle. My preferred method of shredding chicken when making soup is to remove the pieces when cooked and place them in a metal or glass pan with sides, that way any excess liquid from the soup can drip into the container and can be added back into the soup later. When the meat is cool enough, use your hands to shred the meat into the size pieces preferred. Alternatively, cut or chop the cooked meat into smaller pieces with a knife. Some rustic soups are great with larger chunks of meat; in that case separate the leg from the thigh and place back in the broth.

If the choice is to remove the skin, this can be accomplished before or after cooking. Prior to cooking, simply tug the end of the chicken skin, peeling away from the meat. Store any uncooked chicken skin, airtight, in the freezer and add to the next batch of stock (see page 237). When removing chicken skin from cooked chicken, proceed with the same method as raw chicken and discard the cooked skin, or save for stock.

More things chicken

Brining
Brining is never necessary, but a taste bud luxury. Some time ago I had some brined chicken and decided to use it for soup. It produced a more highly seasoned bite when eating the chicken from the soup and was really tasty. Check out the brine recipe in the larder section (see page 237).

Fat
Chicken fat (aka schmaltz) has many uses. Use chicken fat to sauté vegetables when making chicken soup, to roast potatoes or other root vegetables, to sauté livers and make classic Chopped Chicken Liver (page 238), or chill in the freezer then whisk into a soft cloud and serve immediately on fresh baguette with prosciutto. Schmaltz can be rendered when making stock or rendered from making Gribenes (page 238). This is good stuff; don't waste it. To store chicken fat, transfer it to an airtight container and refrigerate for up to one month, or freeze up to six months.

Innards
Some chickens come with a pile of savory goods stuffed into the cavity; sometimes these items are removed and sold separately. If such a prize is stowed inside the chicken cavity, you have lots of options. Innards can be frozen until a collection of the quantity that is needed for a recipe is acquired. All innards can be simmered and eaten with soup. Chicken liver can be cooked in rendered chicken fat to make classic Chopped Chicken Liver (see page 238), puréed with egg yolks and cream to make Chicken Liver Mousse (page 239) or added to a favorite fried rice recipe.

Coxcomb
This is the beautiful, orange-colored fleshy growth on the top of male chickens' (or turkeys' or pheasants') heads. Coxcomb are used in France as a garnish on some dishes, and minced and added to sauces. Italians make a dish called Cimabella con cibreo, where the combs are combined with chicken livers and eggs in a sauce served with tagliatelle.

Skin
When removed prior to cooking, chicken skin can be saved and used to make the most delicious crispy chicken skin (page 238). Enjoy as a crispy snack with crudités, garnish salad with broken crispy bits instead of croutons, crumble over pasta with a meaty ragu, or snack on them like pork rinds. Finely crumble bits of crispy chicken skin into soft butter and fold together for a savory topping on a baked potato or a compound butter for tossing steamy cooked pasta.

Gribenes
The by-product of rendering schmaltz; this is the crispy crackling-like crunchy bits left after slowly cooking the fat from the skin (see page 238).

Africa

NORTH AFRICA

Algeria, Egypt, Libya, Morocco

Maghreb cooking, the cuisine of North African countries bordering the Mediterranean Sea, reflects the area's rich geographical, social, economic, political and cultural diversity. Traditionally including Morocco, Libya, Tunisia, Algeria and Mauritania, this region's food cultures have also been significantly influenced by Italian and French cuisines.

From 600 BC, Arabs contributed a range of spices to the food, while Ottoman Turks brought pastries and bakery items, and the New World shared vegetables such as potatoes, squash (pumpkin), tomatoes and chilies. As this is a predominantly Muslim region, halal meats are usually eaten.

North African cuisine boasts big, bold spice blends, vegetables, pasta and grains. Many North African countries have similar dishes, if not the same, and multiple countries often claim to be the birthplace of a particular dish. It is hard to pin down the exact country of origin, as migration has taken dishes and cooking styles across borders and territories.

Soups play a significant role. They are sometimes eaten for breakfast, as a small first course before dinner or as the main component of a meal. During Ramadan, a cup of Shorba Frik (page 29) is a traditional dish to break the fast and ready one's senses and stomach for a meal. Soups are almost always eaten with bread or flatbread, a staple of the North African diet.

Chorba Bayda

Shorba Baïda

Serves 4–6

2 egg yolks from large eggs
60 ml (2 fl oz/¼ cup) lemon juice
2 tablespoons rendered chicken fat
　　or vegetable oil
15 g (½ oz) butter or smen (fermented
　　butter common in African cuisine)
1 onion, cut into 5 mm (¼ in) cubes
1 large carrot, cut into 5 mm (¼ in) cubes
1 celery rib (stalk), cut into 5 mm
　　(¼ in) cubes
3 garlic cloves, thinly sliced
½ teaspoon ground cinnamon
¼ teaspoon freshly ground black pepper
1 × 1.35 kg (3 lb) chicken, quartered
1450 ml (49 fl oz/6 cups) water
　　or Chicken Stock (page 237)
1 tablespoon salt
40 g (1½ oz/¼ cup) basmati rice
450 g (1 lb/3 cups) cooked chickpeas, drained
1 small bunch cilantro (coriander) or parsley,
　　roughly chopped, to garnish

Chorba bayda translates as white soup. It is traditionally from Algeria, but is also popular in some areas of Morocco. This soup is rich as it is thickened with egg, giving it its namesake white color. It is comforting and nourishing, thanks to ingredients such as chicken, rice and chickpeas. Enhanced with rich butter and aromatic cinnamon, it stands out from others. Broken vermicelli can be used instead of rice. If omitting rice, cook as directed adding the vermicelli during the last 2–3 minutes of cooking.

Combine the egg yolks and lemon juice in a small bowl. Using a whisk, beat until well blended. Alternatively, use a blender until thoroughly combined, then set aside.

Melt the chicken fat or oil and butter in a large pot over a medium–high heat. Add the onion, carrot, celery and garlic and cook slowly, stirring frequently, for 4 minutes, or until the vegetables are tender, but not browned, and the onions are translucent. Stir in the cinnamon and pepper.

Add the chicken pieces, water or stock and the salt. Bring to the boil, then immediately reduce the heat to a very low simmer. Remove the breasts when cooked through, about 7–10 minutes, and the leg/thigh pieces when the meat separates from the bone around the end of the leg, about 15 minutes. (When the chicken is cooked, a thermometer will read 74°C (165°F) when inserted into the thickest part of the thigh or breast and the juices will run clear.) Add the rice to the soup when the breasts are removed and stir to combine.

When the chicken is cooked, remove from the pot and leave until cool enough to handle, then remove the chicken skin and discard. Using your hands, shred all the meat and discard the bones. Add the meat back to the soup with the chickpeas.

Ladle a few spoonfuls of the hot broth into the yolk mixture, then add more broth, a spoonful at a time, until the egg mixture is warm. Adding too much hot liquid to the eggs will curdle the eggs, so do this step slowly.

When the egg mixture is warm, turn off the heat and drizzle the egg mixture into the hot broth, stirring constantly with a spoon. The soup will thicken, become silky, and the broth should turn from brown to white. Season with salt and pepper, garnish with cilantro or parsley and serve.

Hamoud

Serves 4–6

1 × 1.35 kg (3 lb) chicken, quartered
1.9 liters (64 fl oz/8 cups) water
  or Chicken Stock (page 237)
2 tablespoons salt
3 tablespoons rendered chicken fat
  or vegetable oil
3 celery ribs (stalks) with leaves,
  cut into thin half-moons
2 leeks, cut into 1 cm (½ in) cubes
4 garlic cloves, slivered
100 g (3½ oz/½ cup) basmati rice
3 zucchini (courgettes), sliced
  into thin half-moons
1–2 lemons

Traditional in Egyptian cuisine, hamoud is eaten as a soup, and also as a sauce over rice. Serving the meat and vegetables on the side or as a separate course allows for a whole chicken carcass to stretch over several courses, or even several meals. The most essential ingredients of hamoud are chicken, celery, lemon and garlic; other vegetables are often added when in season.

Place the chicken and water or stock into a large pot with the salt. Weigh down the chicken under a few small plates to keep it submerged and simmer gently over a medium heat until the chicken pieces are cooked through, about 7–10 minutes for the breasts and 15–18 minutes for the legs and thighs. The meat should separate from the end of the leg bone when cooked, a thermometer will read 74°C (165°F) when inserted into the thickest part of the thigh or breast and the juices of the chicken will run clear.

When the chicken is cooked, remove from the pot and leave until cool enough to handle, then remove the chicken skin and discard. Using your hands, shred all the meat and discard the bones. Set the meat aside and reserve the broth.

Wipe out the pot, then add the chicken fat or oil and melt over a medium heat. Add the celery, leeks and garlic and cook slowly for 6–8 minutes, stirring constantly, until the vegetables are soft.

Add the reserved broth and bring to a very gentle simmer. Add the rice and cook for 10 minutes, or until tender, adding the zucchini during the last 2 minutes of cooking the rice. Add the reserved chicken to the soup and stir to combine.

Squeeze the lemon juice into the soup, adding as much tangy flavor as possible without it becoming sour. Season with salt and freshly ground black pepper.

Mulukhiya

Molukhia, Molokhia

Serves 6

2 × whole chicken legs (approx. 670 g/1½ lb),
    including drumstick, or 4 chicken
    thighs, skin on
5 cm (2 in) cinnamon stick
2 bay leaves
1.9 liters (64 fl oz/8 cups) Chicken Stock
    (page 237), plus extra as needed
2 teaspoons salt
120 ml (4 fl oz/½ cup) extra-virgin olive oil,
    plus 3–4 tablespoons extra
200 g (7 oz/8 cups) fresh Jew's mallow
    leaves or spinach
1 large yellow onion, chopped
10 garlic cloves, very finely chopped
80 g (2¾ oz) cilantro (coriander),
    finely chopped
½ teaspoon cayenne pepper
2 tablespoons lemon juice

Mallow (Jew's mallow, jute) is very popular in the Middle East and North Africa, if not most widely used in Egyptian, Syrian and Lebanese cooking. The saw-toothed leaves have tendrils at the base of each leaf. Nutritionally, it is a powerhouse: the leaves are packed with three times more calcium and phosphorous than kale, and contain four times the amount of riboflavin. Mallow is a good source for vitamin C, vitamin A and a host of other minerals and vitamins. When cooked, the texture is that of cooked okra and the flavor is slightly bitter. Traditionally, this green is used in stews with protein, such as rabbit, chicken, beef or fish. Bouillon cubes are popular in Middle East cooking, but I prefer to use a good homemade stock.

One of Egypt's rulers from the Fatimid dynasty, Caliph Al-Hakim Abu Ali Mansur, who ruled Egypt from AD 996 to 1021, banned the consumption of molokhia because he believed that it worked as a sexual stimulant in women. After his reign, the ban was lifted and households continued to uphold the traditional meal, regardless of religion, across the country. Serve with steamed basmati rice, pita, vinegar, sliced raw onions and sliced tomatoes.

Combine the chicken legs or thighs, cinnamon, bay leaves, stock and 1 teaspoon salt in a large pot over a medium heat and cook for 30 minutes, or until the chicken is just tender when pierced with a fork or knife. When the chicken is cooked, remove from the pot and leave until cool enough to handle. Strain the broth and set aside, discarding the contents of the pot.

Warm the extra-virgin olive oil in another large pot over a medium heat. Add the Jew's mallow leaves and cook, stirring, for 10 minutes. If the pan seems dry, add 1–2 tablespoons extra oil to prevent the leaves from burning. When the leaves are tender, remove from the pan and set aside. Reduce the heat to low–medium, add 2 tablespoons extra-virgin olive oil, then add the onion and 8 garlic cloves and cook for 5 minutes, or until the onions are translucent and tender, but not gaining any color. If the onions begin to brown, reduce the heat.

Return the Jew's mallow leaves to the pan, then add the strained broth. You need to make it up to 1.9 liters (64 fl oz/8 cups) liquid, so add more stock if needed. Add the remaining salt and simmer slowly for 1 hour, or until the leaves have turned dark green and the stew has become thick.

Meanwhile, using your hands, shred the cooled chicken meat into bite-sized pieces. Discard any skin and bones.

After the leaves have been cooking for 1 hour, add the chicken, cilantro, cayenne and remaining garlic and cook for a further 20 minutes. Add the lemon juice and cook for 10 minutes. Season with salt.

Shurbat Lisan Asfour

Serves 4

1 × 1.35 kg (3 lb) chicken, quartered
1.9 liters (64 fl oz/8 cups) water
   or Chicken Stock (page 237)
12 whole allspice berries
1 large yellow onion, quartered
1 teaspoon paprika
3 bay leaves
10 cardamom pods
1 roma or plum tomato, quartered
2 celery ribs (stalks), cut into
   5 cm (2 in) lengths
30 g (1 oz) mastic rocks
1 tablespoon salt
60 g (2 oz) butter
100 g (3½ oz/1 cup) orzo pasta

Shurbat lisan asfour, or bird's tongue soup, is named for the shape of orzo, the garnish of the soup. This simple and flavorful soup is served before a meal, especially during Ramadan, to gently soften hunger as a precursor to the balance of the meal. Sweetness comes from the butter and balances the tart flavor from the tomato, while the allspice and cardamom add depth. All ages will certainly feel nurtured by this soup.

Combine the chicken, water or stock, allspice, onion, paprika, bay leaves, cardamom pods, tomato, celery, mastic and salt in a large pot. Weigh down the chicken under a few small plates to keep it submerged and simmer gently over a medium heat until the chicken pieces are cooked through, about 7–10 minutes for the breasts and 15–18 minutes for the legs and thighs. The meat should separate from the end of the leg bone when done, a thermometer will read 74°C (165°F) when inserted into the thickest part of the thigh or breast and the juices of the chicken will run clear.

    When the chicken is cooked, remove from the pot and leave until cool enough to handle, then remove the chicken skin and discard. Reserve the meat for another use. Strain the broth and set aside.

    Wipe out the pot, then add the butter and melt over a medium heat. Add the orzo and cook, stirring constantly, for about 3–5 minutes until the pasta is toasted and golden. Add the reserved broth, then stir and cook for a further 9–10 minutes until the pasta is tender. Season with salt and freshly ground black pepper.

Shorba Frik

Serves 4

110 g (4 oz/½ cup) dried chickpeas
1 × 1.35 kg (3 lb) chicken, quartered
1.9 liters (64 fl oz/8 cups) water
    or Chicken Stock (page 237)
2 tablespoons salt
3 tablespoons rendered chicken
    fat or vegetable oil
6 garlic cloves, very finely chopped
2 tablespoons ras el hanout
½ large yellow onion, halved
3 tablespoons tomato paste
170 g (6 oz) canned tomato purée (passata)
1 tablespoon paprika
¼ teaspoon cayenne pepper
150 g (5½ oz/⅔ cup) freekeh (green wheat)
    or use orzo for Tunisian-style chorba
2 celery ribs (stalks), cut into
    5 mm (¼ in) cubes
40 g (1½ oz) cilantro (coriander),
    roughly chopped
1 teaspoon dried mint

This soup, like others that have migrated as people have, has roots in Tunisia, Libya, Algeria and the Middle East. Traditionally a favorite during Ramadan, it is satisfying and flavorful. In Tunisia, the freekeh will be substituted with orzo, a reflection of the large numbers of Italians living there until the 1950s. Shorba (or chorba) is the common North African name for a soup or a stew. The word originated as shurbah, a Middle Eastern term. Freekeh, toasted immature (green) wheat, adds a hearty, toothy texture. Breads and flatbreads are an important part of the meal, so make sure to serve this soup with delicious bread.

Place the dried chickpeas in a large bowl and cover with cool water, to at least 5 cm (2 in) above the legumes. Cover and leave to soak overnight at room temperature. The next day, drain the chickpeas and set aside until ready to use.

Place the chicken and water or stock in a large pot with the salt. Weigh down the chicken under a few small plates to keep it submerged and simmer gently over a medium heat until the chicken pieces are cooked through, about 7–10 minutes for the breasts and 15–18 minutes for the legs and thighs. The meat should separate from the end of the leg bone when cooked, a thermometer will read 74°C (165°F) when inserted into the thickest part of the thigh or breast and the juices of the chicken will run clear.

When the chicken is cooked, remove from the pot and leave until cool enough to handle, then remove the chicken skin and discard. Using your hands, shred all the meat and discard the bones. Set the meat aside and reserve the broth.

Wipe out the pot, then add the chicken fat or oil and melt over a medium heat. Add the garlic, ras el hanout and onion, sauté until tender, but not browned, then add the tomato paste. Cook the paste, stirring, until it darkens slightly. Add the tomato pureé, paprika and cayenne and cook slowly for 4–5 minutes, stirring constantly, until the vegetables are soft. If the bottom of the pot begins to darken, add 2 tablespoons water and stir with a wooden spoon, gently scraping any bits stuck on the bottom of the pot.

Add the freekeh (if using), the celery and chickpeas to the pot, then stir in the reserved broth. Stir to combine and cook at a gentle simmer for 20–30 minutes until the freekeh and chickpeas are cooked. If not using freekeh, simmer for 30 minutes to reduce the broth. If using orzo, cook the pasta in a separate pot for 6–10 minutes until tender, then strain and add to the soup after the 30 minutes of cooking.

Add the reserved shredded chicken, if not saving for another use, to the soup and stir to combine. Stir in the herbs and season with salt and freshly ground black pepper.

Harira

Serves 6

150 g (5½ oz/¾ cup) dried chickpeas
1 × 1.35 kg (3 lb) chicken, quartered
2.4 liters (81 fl oz/10 cups) water
   or Chicken Stock (page 237)
2 tablespoons salt
3 tablespoons rendered chicken fat
   or olive oil
1 yellow onion, cut into 5 mm (¼ in) cubes
2 celery ribs (stalks), cut into 5 mm
   (¼ in) cubes
3 garlic cloves, very finely chopped
2 carrots, cut into 5 mm (¼ in) rounds
2 teaspoons ground cumin
2 teaspoons cumin seeds
1 teaspoon ground coriander
½ teaspoon ground turmeric
pinch of saffron threads, crushed
   and dissolved in 2 tablespoons
   boiling water
150 g (5½ oz/¾ cup) dried brown lentils
100 g (3½ oz/½ cup) basmati rice
1–2 lemons
40 g (1½ oz) cilantro (coriander), leaves
   roughly chopped and stems finely
   chopped
50 g (1¾ oz) parsley, leaves roughly
   chopped and stems finely chopped

This hearty soup is typically served for lunch, or as a starter for dinner. It is a favorite during Ramadan as it provides enough sustenance to satisfy the discomfort after a day of fasting. Often, the rice is substituted with wheat vermicelli noodles; similar soups in bordering countries may use freekeh (toasted green wheat). Traditional accompaniments are smen (fermented butter), plain, thick yogurt and bread or flatbread.

Place the dried chickpeas in a bowl and cover with cool water, to at least 5 cm (2 in) above the legumes. Cover and leave to soak overnight at room temperature. The next day, drain the chickpeas and set aside until ready to use.

Place the chicken and water or stock into a large pot with the salt. Weigh down the chicken under a few small plates to keep it submerged and simmer gently over a medium heat until the chicken pieces are cooked through, 7–10 minutes for the breasts and 15–18 minutes for the legs and thighs. The meat should separate from the end of the leg bone when cooked, a thermometer will read 74°C (165°F) when inserted into the thickest part of the thigh or breast and the juices of the chicken will run clear.

When the chicken is cooked, remove from the pot and leave until cool enough to handle, then remove the chicken skin and discard. Using your hands, shred all the meat and discard the bones. Set the meat aside and reserve the broth.

Wipe out the pot, then add the chicken fat or oil and melt over a medium heat. Add the onion, celery, garlic, carrots and spices, except the saffron, and cook slowly for 4–5 minutes, stirring constantly, until the vegetables are soft. If the bottom of the pan begins to darken, add 2 tablespoons water and gently stir to remove any bits stuck on the bottom.

Add the chickpeas, the reserved broth and the saffron, then stir and cook for 10 minutes. Add the lentils and rice and cook for a further 10–20 minutes until tender. If much of the broth evaporates as the lentils and rice cook, add some more water or stock to achieve a soupy stew that has some brothiness to it.

Add the reserved chicken to the pot and stir to combine, then squeeze in enough lemon juice to add as much tangy flavor as possible without it becoming sour. Season with salt and freshly ground black pepper and garnish with the herbs.

EAST + WEST AFRICA

Ethiopia, Senegal, Tanzania

Richer compared to those of North Africa, the soups of Ethiopia, Senegal and Tanzania are fortified with peanuts, lentils and coconut. The flavors are warm, complemented by curry spice blends, Berbere (page 35) and chilies. Some African regions remained closed to culinary influences until the 1600s, when the slave trade brought outside contact. Cassava, peanuts and chilies were introduced, but they did not impact the cooking methods.

Cuisine in parts of East Africa has been influenced by the Swahili culture, a blending of local customs evolving from the East African slave trade, and Portuguese culture. As in many poorer nations, the diets of this region are based heavily on starch, including a popular rice-based pilaf, as well as sambusas – savory fried pastries filled with potatoes, peas and spices. East African cultures tend to eat less meat; larger animals are used as a form of currency rather than for food. Ugali, a maize-based porridge, is sometimes served with meat or vegetable stews. Steamed green bananas are also often eaten as a starchy filler.

Fufu is the staple starch in some West African cuisines. It is a combination of pounded cassava and green plantain flour mixed with water to make a dough, which is then often eaten with peanut stew. Variations include other starchy vegetables, such as yam, and cereal grains such as millet or sorghum.

Each region enjoys varied soups and stews. Many include meat, while others focus on vegetables. Some East African soups feature varieties of lentils as the base, such as the Ethiopian Ye Misir Shorba Be Doro (page 37), while others use peanuts or plantains (Supu Ya Kuku, page 41). West African dishes also favor peanuts and combine them with local root vegetables, as in Senegalese Chicken Mafé (page 38).

Doro Wat

Serves 4

2 tablespoons vegetable oil
2 large yellow onions, cut into 1 cm
    (½ in) cubes
3 garlic cloves
2.5 cm (1 in) piece ginger, peeled
2½ tablespoons Berbere (page 35)
½ tablespoon smoked paprika
½–1 teaspoon cayenne pepper
1 tablespoon tomato paste
60 ml (2 fl oz/¼ cup) red wine
175 ml (6 fl oz/¾ cup) Chicken Stock
    (page 237)
20 g (¾ oz) butter
4 × whole chicken legs (approx. 1.3 kg/
    2 lb 14 oz), leg and thigh attached, skin on
4 large Hard-boiled Eggs (see below),
    peeled

I am happy to be challenged that this is not a soup, but rather a stew. It really is a fair argument. Nonetheless, doro wat (chicken stew) is the iconic chicken dish of Ethiopia, and it deserves its place. I was lucky enough to learn how to make it when I was traveling in Ethiopia in 2017. After visiting the market in Addis Ababa and gathering spices needed to make the national spice blend berbere, we headed to the local mill house where locals grind spices to use at home. The freshly ground berbere, a blend of the dried berbere chili, ginger, coriander and cardamom, is the base of this incredible stew. In this dish, it doesn't matter which came first, the chicken or the egg. You get both. Serve with injera, a fermented flatbread made with teff.

Heat the oil in a large pot over a medium heat. Add the onions, garlic and ginger and cook gently for 15–20 minutes until the onions are very tender. Add the berbere, smoked paprika, cayenne and tomato paste, then stir to combine and gently toast on the bottom of the pan for about 2–3 minutes. Add the red wine, stir and scrape the caramelized bits from the bottom of the pan, then cook for 2–4 minutes until the wine has evaporated. Add the stock, butter and chicken, bring to a gentle simmer and cook for about 30 minutes, or until the chicken is tender, the leg meat begins to pull from the bone and the juices run clear when a skewer is inserted into the thickest part of the thigh. Add the eggs and stir to combine. Warm the eggs in the broth and season with salt. The broth should be thickened and rich.

Makes 4 eggs

4 large eggs, cold

Hard-boiled Eggs

Bring a pot of water to the boil, then lower to a rapid simmer. Carefully add the eggs, one at a time, and gently boil for 7–9 minutes. Drain the eggs and transfer to a bowl of ice-cold water to stop them cooking. Leave to cool, then peel and set aside.

AFRICA

Ye Ocholoni Ina Doro Shorba

Serves 6

2 tablespoons rendered chicken
    fat or vegetable oil
2 yellow onions, cut into 2 cm (¾ in) cubes
2 carrots, cut into 2.5 cm (1 in) rounds
1 sweet potato (about 450 g/1 lb), peeled
    and cut into 2 cm (¾ in) cubes
2 tablespoons Berbere (see opposite),
    plus extra to garnish
1 tablespoon salt
1.9 liters (64 fl oz/8 cups) water
    or Chicken Stock (page 237)
450 g (1 lb) boneless, skinless
    chicken breasts or tenders
255 g (9 oz/1 cup) natural smooth
    peanut butter
65 g (2¼ oz/⅓ cup) basmati rice
30 g (1 oz) chopped roasted peanuts,
    to garnish

Variations of peanut soup are popular throughout East and West Africa. Ingredients will vary depending on the region, adding or subtracting collard greens (spring cabbage), chickpeas, tomatoes, spices and squash. It is a hearty and flavorful soup, rich from the peanut butter and spicy from the berbere.

Melt the chicken fat or oil in a large pot over a medium–high heat. Add the onion, carrot and sweet potato and cook for 3–4 minutes until the onion becomes translucent. Stir in the berbere and salt, then add the water or stock and bring to a very gentle simmer. Place the chicken in the soup and cook gently until just cooked through, 2–3 minutes for the tenders and 6–8 minutes for the breasts. Remove the chicken from the soup, then continue cooking at a gentle simmer for 8–10 minutes until all the vegetables are very tender. Cut the chicken into bite-sized pieces and set aside on a plate.

Using a blender or an immersion blender, purée the soup with the peanut butter until very smooth. If using a blender, take care to remove the center piece on the blender cover – the hot soup will splatter without a vent. Pour the soup back into the pot; it will be thin. Add the rice and cook at a very slow simmer, stirring with a whisk, for 10 minutes, or until the rice is tender. Make sure the rice does not stick to the bottom of the pot, and the soup does not become too thick and burn. Thin the soup with a little water or stock as needed.

When the rice is cooked, season with salt and ladle into bowls. Garnish with the chicken pieces, a sprinkle of berbere and peanuts.

Makes 35 g (1¼ oz)

6 green cardamom pods
8 cloves
1 teaspoon coriander seeds
½ teaspoon ground allspice
½ teaspoon fenugreek seeds
1 tablespoon chili powder, such as ancho
    or New Mexico
1 tablespoon salt
1 teaspoon ground ginger
¼ teaspoon ground cinnamon

Berbere Spice

Place the cardamom, cloves, coriander, allspice and fenugreek in a small pan and toast over a high heat, making sure not to burn the spices, until fragrant. Set aside to cool.

When cool, grind finely in a spice grinder or coffee grinder, transfer to a bowl and stir in the remaining ingredients. Store in an airtight container for up to 6 months.

Ye Misir Shorba Be Doro

Ethiopia

Serves 4

1 × 1.35 kg (3 lb) chicken, quartered
1450 ml (49 fl oz/6 cups) water
  or Chicken Stock (page 237)
2 tablespoons salt
2 tablespoons rendered chicken
  fat or vegetable oil
40 g (1½ oz) butter
2 large red onions, cut into 5 mm
  (¼ in) cubes
3 garlic cloves, very finely chopped
2½ tablespoons Berbere (page 35)
2.5 cm (1 in) piece ginger, peeled
  and very finely chopped
60 ml (2 fl oz/¼ cup) dry red wine
200 g (7 oz) canned diced tomatoes
250 g (9 oz/1 cup) red lentils,
  thoroughly rinsed
1 lemon

Ethiopia is home to rich and complex stewed meats and vegetables. Most often, each dish starts with butter. Ethiopians have a graded system from fresh butter to several levels of fermented butter, making sure that they can preserve what they do not use immediately. This process of fermenting butter – similar to injera, their staple fermented flatbread made with teff – provides health as well as preservation benefits. This stew is always eaten with injera. Ethiopians use their hands to eat, scooping up sauce and meat with the flatbread as their tool. Injera is less commonly found outside of Ethiopia. Ethiopian dishes are served with rice when injera is not available, although rice is not a native grain to the country and is rarely eaten there.

Place the chicken and water or stock in a large pot with the salt. Weigh down the chicken under a few small plates to keep it submerged and simmer gently over a medium heat until the chicken pieces are cooked through, about 7–10 minutes for the breasts and 15–18 minutes for the legs and thighs. The meat should separate from the end of the leg bone when cooked, a thermometer will read 74°C (165°F) when inserted into the thickest part of the thigh or breast and the juices of the chicken will run clear.

When the chicken is cooked, remove from the pot and leave until cool enough to handle, then remove the chicken skin. Cut large chunks of the chicken on the bone (leg, thigh, half breasts) and reserve to serve larger pieces of chicken in the broth. Alternatively, shred all the meat and set aside. Strain the broth and reserve.

Wipe out the pot, then add the chicken fat or oil and butter and melt over a medium heat. Add the onions, garlic, berbere and ginger and cook slowly for 3–4 minutes, stirring constantly, until the vegetables are soft. Add the red wine and cook, stirring, for 2–4 minutes until the wine evaporates. Add the tomatoes and lentils and stir to combine. Add the reserved stock, then bring to a very gentle simmer and cook for 10 minutes, or until the lentils are tender. Add the reserved chicken to the soup and stir to combine.

Squeeze the lemon juice into the soup, adding as much tangy flavor as possible without it becoming sour. Season with salt and freshly ground black pepper and serve.

AFRICA

Chicken Mafé

Serves 6

1 × 1.35 kg (3 lb) chicken, quartered
1.9 liters (64 fl oz/8 cups) water
  or Chicken Stock (page 237)
2 tablespoons salt
3 tablespoons vegetable oil
½ yellow onion, cut into 1 cm (½ in) cubes
3 garlic cloves, very finely chopped
4 cm (1½ in) piece ginger, peeled
  and very finely chopped
1 small jalapeño chili, very finely chopped
1 small eggplant (aubergine), cut into
  1 cm (½ in) cubes
2 tablespoons curry powder
1 tablespoon chili powder
2 tablespoons tomato paste
250 g (9 oz/1 cup) smooth peanut butter
500 g (1 lb 2 oz/2 cups) canned
  diced tomatoes
1 butternut squash (pumpkin),
  zucchini (courgette) or other squash,
  cut into 2.5 cm (1 in) cubes
1 large potato or sweet potato, peeled
  and cut into 2.5 cm (1 in) cubes
140 g (5 oz) frozen okra, cut into
  1 cm (½ in) rounds
1 lime

A version of this soup is found all over West Africa. And, for that reason, this soup is often lumped into a category called West African peanut soup. Chicken mafé is bold, nutritious and filling, and begs for a squeeze of lime just before serving to lighten the richness. Chicken mafé is typically served alongside or over steamed white rice.

Place the chicken and water or stock into a large pot with the salt. Weigh down the chicken under a few small plates to keep it submerged and simmer gently over a medium heat until the chicken pieces are cooked through, about 7–10 minutes for the breasts and 15–18 minutes for the legs and thighs. The meat should separate from the end of the leg bone when cooked, a thermometer will read 74°C (165°F) when inserted into the thickest part of the thigh or breast and the juices of the chicken will run clear.

When the chicken is cooked, remove from the pot and leave until cool enough to handle, then remove the chicken skin and discard. Using your hands, shred all the meat and discard the bones. Set the meat aside and reserve the broth.

Wipe out the pot, add the oil and warm over a medium heat. Add the onion, garlic, ginger, jalapeño, eggplant, curry powder, chili powder and tomato paste and cook slowly for 4–5 minutes, stirring constantly, until the vegetables are soft.

In a blender, carefully process the warm broth and peanut butter until smooth. Add the tomatoes, squash, potato and peanut broth to the soup and stir to combine. Bring to a simmer and cook slowly for 8–10 minutes until the vegetables are tender. If the soup is too thick, add some water as needed.

Add the chicken meat and okra and cook for 1–2 minutes until the okra is tender, then season with salt and freshly ground black pepper. Squeeze the lime juice into the soup, adding as much tangy flavor as possible without it becoming sour.

Supu ya Kuku

Serves 4

2 tablespoons rendered chicken
    fat or peanut oil
1 yellow onion, cut into 1 cm (½ in) cubes
3 garlic cloves, thinly sliced
2 tablespoons curry powder
1 tablespoon chili flakes
2 teaspoons freshly ground black pepper
115 g (4 oz/1¼ cups) unsweetened
    shredded (desiccated) coconut
1.9 liters (64 fl oz/8 cups) Chicken
    Stock (page 237)
670 g (1½ lb) boneless, skinless
    chicken breast or tenders
1 tablespoon salt
4 roma or plum tomatoes, roughly chopped
3 ripe plantains, sliced into 2.5 cm
    (1 in) rounds

The flavors in this soup are an unexpected treat. Traditionally, the soup features plantains. If you can't find plantains, then substitute bananas. Bananas have more residual sugar, bring a softer texture and perfume the broth for a tropical feel. The coconut adds a little sweetness and the curry is a wonderful addition of sharpness. There's a certain earthiness and warmth to this soup that is surprising and different.

Melt the chicken fat or oil over a medium–high heat in a large pot. Add the onion and garlic, then stir in the curry powder, chili flakes and pepper and cook for 3–4 minutes until the onion becomes tender and translucent. If the onion starts to brown, reduce the heat. Add the coconut and stir for 1 minute to toast.

Add the stock and chicken and bring to a very gentle simmer. Season the broth with the salt, then add the tomatoes and cook for 3 minutes, or just until the chicken is cooked through.

When the chicken is cooked, remove from the pot and leave to cool, then cut into bite-sized chunks. Stir the chicken into the soup with the plantain pieces and season with salt and pepper.

The Americas

NORTH AMERICA

Canada, Mexico, USA

While most soups and stews in the United States and Canada mirror their European roots, the soups of Mexico are more indicative of the warmer weather the country enjoys all year round.

Canadian and American fare features a variety of ethnic foods, including European and Asian cuisines, and everything in between. Due to the great number of cultures present in Canada and the US, the types of food available reflect many traditions. Border towns between the US and Canada share similarities, as do their counterparts along the US–Mexican border. Mexico has distinct cuisines of its own, with variations and specialties in every region.

Many US and Canadian soups are based on simple ingredients, such as carrots, onions, celery, potatoes and herbs. Yet, there is also significant regional variety. The wonderful Chicken Gumbo (page 59) from the American South features flavors brought to the US from the African continent during the slave trade, and Green Chili Chicken Stew (page 65) is influenced by America's neighbor to the south.

Soups from Mexico and the southern US border states use chilies and bright citrus fruits. Mexico's cuisine utilizes the heat of local chilies, with each region taking pride in the chili specific to that area, and Mexican soups form a traditional cuisine of their own. Pozole Verde (page 54) and Pozole Rojo (page 52) show the flexibility of Mexican cooking and the use of ingredients as they are available.

Chicken Fricot

Serves 6

Dumplings

140 g (5 oz/1 cup) all-purpose (plain) flour
1 tablespoon chopped savory sprigs
2 teaspoons baking powder
1½ teaspoons salt
120 ml (4 fl oz/½ cup) whole (full-cream)
   milk

Soup

2 tablespoons rendered chicken fat
   or butter
3 garlic cloves, thinly sliced
1 large yellow onion, cut into 1 cm
   (½ in) cubes
1 carrot, cut into 1 cm (½ in) cubes
1 celery rib (stalk), cut into 1 cm
   (½ in) cubes
115 g (4 oz) bacon or salt pork,
   finely chopped
4 savory sprigs
1.9 liters (64 fl oz/8 cups) Chicken
   Stock (page 237)
1 tablespoon salt
670 g (1½ lb) boneless, skinless chicken
   breast, cut into bite-sized pieces
1 large russet potato, peeled and cut
   into 2.5 cm (1 in) cubes

Fricot is a traditional Acadian dish. The word fricot originated in eighteenth-century France, where it was the term referring to a feast. Then, as time passed, fricot referred to a stew, made either with meat or fish. This variation of chicken soup with dumplings is a classic comfort dish: a savory, warm stew garnished with dumplings that puff when dropped into simmering broth. Fluffy dumplings, also called doughboys, are cooked atop the stew, not unlike chicken and dumplings in the Southern US (see page 63). In lean times, a meatless fricot would be made. Fricot à la belette was one term for this. It means weasel stew, the reference being made to the cook, who is as sly as a weasel for leaving out the meat. Prince Edward Island Acadians use the term fricot à la bazette, which means 'stupid cook's stew', implying that the meat was forgotten.

For the dumplings, combine the flour, savory, baking powder and salt in a bowl. Stir in the milk to make a thick batter and set aside.

For the soup, heat a large pot over a medium–high heat. Add the chicken fat or butter, then add the garlic, onion, carrot, celery and bacon or salt pork and sauté for 3–4 minutes until tender. Add the savory and stock and season with the salt. Bring to a gentle simmer, then add the chicken and potato. Drop teaspoonfuls of the dumpling dough into the pot and simmer very gently for 10 minutes. Season with salt and freshly ground black pepper.

Caldo Tlalpeño

Serves 4–6

85 g (3 oz/½ cup) dried chickpeas
1 × 1.35 kg (3 lb) chicken, quartered
1.9 liters (64 fl oz/8 cups) water
    or Chicken Stock (page 237)
2 tablespoons salt
4 roma or plum tomatoes, quartered
2 chipotle peppers in adobo
¼ white onion, roughly chopped
2 garlic cloves
7 g (¼ oz/¼ cup) fresh epazote,
    loosely packed, or 1 teaspoon dried
1 teaspoon dried oregano
2 bay leaves
3 large carrots, cut into 5 mm (¼ in) rounds
225 g (8 oz) green beans, cut into
    2.5 cm (1 in) pieces
2 zucchini (courgettes), cut into 1 cm
    (½ in) cubes

To garnish
2 ripe avocados, cubed
170 g (6 oz) panela cheese, paneer
    or firm ricotta, cubed
½ bunch cilantro (coriander),
    roughly chopped
1 lime, cut into wedges

The recipe for Tlalpeño soup was born in the early 1900s in the village of Tlalpan, a suburb of Mexico City. At one of the many food stalls at the suburb's tram stop, a woman sold chicken soup. Her soup became so beloved, her fans named it Tlalpeño soup. Traditionally, vegetable garnishes varied: turnips, green beans and a few other seasonal vegetables can be added. Long-grain rice is often served alongside, and sometimes served in the soup itself. Serve with warm corn tortillas or crispy tostadas.

Place the dried chickpeas in a bowl and cover with cool water, to at least 5 cm (2 in) above the legumes. Cover and leave to soak overnight at room temperature. The next day, drain the chickpeas and cook in a pan of gently simmering water for 20–30 minutes until tender. Season the beans with salt while still in the cooking water, then reserve.

Place the chicken and water or stock in a large pot with the 2 tablespoons salt. Weigh down the chicken under a few small plates to keep it submerged and simmer gently over a medium heat until the chicken pieces are cooked, about 7–10 minutes for the breasts and 15–18 minutes for the legs and thighs. The meat should separate from the end of the leg bone when cooked, a thermometer will read 74°C (165°F) when inserted into the thickest part of the thigh or breast and the juices of the chicken will run clear.

When the chicken is cooked, remove from the pot and leave until cool enough to handle, then remove the chicken skin and discard. Using your hands, shred all the meat and discard the bones. Set the meat aside. Strain the broth and reserve.

Place the tomatoes, chipotle, onion, garlic, epazote, and 475 ml (16 fl oz/2 cups) of the reserved broth in a blender and process until smooth.

Wipe out the pot and place over a medium–high heat. Pour the purée into the pot, then add the oregano and bay leaves and cook slowly, stirring, for 3–5 minutes. Add the reserved broth, bring to a gentle simmer, then add the carrots and green beans and cook for 3–4 minutes until tender, adding the zucchini during the last 1–2 minutes of cooking. Drain the chickpeas and stir into the soup.

Add the reserved chicken to the soup and stir to combine. Season with salt and freshly ground black pepper and serve the soup garnished with avocado, cheese, cilantro and lime.

Sopa de Albóndigas de Pollo y Masa

Serves 4

Broth
½ × 1.35 kg (3 lb) chicken (the other
    half will be used for the meatballs)
¾ yellow onion, roughly chopped
½ green bell pepper (capsicum), seeded
    and quartered
3 garlic cloves, smashed
3 tablespoons sour orange juice
40 g (1½ oz) culantro,
    or cilantro (coriander)
3 mint sprigs, leaves and stems
2.9 liters (97½ fl oz/12 cups) water
    or Chicken Stock (page 237)
½ teaspoon whole black peppercorns
4 whole cloves
1 tablespoon salt

Meatballs
¼ yellow onion, roughly chopped
½ green bell pepper (capsicum), seeded
    and roughly chopped
2 garlic cloves
1½ tablespoons unsalted butter
1 teaspoon achiote paste
55 g (2 oz/⅓ cup) dry corn masa
    or masa arepa
280 g (10 oz) ground (minced) chicken
    from the remaining ½ chicken (breast,
    leg and thigh)
40 g (1½ oz) culantro, or cilantro
    (coriander), finely chopped
3 mint sprigs, leaves picked and
    finely chopped
2 tablespoons sour orange juice
1 teaspoon salt

Mexican sunshine radiates through the country's cuisine. I grew up just north of Mexico, and Mexican food became just as much a part of my cultural cuisine as that of my family. Rich, bright and satisfying, this soup isn't spicy; it is lively and deeply pleasing. Read the recipe carefully: the whole chicken is divided between the broth and the meatballs. If you are not able to locate sour oranges, substitute 2 tablespoons orange juice and 1 tablespoon lime juice in the soup. For the meatball portion, substitute sour orange juice with 1 tablespoon orange juice and 2 teaspoons lime juice. Culantro is an herb commonly used in Latin America and the Caribbean; it is sometimes referred to as serrated coriander and is available in some Latin American markets. Its flavor is similar to cilantro (coriander), but much more pungent. If you can't find it, substitute with cilantro (coriander) leaves and stems.

For the broth, place all ingredients in a large pot. Bring to the boil over a high heat, then immediately reduce the heat to a gentle simmer and cook until each piece of chicken is cooked through, about 5–7 minutes for the breast and 15 minutes for the thigh and leg, when the meat separates from bone.

Leave the chicken until cool enough to handle, then remove the chicken skin and discard. Using your hands, shred the chicken into bite-sized pieces and discard the bones. Set the meat aside.

Strain the broth into a large bowl, discarding the solids, and return the broth to the pot and bring to a gentle simmer over a medium heat.

Meanwhile, for the meatballs, place the onion, bell pepper and garlic in a food processor and pulse until the mixture is finely ground. Scrape the sides of the mixer a few times to ensure even processing. Melt the butter in a large pan over a medium heat. Add the onion mixture and achiote paste and cook for 5–7 minutes, stirring occasionally, until most of the liquid has evaporated. Transfer to a large bowl and leave to cool completely.

When the onion mixture is cool, add the masa, ground (minced) chicken, culantro, mint, sour orange juice and salt and stir until thoroughly combined. Form the mixture into a ball of dough, then shape the dough into 16 × 4 cm (1½ in) balls and add them to the very gently simmering broth. Cook for 4–6 minutes until the meatballs float to the surface, stirring gently once or twice. Return the remaining chicken to the broth to heat through.

Sopa Azteca

Tortilla Soup

Serves 4

2 large ancho chilies
2 chipotle chilies in adobo
420 g (15 oz/2 cups) whole canned
    tomatoes, puréed
240 ml (8 fl oz/1 cup) water
3 tablespoons vegetable oil
1 yellow onion, cut into 5 mm (¼ in) cubes
3 garlic cloves, very finely chopped
1 × 1.35 kg (3 lb) chicken, skinned
    and quartered
950 ml (32½ fl oz/4 cups) water
    or Chicken Stock (page 237)

To serve
tortilla chips
lime wedges
shaved radish
corn, when in season
sour cream
cotija cheese, or other Mexican
    crumbly cheese

In Mexico, you will see this recipe vary by region. You might see it made with tomatillos in the state of Hidalgo, but it's usually done with tomatoes in most regions. The chilies will always vary depending on the area, from dark and smoky to lighter and pungent. Chilies are the most important ingredient in this soup as they are responsible for the fortifying flavor. I prefer chilies on the smokier side of the spectrum for this recipe. Garnish this soup with a squeeze of lime, and add corn, sliced right off the cob, when in season.

Place a heavy-bottomed pan, such as a cast-iron frying pan, over a medium–high heat. Add the ancho chilies and weigh down lightly with a plate or small pan. Toast the chilies, turning to toast all sides, until their color becomes darker. Leave to cool, then discard the stems and inner seeds. Place the chilies in a blender with the chipotle chilies, tomatoes and water and process until smooth. Set aside.

Heat the oil in a large pot over a medium–high heat. Add the onion and garlic and cook for 4 minutes, stirring occasionally, until the onions are translucent. Stir in the chili-tomato mixture, then reduce the heat to medium and cook for 3 minutes, or just until the purée starts to thicken. Add the chicken and water or stock and bring to a very gentle simmer. Cook for 20 minutes, or until the chicken is cooked through.

When the chicken is cooked, remove from the soup with tongs or a slotted spoon and leave to cool. Using your hands, shred all the meat and discard the bones. Add the chicken to the soup and gently warm all together. Serve with the accompaniments.

Pozole Rojo

Serves 4–6

2 dried ancho chilies
2 dried guajillo chilies
700 g (1 lb 9 oz) canned hominy,
    drained and rinsed
1 × 1.35 kg (3 lb) chicken, quartered
1 garlic head, papery outer layers removed
1.9 liters (64 fl oz/8 cups) water
    or Chicken Stock (page 237)
2 tablespoons salt
1 white onion, halved
5 cilantro (coriander) sprigs
3 roma or plum tomatoes
3 garlic cloves, chopped
1 tablespoon ground cumin
1 teaspoon ground allspice
3 whole cloves, ground

To serve
½ head iceberg, romaine lettuce
    or green cabbage, finely shredded
1 bunch radishes, thinly sliced, greens
    discarded
2 avocados, diced
1 bunch cilantro (coriander),
    roughly chopped
½ white onion, very finely chopped
3 limes, cut in wedges
2 tablespoons dried oregano
dried ground chili, such as piquín,
    or a Mexican mix, such as Tajín
12 tostadas or 420 g (15 oz) tortilla chips

Pozole means hominy (maize) and is a traditional soup from Mexico, typically made with pork or chicken as the base protein. A celebratory dish on New Year's Eve, this is now a meal that is commonplace all year round, but especially for special occasions and celebrations, such as birthdays and Christmas. Maize (corn) is considered to be very holy. The soup is rich and flavorful and the garnishes are fun to add, changing every bowl according to the personal tastes and preferences of the diner.

Preheat the oven to 200°C (400°F). Toast the dried chilies in the oven, turning them over once when the first side is toasted. The chilies should not be blackened. Remove from the oven and leave to cool. Once cool, place in a bowl and cover with hot water, weighing the chilies down with a plate to make sure they are submerged. Set aside.

Place the hominy in a large pot. Add the chicken, garlic, water or stock and salt. Bring to the boil, then reduce the heat to a gentle simmer and simmer for 30 minutes, removing the breast portions after 15 minutes. The juices of the chicken should run clear.

Remove the chicken from the pot and leave until cool enough to handle, then remove the chicken skin and discard. Using your hands, shred all the meat and discard the bones. Set the meat aside. Alternatively, don't shred the chicken and just cut it into pieces.

Drain the soaking chilies and remove the stems and inner seeds. Place in a blender with the onion, cilantro, tomatoes, garlic, cumin, allspice, cloves, and 240 ml (8 fl oz/1 cup) of the broth from cooking the chicken. Process until puréed as finely as possible.

Add the purée to the pot with the hominy and simmer for 15–20 minutes over a low heat. Add the chicken to the soup and season with salt and freshly ground black pepper. Serve with the accompaniments.

Pozole Verde

Serves 4–6

2 poblano peppers
700 g (1 lb 9 oz) canned hominy,
 drained and rinsed
1 × 1.35 kg (3 lb) chicken, quartered
1 garlic head, cut in half along the equator
1.9 liters (64 fl oz/8 cups) water
 or Chicken Stock (page 237)
2 tablespoons salt
450 g (1 lb) tomatillos, halved
80 g (2¾ oz) cilantro (coriander),
 roughly chopped
1 white onion, quartered
1–3 serrano peppers (chilies)
1 bunch radishes
40 g (1½ oz/⅓ cup) pepitas
 (pumpkin seeds), toasted
1 tablespoon ground cumin
1 tablespoon dried oregano
3 whole cloves, ground

To serve
½ head iceberg, romaine lettuce
 or green cabbage, finely shredded
2 avocados, diced
1 bunch cilantro (coriander),
 roughly chopped
½ white onion, very finely chopped
3 limes, cut into wedges
2 tablespoons dried oregano
dried ground chili, such as piquín,
 or a Mexican mix, such as Tajín
12 tostadas or 420 g (15 oz) tortilla chips

Pozole verde is a typical dish from the state of Guerrero, although there are many versions in other states of Mexico. Other variations of green pozole include epazote, a fragrant herb widely used in Mexico. The soup can vary in its intensity based on how many serrano peppers (chilies) are used. Adding one will flavor the soup, while adding two or three will intensify the heat level. The accompaniments are the most fun part of eating pozole verde. Everyone can alter the soup to their personal tastes, or even change the flavors and garnishes between starting and finishing the bowl.

Place the poblano peppers under a broiler (grill) until they are charred, turning them over once the first side is charred. Remove and leave to cool. Once cool, remove and discard the stems and inner seeds. Set aside.

Place the hominy in a large pot. Add the chicken, garlic, water or stock and 2 tablespoons salt. Bring to the boil, then reduce the heat to a gentle simmer and simmer for 30 minutes, removing the breast portions after 15 minutes. The juices of the chicken should run clear.

When the chicken is cooked, remove from the pot and leave until cool enough to handle, then remove the chicken skin and discard. Using your hands, shred all the meat and discard the bones. Set the meat aside. Alternatively, don't shred the chicken and just cut it into pieces.

Place the poblano peppers, tomatillos, cilantro, onion, serrano peppers, radish greens (slice and reserve the radishes as an accompaniment), pepitas, cumin, oregano, cloves, and 240 ml (8 fl oz/1 cup) of the broth from cooking the chicken in a blender and process until puréed as finely as possible.

Add the purée to the pot with the hominy and simmer for 15–20 minutes over a low heat until the salsa changes in color from bright green to olive green. Add the chicken to the soup and season with salt and freshly ground black pepper. Serve with the accompaniments, including the radishes reserved from the soup.

Sopa de Lima

Serves 4

1 × 1.35 kg (3 lb) chicken, quartered
1450 ml (49 fl oz/6 cups) water
  or Chicken Stock (page 237)
1 large white onion, halved
8 garlic cloves (4 peeled, 4 unpeeled)
2 dried bay leaves
4 whole cloves
7.5 cm (3 in) piece cinnamon stick
15 whole black peppercorns
¼ teaspoon dried oregano
2 tablespoons salt
2 roma or plum tomatoes, halved
1 small green bell pepper (capsicum),
  seeded and chopped
3 tablespoons lime juice, plus 1 extra lime,
  to garnish
3 tablespoons grapefruit juice
40 g (1½ oz) cilantro (coriander),
  roughly chopped
Tortilla Chips (see below)

Sopa de lima is the Mayan poultry and lime soup that's popular up and down the Yucatán. The soup is a light meal, with bright and refreshing flavors. A combination of lime and grapefruit juice provides the acidity and bitterness of the native Mexican lima ágria, typically unavailable in other parts of the world. However, if you are lucky enough to be able to source fresh lima ágria, omit the lime and grapefruit and add about 4 tablespoons of the fresh juice. If the soup is not perky enough, add lime juice, a little at a time, until the flavor is sufficiently bright. Occasionally, this soup is made from beef or pork. Tortilla chips are served on the side, providing a crunch throughout the meal.

Place the chicken, water or stock, ½ onion, 4 peeled garlic cloves, bay leaves, cloves, cinnamon, peppercorns and oregano in a large pot with the salt. Weigh down the chicken under a few small plates to keep it submerged and gently simmer over a medium heat until the chicken pieces are cooked through, about 7–10 minutes for the breasts and 15–18 minutes for the legs and thighs. The meat should separate from the end of the leg bone when cooked, a thermometer will read 74°C (165°F) when inserted into the thickest part of the thigh or breast and the juices of the chicken will run clear.

When the chicken is cooked, remove from the pot and leave until cool enough to handle, then remove the chicken skin and discard. Using your hands, shred all the meat and discard the bones. Set the meat aside. Strain the broth and reserve.

Meanwhile, char the remaining unpeeled garlic and halved tomatoes in a cast-iron or heavy-bottomed pan placed over a high heat for 4–6 minutes. When both have blackened, remove from the heat and leave to cool. Peel the garlic and tomatoes and finely chop with the remaining onion and the bell pepper.

Wipe out the pot, then place over a medium–high heat and cook the chopped tomato mixture into the hot pan. Cook for 3–5 minutes until the vegetables are tender, but not browned. Add the reserved strained broth and bring to a gentle simmer.

Add the citrus juices, the reserved shredded chicken and cilantro to the soup and stir to combine. Season with salt and serve garnished with Tortilla chips.

Tortilla Chips

Serves 4

60 ml (2 fl oz/¼ cup) vegetable oil
4 small corn tortillas, sliced into strips

Warm the oil in a frying pan over a medium heat. When hot, add the tortilla strips and fry for 3 minutes, stirring frequently, until the tortilla strips are mostly crisp all over. Transfer the tortilla strips to a plate lined with paper towel to drain. Season with salt.

THE AMERICAS

Bott Boi

Serves 4

1 × 1.35 kg (3 lb) chicken
1.9 liters (64 fl oz/8 cups) water
   or Chicken Stock (page 237)
2 tablespoons salt
1 yellow onion, cut into medium dice
4 carrots, cut into 5 mm (¼ in) rounds
4 celery ribs (stalks), cut into
   5 mm (¼ in) cubes
pinch of saffron threads
3 large potatoes, peeled and sliced
   as thinly as possible

Noodles
350 g (12½ oz/2½ cups) all-purpose
   (plain) flour, plus extra for dusting
15 g (½ oz) unsalted butter
½ teaspoon baking powder
2 large eggs
120 ml (4 fl oz/½ cup) whole (full-cream)
   milk, plus extra as needed

A relative of the American South's Chicken and Dumplings (page 63), bott boi was created in central and southeastern Pennsylvania. This dish can be made in big quantities, making it convenient for large community events in these rural farming areas. Featured meat may vary from chicken and can include ham or beef simmered in stock, with the same dish preparation. The noodles or dumplings are a characteristic staple of the Pennsylvania Dutch and English diets; the region is rich in immigrants from these backgrounds.

Place the chicken and water or stock in a large pot with 2 tablespoons salt. Weigh down the chicken under a few small plates to keep it submerged and simmer gently over a medium heat until the chicken pieces are cooked through, about 7–10 minutes for the breasts and 15–18 minutes for the legs and thighs. The meat should separate from the end of the leg bone when cooked, a thermometer will read 74°C (165°F) when inserted into the thickest part of the thigh or breast and the juices of the chicken will run clear.

Meanwhile, make the dough for the noodles. Place the flour, butter and baking powder in a bowl and, using your fingers, break the butter into tiny bits into the flour. Add the eggs and milk and mix with a spoon until the dough comes together. If the dough is too dry, add more milk, 1 teaspoon at a time, until all the ingredients are incorporated and the dough is cohesive and soft. Do not knead more than is necessary or the noodles will be tough.

Roll the dough out on a lightly floured work surface as thinly as possible, then cut into 5 cm (2 in) squares. Place on a baking tray and freeze for 30 minutes.

When the chicken is cooked, remove from the pot and leave until cool enough to handle, then remove the chicken skin and discard. Using your hands, shred all the meat and discard the bones. Set the meat aside. Strain the broth and reserve.

Wipe out the pot, then place over a medium heat, add the onion, carrot, celery and saffron and cover with just enough of the reserved broth to cover. Cook for 3–5 minutes until the vegetables are soft.

Remove the pot from the heat and stir the reserved chicken into the cooked vegetables in the pot, then add a layer of noodles, making sure the noodles aren't touching. Add just enough broth to barely cover the noodles, then add a layer of potatoes and another layer of broth. Repeat with the noodles, potatoes and broth, finishing with a layer of noodles.

Place the pot back on the stove and cook over a medium–high heat until the bott boi simmers, then reduce the heat to very low. Cover with a lid and cook for 20–30 minutes until the noodles are cooked through and the potatoes are tender. Stir to combine the ingredients and season with salt and freshly ground black pepper.

Chicken and Slicks

Serves 4–6

1 × 1.35 kg (3 lb) chicken, quartered
1 yellow onion, halved
1 garlic head, cut in half on the equator
½ teaspoon black peppercorns
80 g (2¾ oz) parsley, stems reserved
    and leaves chopped
1½ teaspoons salt
1.9 liters (64 fl oz/8 cups) water
    or Chicken Stock (page 237)
juice of 1 lemon
pinch of ground nutmeg

Dumplings
140 g (5 oz/1 cup) all-purpose (plain)
    flour, plus extra for dusting
45 g (1½ oz) unsalted butter, softened
1 teaspoon baking powder
½ teaspoon salt
60 ml (2 fl oz/¼ cup) whole (full-cream) milk,
    plus extra as needed

Somewhere between noodles and dumplings, slicks are old-school Carolina Appalachian fare at its best. They are basically thin, poached biscuits (scones), and this recipe is as tender as it gets. Chill the rolled and cut dough before poaching, and serve as soon as they are ready; these slicks are perfectly tender and will not hold up like sturdier noodles. The bits of excess flour on the slicks will slightly thicken the broth, giving the soup more body. Some slicks are cut into squares, while other recipes call for cutting slicks into long, thick noodle-like shapes. Slicks earned their name from their texture – slick and slippery.

Place the chicken, onion, garlic, peppercorns, parsley stems, and salt in a large pot. Add the water or stock and bring to the boil over a medium–high heat, then reduce the heat to medium and simmer gently until the chicken pieces are cooked through, about 7–10 minutes for the breasts and 15–18 minutes for the legs and thighs. The meat should separate from the end of the leg bone when cooked, a thermometer will read 74°C (165°F) when inserted into the thickest part of the thigh or breast and the juices of the chicken will run clear.

Meanwhile, make the dumpling dough. Stir the flour, butter, baking powder and salt together in a bowl, mashing with a fork until the mixture resembles coarse wet crumbs. Stir in the milk until it forms a dough. Knead the dough a couple of times, just to make it into a cohesive ball. If the dough seems dry, add more milk, 1 teaspoon at a time, until it comes together. Cover with plastic wrap and leave for about 20 minutes.

When the chicken is cooked, remove from the pot and leave until cool enough to handle, then remove the chicken skin and discard. Using your hands, shred all the meat and discard the bones. Set the meat aside. Strain the broth, pour back into the pot and bring to a gentle simmer over a medium heat.

Roll the dumpling dough out on a floured work surface into a rough 25 cm (10 in) square, about 5 mm (¼ in) thick. Cut the dough into 4 cm (1½ in) wide strips, then cut each strip into 4 cm (1½ in) squares.

Add the reserved chicken and the dumplings to the broth, one at a time. Cover and simmer for 2–4 minutes until the dumplings have puffed slightly and are cooked through. Stir gently once or twice to make sure that they don't stick to each other. Stir in the chopped parsley leaves, lemon juice and nutmeg and serve.

Chicken Gumbo with Okra

Serves 4–6

210 g (7½ oz/1½ cups) all-purpose
   (plain) flour
1 teaspoon finely ground black pepper
1¼ teaspoons finely ground white pepper
1 teaspoon mild mustard powder
1½ teaspoons cayenne pepper
1½ teaspoons paprika
1 teaspoon filé powder
1 × 1.35 kg (3 lb) chicken, quartered
1450 ml (49 fl oz/6 cups) water
   or Chicken Stock (page 237)
2 tablespoons salt
225 g (8 oz) bacon drippings or butter
1 yellow onion, cut into 5 mm (¼ in) cubes
2 celery ribs (stalks), cut into
   5 mm (¼ in) cubes
3 garlic cloves, very finely chopped
1 green bell pepper (capsicum), seeded and
   cut into 5 mm (¼ in) cubes
2 bay leaves
225 g (8 oz) andouille or kielbasa
   sausage, cut into 1 cm (½ in) pieces
100 g (3½ oz/1½ cups) okra, cut
   into 1 cm (½ in) pieces
225 g (8 oz) prawns,
   peeled and deveined

Creole gumbo is the state dish of Louisiana and has roots in France (bouillabaisse) and West Africa (okra). The dish can be made from fish or fowl, but smoked sausage is added to either variation. The traditional base is made from onion, celery and green bell pepper (capsicum), to which flour and fat (butter, oil) are added to make a roux. The roux is cooked until it is very toasted and dark before stock is added. Filé (dried and ground sassafras leaves) is a traditional thickening agent. This stewy dish is always served with steamed white rice and/or potato salad, placed in the same bowl. Other variations include rabbit and snails, various available fish and Southern fowl.

Mix the flour, peppers, mustard, cayenne, paprika and filé together in a bowl. Set aside.

Place the chicken and water or stock in a large pot with the salt. Weigh down the chicken under a few small plates to keep it submerged and simmer gently over a medium heat until the chicken pieces are cooked, about 7–10 minutes for the breasts and 15–18 minutes for the legs and thighs. The meat should separate from the end of the leg bone when cooked, a thermometer will read 74°C (165°F) when inserted into the thickest part of the thigh or breast and the juices of the chicken will run clear.

When the chicken is cooked, remove from the pot and leave until cool enough to handle, then remove the chicken skin and discard. Using your hands, shred all the meat and discard the bones. Set the meat aside and reserve the broth.

Wipe out the pot, then melt the bacon drippings or butter over a medium heat. Add the onion, celery, garlic, green bell pepper and bay leaves and cook slowly, stirring constantly, for 3–4 minutes until the vegetables are soft. Stir in the reserved flour mix and cook for 8–10 minutes until the flour is golden brown. Season lightly with salt and freshly ground black pepper, then add the reserved stock and the sausage and cook at a slow simmer for 5–8 minutes until the soup thickens. Add the okra, prawns and reserved chicken and cook for a further 3–4 minutes just until the prawns are cooked and the okra is tender. Adjust the seasoning and serve.

MATZO BALLS

One large or a couple small? Matzo/matzah balls: one size does not fit all. Like a perfectly cooked steak or a favorite style of eggs for breakfast, everyone will have their ideal. Considerations of size include aesthetic (how the balls fit in the bowl), managing ball to broth ratio, and when one is gone, will you have another left to enjoy?

Texture is the question of the century. You like what you like, just as with anything else. Some like it pillowy and tender, others prefer tender on the outside with a little chew in the inside. Dense matzo balls show novice skill.

Use matzo or matzo meal? Matzo meal will provide the same consistency every time; if you grind your own, you may have variation.

60

Isabel's Matzo Ball Soup

Serves 4

2 tablespoons rendered chicken
   fat or olive oil
2 large eggs
125 g (4½ oz/½ cup) matzo meal
2 tablespoons water
1 teaspoon salt
1.9 liters (64 fl oz/8 cups)
   Chicken Stock (page 237)
2 tablespoons roughly chopped
   dill, to garnish

The story goes like this: My mom's (Isabel's) matzo balls were never as tender as she wished until she made a batch of matzo balls, turned off the heat and left them in the poaching liquid while we went to services at the synagogue. When we returned to eat dinner, the balls, sitting in the warm water for an hour or two, softened and plumped up. Her, and now my, cooking method was changed forever. I find that the perfect balance is poaching for 30 minutes, then letting the matzo balls rest in the poaching liquid, covered, for a further 30 minutes. The centers of the balls become a little chewy and the exteriors are soft and fluffy, just the way I like them.

Place the chicken fat or olive oil, eggs, matzo meal, water and salt in a large bowl and stir until completely combined. Cover with plastic wrap and chill for 30 minutes.

Bring a large pot of very well salted water to a simmer. Scoop the batter into soft but not packed golf-ball-sized balls, then lightly drop into the simmering water, partially cover with a lid and simmer for 30 minutes. Turn off the heat and leave to stand, still covered with a lid, for 30 minutes.

Gently heat the stock until hot, season with salt and ladle into serving bowls with 2 matzo balls each. Garnish with dill.

My Neighbor's Chicken Soup

Serves 6

3 tablespoons vegetable oil
900 g (2 lb) boneless, skinless chicken thighs
3 large carrots, cut into 1 cm
    (½ in) rounds
1 large yellow onion, cut into 5 mm
    (¼ in) cubes
8 celery ribs (stalks), cut into 1 cm
    (½ in) cubes
3 garlic cloves, very finely chopped
15 cm (6 in) rosemary sprig, leaves
    very finely chopped
6 sage leaves, very finely chopped
1 tablespoon garlic powder
1 teaspoon dried thyme
½ teaspoon fennel seeds, ground
3 yellow potatoes, such as yukon gold,
    peeled and cut into 1 cm (½ in) cubes
2.4 liters (81 fl oz/10 cups) Chicken
    Stock (page 237)
115 g (4 oz) extra-wide egg noodles

I live in a really special neighborhood. I've known most of the kids since birth or from a really young age, and the adults and kids all hang out in our front yards and spend time together. We celebrate holidays together, share meals and are good friends. My next-door neighbor, Matt, makes awesome chicken soup. It is a classic Eastern European style, adding rosemary and using boneless chicken to speed up the cooking process. I have been the lucky recipient of a container of this soup sitting on my porch when I have come home from working at my restaurant, late at night. Sometimes it is still hot, sometimes it has cooled off, sometimes I heat it up, and other times I eat it cold. It's the best. If you are not planning on eating the soup the day you make it, Matt recommends cooking the noodles in the soup when you reheat it. It tastes better the next day anyway, he insists. I have never been able to wait until the next day to eat my ration!

Heat the oil in a large pot over a medium heat. Add the chicken and season lightly with salt and freshly ground black pepper. Cook for 4–6 minutes until the chicken is lightly browned all over. Add the carrots, onion, celery and garlic to the pot and stir to combine. Add the rosemary, sage, garlic powder, thyme and fennel. Stir and cook for 3–4 minutes until the vegetables just start to become tender. Add the potatoes and stock, then stir and bring to a simmer. Cook for 20 minutes, or until the vegetables and chicken are tender.

When the chicken is cooked, remove from the pot and, using your hands, shred the meat. Return the meat to the pot, add the noodles and cook for a further 9–10 minutes. Season with salt and pepper.

Chicken and Dumplings

Serves 4

1 × 1.35 kg (3 lb) chicken, quartered
1.9 liters (64 fl oz/8 cups) water
   or Chicken Stock (page 237)
2 tablespoons salt
70 g (2½ oz) butter
1 yellow onion, cut into 5 mm (¼ in) cubes
2 carrots, cut into 5 mm (¼ in) cubes
2 celery ribs (stalks), cut into 5 mm
   (¼ in) cubes
3 garlic cloves, very finely chopped
1 thyme sprig
2 bay leaves
85 g (3 oz) extra all-purpose
   (plain) flour
120 ml (4 fl oz) heavy (double) cream
230 g (8 oz/1½ cups) peas, fresh or frozen
4 tablespoons very finely chopped parsley

Dumplings
300 g (10½ oz/2 cups) all-purpose
   (plain) flour
1 tablespoon baking powder
1 teaspoon salt
320 ml (11 fl oz) heavy (double) cream

The iconic dish of the American South and Midwest, chicken and dumplings, is an easily loved comfort food. It is easy to make, inexpensive, and there are simple variations. Some claim that chicken and dumplings is native to the American South or Midwest, but similar dishes have been made by French Canadians, and even in Ireland and Germany. All variations feature a chicken broth base, sometimes with vegetables, sometimes without, with a pastry or biscuit (scone) topping that is steamed on top of the soup. Salt and pepper tend to be the only seasoning, but sometimes, a few fresh herbs such as thyme, dill and parsley are included. Chicken and Slicks (page 57), from the American Appalachians, is another variety, while the Pennsylvania Dutch's version is called Bott Boi (page 56).

Place the chicken and water or stock in a large pot with the salt. Weigh down the chicken under a few small plates to keep it submerged and simmer gently over a medium heat until the chicken pieces are cooked through, about 7–10 minutes for the breasts and 15–18 minutes for the legs and thighs. The meat should separate from the end of the leg bone when cooked, a thermometer will read 74°C (165°F) when inserted into the thickest part of the thigh or breast and the juices of the chicken will run clear.

When the chicken is cooked, remove from the pot and leave until cool enough to handle, then remove the chicken skin and discard. Using your hands, shred all the meat and discard the bones. Set the meat aside and reserve the broth.

Wipe out the pot, then add the butter and melt over a medium heat. Add the onion, carrots, celery, garlic, thyme and bay leaves and cook slowly, stirring constantly for 3–4 minutes until the vegetables are soft. Stir in the flour and season lightly with salt and freshly ground black pepper. Add the reserved stock, which should measure 1450 ml (49 fl oz/6 cups), adding water if necessary to make the correct volume. Stir in the cream and cook at a slow simmer for 3–5 minutes until the soup thickens slightly.

To make the dumplings, mix the flour with the baking powder and salt in a small bowl. Add the cream and stir just until a dough forms. The texture of the dough should be slightly wetter than biscuit (scone) dough.

Add the reserved chicken, peas and parsley to the soup, then adjust the seasoning. Using two spoons, make small dumplings and add directly to the soup. Simmer gently for a further 3–4 minutes until the dumplings are cooked.

Green Chili Chicken Stew

Serves 4–6

3 tablespoons vegetable oil
1 yellow onion, cut into 1 cm (½ in) cubes
4 garlic cloves, very finely chopped
2 bay leaves
2 teaspoons ground cumin
½ teaspoon dried oregano
950 ml (32½ fl oz/4 cups) Chicken Stock
   (page 237)
225 g (8 oz) fire-roasted hatch green chilies,
   cut into 1 cm (½ in) cubes
670 g (1½ lb) boneless, skinless
   chicken breasts
1 large potato, peeled and cut into 1 cm
   (½ in) cubes
150 g (5½ oz/1 cup) frozen corn kernels
80 g (2¾ oz) cilantro (coriander),
   roughly chopped
2 limes, cut into wedges
240 ml (8 fl oz/1 cup) sour cream
flour tortillas or tortilla chips, to serve

Specific to the American Southwest, Hatch green chilies are harvested and fire-roasted in autumn. This notable pepper, similar to the more common Anaheim chili, hails from the Hatch Valley in southern New Mexico and has an enthusiastic fan base. Frozen and jarred hatch chilies are marketed nationwide in the US. Green chili stew is a favorite dish in the Hatch Valley and throughout New Mexico. Serve with corn or flour tortillas, or tortilla chips for an added crunch. If a less spicy dish is preferred, remove the seeds from the chilies before adding to the stew.

Heat the oil in a large pot over a medium–high heat. Add the onion, garlic, bay leaves, cumin and oregano and stir to combine. Cook for 3–4 minutes until the onion is translucent. Add the stock, chilies and chicken and simmer gently for 6–9 minutes until the chicken is cooked through. Rapid cooking of chicken breasts will yield tough and dry meat, so make sure to keep the simmer slow and gentle. Add the potato 4–5 minutes before the chicken is cooked.

When the chicken is cooked, remove from the pot and leave until cool enough to handle. Using two forks, shred the chicken and return the meat to the pot.

Add the corn and cilantro, then season with salt and freshly ground black pepper. Serve with lime wedges, sour cream and tortillas.

Pennsylvania Dutch Rivel

Serves 4

2 × whole skinless chicken legs (approx.
 670 g/1½ lb), legs and thighs on the bone,
 or 4 boneless, skinless chicken thighs
1.9 liters (64 fl oz/8 cups) water
 or Chicken Stock (page 237)
1 yellow onion, cut into medium dice
1 celery rib (stalk), cut into medium dice
1 large carrot, cut into medium dice
1 tablespoon salt
600 g (1 lb 5 oz/3 cups) fresh corn kernels,
 cut off cob from about 8 ears
3 parsley sprigs, roughly chopped

Rivels
140 g (5 oz/1 cup) all-purpose (plain) flour
1 teaspoon salt
¼ teaspoon black pepper
1–2 large eggs

Think corn chowder, then add in chunks of chicken and hearty, doughy dumplings. This is the foundation of Pennsylvania Dutch rivel soup, found in the Mennonite and Amish culture in Pennsylvania. Their tradition of farming and their need for sturdy meals accompanying a day of hard physical work is met with a solid culinary culture. In more frugal times, the soup would simply feature a meat broth with dumplings, omitting any of the more costly ingredients.

Bring the chicken, water or stock, onion, celery, carrot and salt to a simmer in a large pot over a medium–high heat. Reduce the heat and maintain a gentle simmer. Cook for 20 minutes, or until the chicken is cooked through and the meat separates from the end of the leg bone.

Meanwhile, make the rivels. Mix the flour, salt and black pepper together in a bowl. Whisk the eggs in a separate bowl, then drizzle the eggs into the flour mixture, stirring with a fork, until the flour mixture makes pea-sized (and some larger) dumplings. All the egg mixture may not be needed – the dough should not be too wet.

When the chicken is cooked, remove from the pot and leave until cool enough to handle. Add the rivels and corn to the soup and simmer gently for 5 minutes. Halfway through cooking the rivels, shred the chicken meat and add to the soup. Season with salt and pepper, then garnish with parsley and serve.

CENTRAL + SOUTH AMERICA + THE CARIBBEAN

Argentina, Belize, Brazil, Colombia, Cuba, Dominican Republic, Guatemala, Haiti, Panama, Peru, Puerto Rico, Suriname, Trinidad

Latin American cuisine is highly diverse, varying in style from country to country. Many countries utilize corn (fresh and dried) as a staple, as well as a wide variety of root vegetables, tomatoes, beans and chilies. Long-grain rice and potatoes are common in most soups. While some regional cuisines feature more intense and fiery chilies, others use milder local varieties.

Sofrito is the foundation of most soups and stews. It is a combination of sautéed onions, garlic, green bell peppers (capsicum), herbs and tomatoes. This combination of savory vegetables gives a recognizable flavor to Latin cuisine, creating a distinctive profile.

Some of the sweetest soup broths come from this region, using various combinations of simmered starchy root vegetables and corn to add sweetness to the dish, while chilies are used to warm the soup rather than create any intense heat.

Belize serves Escabeche (page 70), a chicken soup with bright, acidic flavors that wake up the palate in the warmer weather. The root vegetables in Colombia's and Panama's Sancocho (pages 76 and 88) make a sweet and comforting broth. This region's soups vary in flavor and texture, and all are shaped by the local produce they are based on.

Cazuela Gaucho

Serves 6

90 ml (3 fl oz) vegetable oil,
    plus extra, if needed
12 chicken legs
280 g (10 oz/2 cups) all-purpose (plain) flour
2 large carrots, cut into 5 mm (¼ in) rounds
225 g (8 oz) winter squash (pumpkin),
    such as butternut, cut into 2.5 cm (1 in)
    pieces
1 parsnip, cut into 5 mm (¼ in) rounds
2 yellow onions, cut into 1 cm (½ in) cubes
2 garlic cloves, very finely chopped
2 teaspoons paprika
2 bay leaves
60 g (2 oz/⅓ cup) pearl barley
120 ml (4 fl oz/½ cup) white wine
1.9 liters (64 fl oz/8 cups) Chicken Stock
    (page 237)
4 yellow potatoes, peeled and cut into
    large wedges
2 ears fresh corn, quartered
140 g (5 oz) frozen peas
115 g (4 oz) green beans, cut into 2.5 cm
    (1 in) pieces

Variations of this soup are typical throughout much of South America. The root vegetables lend hearty and rich components, while at the same time sweetening the broth. Vegetables may vary, depending on region, season and availability, but this is a standard collection. Leftovers may need an addition of stock, as the starchy vegetables may absorb some liquid.

Heat a large pot over a medium–high heat and add the oil. Season the chicken legs with salt and dredge in flour. When the oil is hot, shake off the excess flour and sear the chicken legs for 4–6 minutes on all sides until golden brown. Remove the chicken legs from the oil and set aside.

Add more oil to the pot, if needed, then add the carrots, squash and parsnip and cook, stirring constantly, for a few minutes. Add the onions, garlic, paprika, bay leaves and barley. Stir and cook for a few minutes until the vegetables have softened and the onions are translucent. Add the wine and cook for a further 2–4 minutes until it evaporates. Add the stock and bring to a simmer, then add the chicken back into the pot. Season the soup with salt and simmer for 20–25 minutes until the barley is almost tender, then add the potatoes and corn and simmer slowly for a further 5 minutes, or until the potatoes are almost tender. Add the peas and green beans, stir and cook for 3–4 minutes. Make sure the potatoes are cooked through. Season with salt and freshly ground black pepper and serve.

Escabeche

Serves 4

1 × 1.35 kg (3 lb) chicken, quartered
  or 4 whole chicken legs (leg and
  thigh connected)
1.9 liters (64 fl oz/8 cups) water or
  Chicken Stock (page 237)
10 whole allspice berries
6 Belizean oregano leaves or 4 teaspoons
  dried oregano
12 cloves
2 teaspoons cumin seeds
3 teaspoons black peppercorns
2 bay leaves
2 cinnamon sticks
4 garlic cloves, smashed
2 tablespoons salt
2 large white onions, thinly sliced
120–240 ml (4–8 fl oz/½–1 cup)
  distilled white vinegar
Pickled Jalapeños Peppers (see opposite)
2 tablespoons vegetable oil

This soup is eaten with chicken on Sundays, or on special occasions. It is delicate, bright and acidic. The onions, when steeped in the soup after being lightly cooked in boiling water, add sweetness to the broth. This sweetness is counterbalanced by the white vinegar, which adds a pickled flavor. The two juxtapose and complement one another. Typically eaten with warm corn tortillas, and a glass of cola, this is a casual and special meal.

Place the chicken, water or stock, allspice, oregano, cloves, cumin, pepper, bay leaves, cinnamon sticks and garlic in a large pot with the salt. Weigh down the chicken under a few small plates to keep it submerged and simmer gently over a medium heat until the chicken pieces are cooked through, about 7–10 minutes for the breasts and 15–18 minutes for the legs and thighs. The meat should separate from the end of the leg bone when cooked, a thermometer will read 74°C (165°F) when inserted into the thickest part of the thigh or breast and the juices of the chicken will run clear.

When the chicken is cooked, remove from the pot and set aside. Strain the broth and pour back into the pot.

Meanwhile, place the sliced onions in a bowl and cover with boiling water. Leave for 5 minutes, then strain the water and pour fresh boiling water over the onions and leave for a further 5 minutes. Strain again, then add the onions to the broth. Season with salt and add 120 ml (4 fl oz/½ cup) of the vinegar, adding extra as needed to taste. Do the same with the pickled jalapeños and some of the pickle brine from the jalapeños. The broth should taste somewhat like pickle brine (vinegar) with some spicy heat (jalapeños) and sweetness (onions).

Season the cooked chicken pieces with salt and freshly ground black pepper and drizzle with the oil. Place the chicken pieces on a baking tray and cook under the broiler (grill) for 2–5 minutes until the skin is golden and crispy. Keep an eye on the chicken to make sure it doesn't burn.

Season the soup, then ladle the broth and the onions and jalapeños into bowls and serve with a piece of chicken in the broth.

Serves 4

450 g (1 lb) green jalapeño chilies, stemmed
    and cut into 5 mm (¼ in) rounds
480 ml (16 fl oz/2 cups) distilled white
    vinegar
½ teaspoon salt

Pickled Jalapeño Peppers

Place the sliced peppers into a plastic or glass container, add the vinegar and salt and mix to combine. Cover and shake to disperse the salt. Store in an airtight container in the refrigerator for 1 week before serving, and up to 1 year.

71

Canja de Galinha

Serves 4–6

2 tablespoons olive oil
1 yellow onion, cut into 5 mm (¼ in) cubes
2 garlic cloves, thinly sliced
1 × 1.35 kg (3 lb) chicken, quartered
150 g (5½ oz/¾ cup) white long-grain rice
1.9 liters (64 fl oz/8 cups) water or
    Chicken Stock (page 237)
1 large potato, peeled and cut into 4 cm
    (1½ in) cubes
2 large carrots, cut into 1 cm (½ in) rounds
1 tablespoon salt
½ bunch parsley, roughly chopped,
    to garnish

Brazilian canja de galinha is often referred to as Brazilian congee. Thick with very tender grains of rice, this soup's rice is not as broken down as Asian congee. Portuguese canja de galinha varies slightly (see page 232) and will tend to have a hard poached egg in the soup, with the addition of sausage or lemon. Brazilians lightly flavor their soup with olive oil, salt, pepper, parsley and sometimes mint. It is not unusual to see corn as an addition to this soup.

Heat the oil in a large pot over a medium–high heat. Add the onion and cook for 3–4 minutes until the onion is translucent. Add the garlic and sauté for 20 seconds, then add the chicken, rice, water or stock, the vegetables and the salt and stir to combine. Bring to the boil, then reduce the heat to a gentle simmer. Place a few small plates on top of the chicken, making sure it remains submerged, and simmer gently over a medium heat for 20–30 minutes until the chicken is cooked through. When the chicken is cooked, a thermometer will read 74°C (165°F) when inserted into thickest part of the thigh or into the breast meat and the juices of the chicken will run clear.

Remove the chicken from the pot and leave until cool enough to handle, then remove the chicken skin and discard. Using your hands, shred all the meat and discard the bones. Add the meat to the soup and stir to combine. Season with salt and freshly ground black pepper. Serve the soup warm with chopped parsley sprinkled on top.

Ajiaco Bogotano

Serves 4–6

1 × 1.35 kg (3 lb) chicken, quartered
1.9 liters (64 fl oz/8 cups) water or
    Chicken Stock (page 237)
2 tablespoons salt
1 leek, cut into thin half-moons
1 green bell pepper (capsicum), cut into
    1 cm (½ in) cubes
2 ears fresh corn, quartered
2 celery ribs (stalks), cut into 1 cm
    (½ in) cubes
2 large carrots, cut into 2.5 cm (1 in) lengths
900 g (2 lb) assorted potatoes, peeled
    and quartered
6 garlic cloves, very finely chopped
2 thyme sprigs
2 bay leaves
1 teaspoon dried oregano
115 g (4 oz) green beans, cut into 1 cm
    (½ in) lengths
40 g (1½ oz) cilantro (coriander), roughly
    chopped, including stems
1 lime

To serve
Aji Picante (see opposite)
1 avocado, diced
1 tablespoon capers
240 ml (8 fl oz/1 cup) cream

There are different versions of ajiaco, variations based on the three countries it is served in: Colombia, Cuba and Peru. It is usually made with chicken and three kinds of potatoes, corn and an herb called guascas. This herb gives the soup a wonderful flavor, but is difficult to find outside of these countries. It is very important to use guascas and papa criolla when available – they are the key ingredients in this dish. Even if you do not have access to guascas, try to find a few varieties of potatoes for this soup.

Place the chicken and water or stock in a large pot with the salt. Weigh down the chicken under a few small plates to keep it submerged and simmer gently over a medium heat until the chicken pieces are cooked through, about 7–10 minutes for the breasts and 15–18 minutes for the legs and thighs. The meat should separate from the end of the leg bone when cooked, a thermometer will read 74°C (165°F) when inserted into the thickest part of the thigh or breast and the juices of the chicken will run clear.

When the chicken is cooked, remove from the pot and leave until cool enough to handle, then remove the skin and discard. Using your hands, shred all the meat and discard the bones. Set the meat aside.

Keep the broth in the pot and add the leek, bell pepper, corn, celery, carrots, potatoes and garlic. Add the thyme, bay leaves and oregano and season lightly with salt. Cook slowly, stirring constantly for 10 minutes, or until the vegetables are soft. When the potatoes are tender, mash with a spoon to break them up and thicken the broth. Add the green beans and cilantro, then stir to combine and cook for another 2 minutes.

Add the chicken to the soup and season with salt and freshly ground black pepper. Squeeze the lime juice into the soup, adding as much tangy flavor as possible without it becoming sour. Serve with aji picante and accompaniments.

Aji Picante (Salsa)

4 spring (green) onions, finely chopped
2 roma or plum tomatoes, finely chopped
1 jalapeño chili, very finely chopped
40 g (1½ oz) cilantro (coriander),
    roughly chopped, including stems
3 tablespoons distilled white vinegar

Place all the ingredients in a bowl, season with salt and stir to combine. Store in an airtight container in the refrigerator for 2–3 days.

Sancocho

Serves 6

3 tablespoons vegetable oil
6 spring (green) onions, cut into 1 cm
(½ in) lengths
1 yellow onion, cut into 1 cm (½ in) cubes
4 garlic cloves, very finely chopped
2 teaspoons ground cumin
1 roma or plum tomato, cut into 1 cm
(½ in) cubes
6 × boneless, skinless chicken thighs
(approx. 420 g/15 oz)
950 ml (32½ fl oz/4 cups) water or
Chicken Stock (page 237)
4 potatoes, peeled and quartered
2 whole yucca or green plantains
2 ears fresh corn
1 small green plantain, peeled and cut into
2.5 cm (1 in) pieces
80 g (2¾ oz) cilantro (coriander),
roughly chopped

Sancocho is a hearty soup with variations throughout Central and South America. Some regional recipes feature beef, pork or chicken, while others combine several meats. The vegetables in regional variations are dictated by what is grown in the specific area. This rendition is traditional in the region of Antioquia, Colombia, and combines potatoes, yucca, corn, plantains and meat. Root vegetables cooked with meats are foundations of many cuisines, as seen with French poule au pot (see page 211).

Heat the oil in a large pot over a medium–high heat. Add the spring onions, onion, garlic and cumin and season lightly with salt. Cook for 3 minutes, or until the vegetables begin to become tender and the onion is translucent. Stir in the tomato and cook for another minute.

Add the chicken and water or stock and stir to combine, then bring to a simmer. Cook for 20 minutes, then add the potatoes, yucca, corn and plantain and cook for another 10 minutes, or until all the vegetables are tender. Stir in the cilantro and season with salt.

Sudado de Pollo

Serves 4–6

1 teaspoon cumin seeds
2 tablespoons rendered chicken fat
1 yellow onion, cut into 1 cm (½ in) cubes
½ red bell pepper (capsicum), cut into
    10 mm (½ in) cubes
2 garlic cloves, sliced
pinch of saffron threads
1 tablespoon achiote paste
320 g (11½ oz/2 cups) chopped tomatoes,
    or whole canned tomatoes, puréed
950 ml (32½ fl oz/4 cups) water or
    Chicken Stock (page 237)
1 tablespoon salt
8 × boneless, skinless chicken thighs
    (approx. 520 g/1 lb 2 oz)
8 small yellow potatoes, such as yukon
    gold, peeled and halved
20 g (¾ oz) cilantro (coriander),
    roughly chopped

Sudado de pollo translates as 'sweaty chicken'. This stewy soup, as other soups and stews in Colombia, is enjoyed daily by many, at any time of day. It is served with a side of rice, sliced avocado and sometimes a small salad. Variations may include yucca, green beans, carrots, corn or peas. And, while sometimes the dish is made as a stew, other times it is made with more liquid and is served as a soup.

Toast the cumin in a small sauté or frying pan over a high heat until the seeds become fragrant and just begin to pop. Remove from the heat immediately so that they do not burn and leave to cool completely, then grind to a powder in a spice grinder or spice mill. Set aside.

Melt the chicken fat in a large sauté or frying pan over a high heat. Add the onion, bell pepper, garlic, saffron and achiote and cook for 2–3 minutes until the onions are translucent. Add the cumin and tomatoes and stir to combine. Add the water or stock and the salt and bring to a simmer. Add the chicken and cook at a very gentle simmer for 20–25 minutes until the chicken is cooked through. Add the potatoes to the soup 10 minutes after adding the chicken; they should be tender when the chicken is cooked. Stir in the cilantro and season with salt and freshly ground black pepper.

Ajiaco

Cuba

Serves 6

225 g (8 oz) tasajo (dried beef), cut into 4 pieces
333 g (12 oz) beef stew meat (shoulder, chuck), cut into 2.5 m (1 in) cubes
225 g (8 oz) pork stew meat (shoulder), cut into 2.5 cm (1 in) cubes
2 tablespoons salt
1.9 liters (64 fl oz/8 cups) water or Chicken Stock (page 237)
1 large yellow onion, very finely chopped
4 garlic cloves, very finely chopped
1 green bell pepper (capsicum), very finely chopped
280 g (10 oz/1½ cups) whole canned tomatoes, puréed
2 × whole chicken legs (approx. 670 g/1½ lb), legs and thighs attached
2 ears fresh corn, cut into thirds
225 g (8 oz) yucca, cut into 5 cm (2 in) pieces
225 g (8 oz) sweet potato, cut into 5 cm (2 in) pieces
225 g (8 oz) boniato (white root yam), cut into 5 cm (2 in) pieces
2 green plantains, peeled and cut into 1 cm (½ in) rounds
225 g (8 oz) cooked chorizo, cut into 1 cm (½ in) rounds

Like a good Italian ragu, the recipe for ajiaco will vary from village to village and from home to home. Cuban ajiaco features many types of meat, while Colombian ajiaco typically only includes chicken and is garnished with cream and capers. Peru's ajiaco, on the other hand, is mostly made of potatoes cooked with garlic and a mix of yellow and red chilies. The richness of the root vegetables and the heartiness of the meats make this a filling and substantial meal.

Soak the tasajo in a bowl of cold water overnight. The next day, drain and discard the water.

Bring the tasajo, beef, pork, salt and the water or stock to the boil in a large pot over a medium–high heat. Reduce the heat to a simmer, cover with a lid and cook for 1 hour at a gentle simmer. Skim any scum that forms on the top of the pot and discard. Add the onion, garlic, bell pepper and tomatoes and cook for a further 30 minutes.

Add the chicken and cook for 15 minutes, then add the corn, yucca, sweet potato, boniato and plantains and cook for a further 10 minutes.

Stir in the chorizo and season with salt. To thicken the soup, mash a little of the cooked vegetables in the pot with a fork.

Sopa de Pollo

Cuba

Serves 4

60 ml (2 fl oz/¼ cup) vegetable oil
1 yellow onion, cut into 1 cm (½ in) cubes
3 carrots, cut into 1 cm (½ in) rounds
4 garlic cloves, thinly sliced
2 large bay leaves
1 tablespoon salt
large pinch of saffron threads
1450 ml (49 fl oz/6 cups) water or Chicken Stock (page 237)
225 g (8 oz) Tomato Sauce (page 239), or use store-bought
1 × 1.35 kg (3 lb) chicken, quartered
2 russet potatoes, peeled and cubed
2 taro roots (malanga), plantain or winter squash (pumpkin), peeled and cubed
140 g (5 oz) fideos or vermicelli/angel hair pasta, broken into quarters
3 tablespoons lime juice

Not unlike many chicken soups of Central and South America, this soup features rich and satisfying root vegetables that make it rib-sticky good. Based on exact region or personal preference, plantains, calabaza (orange-fleshed winter squash/pumpkin) and corn may be added to this dish. If making ahead, omit the noodles and cook in the broth just before serving.

Heat the oil in a large pot over a medium–high heat. Add the onions, carrots, garlic, bay leaves, the salt and saffron and cook for 3–4 minutes until the onions begin to become translucent. Add the water or stock, tomato sauce, chicken, potato and taro root. Weigh down the chicken under a few small plates to keep it submerged and bring to the boil, then immediately reduce the heat to a very low simmer. Cook for 20–30 minutes until the chicken is cooked through, a thermometer reads 74°C (165°F) when inserted into the thickest part of the thigh or breast and the juices of the chicken run clear.

When the chicken is cooked, remove from the pot and leave until cool enough to handle, then remove the chicken skin and discard. Using your hands, shred all the meat and discard the bones. Add the chicken to the soup with the fideos or pasta and cook at a low simmer for 3–4 minutes until the noodles are tender. Season with lime juice, salt and freshly ground black pepper and serve.

Caldo de Gallina
Criolla o Pollo

Dominican Republic

Serves 4

1 × 1.35 kg (3 lb) chicken, quartered
2 carrots, cut into 2.5 cm (1 in) pieces
1 yellow onion, cut into 1 cm (½ in) cubes
3 garlic cloves, halved
2 bay leaves
1.9 liters (64 fl oz/8 cups) water or
   Chicken Stock (page 237)
1 tablespoon salt
2 tablespoons rendered chicken fat
   or vegetable oil
3 celery ribs (stalks), cut into 1 cm
   (½ in) cubes
3 garlic cloves, thinly sliced
1 calabaza or winter squash (pumpkin),
   such as butternut, peeled, seeded and
   cut into 1 cm (½ in) cubes
115 g (4 oz) vermicelli or angel hair pasta,
   broken into 7.5 cm (3 in) pieces
½ bunch cilantro (coriander) leaves,
   roughly chopped, to garnish

Dominicans believe, like most cultures, that their chicken soup heals the sick. Like many chicken soups around the world, this one is brothy and comforting. Add noodles and the sweetness of squash, and you have a nutritious, tasty and satisfying dish. Noodles may absorb liquid from the broth; the soup will become thick. Add more stock as needed, or cook the noodles separately and add to individual bowls of soup. Other traditional additions to this soup are potato, carrots, yucca and oregano.

Place the chicken, carrots, onion, garlic and bay leaves in a pot large enough to snugly fit the chicken with the vegetables. Add the water or stock and the salt and weigh down the chicken under a few small plates to keep it submerged. Bring to the boil, then immediately reduce the heat to a very gentle simmer and cook, uncovered, for 20–30 minutes until the chicken is cooked through, a thermometer reads 74°C (165°F) when inserted into the thickest part of the thigh or breast and the juices of the chicken run clear.

When the chicken is cooked, strain the liquid to remove any solids and reserve the broth. Leave the chicken until cool enough to handle, then remove the chicken skin and discard. Using your hands, shred all the meat and discard the bones. Set the chicken aside.

Rinse and dry the pot, then add the chicken fat or oil and melt over a medium–high heat. Add the celery, garlic and calabaza or squash and cook for 4 minutes, stirring frequently, until the vegetables begin to soften. The calabaza should still be slightly undercooked. Season the vegetables with salt, add the reserved broth and bring to a gentle simmer. Cook for 3–5 minutes until the calabaza is tender. Add the pasta and chicken meat and simmer gently for a further 3–4 minutes until the pasta is cooked. Season with salt and garnish with cilantro.

Pepián

Serves 4

1 × 1.35 kg (3 lb) chicken, quartered
950 ml (32½ fl oz/4 cups) water or
    Chicken Stock (page 237)
3 yellow onions, 1 quartered,
    1 halved and 1 sliced
1 tablespoon salt
2 dried guaque chilies (guajillo)
2 dried pasa chilies (poblano/mulato)
55 g (2 oz/½ cup) raw pepitas (pumpkin
    seeds), plus extra to garnish
55 g (2 oz/scant ½ cup) sesame seeds,
    plus extra to garnish
40 g (1½ oz) coriander seeds
½ teaspoon black peppercorns
3 whole cloves
4 roma or plum tomatoes
1 tablespoon dried oregano
½ small cinnamon stick
720 ml (24½ fl oz/3 cups) water
2 garlic cloves
1 güisquil (chayote) squash, peeled and
    cut into 1 cm (½ in) cubes
450 g (1 lb) potatoes or combination of root
    vegetables, peeled and cut into 1 cm
    (½ in) cubes

Served at home, in restaurants and street carts, this is one of the iconic dishes of Guatemala. Hearty with chicken, or sometimes beef or pork, vegetables and chilies, pepián is a blend of Mayan and Spanish cultures. Variations of this soup include pear, carrot and corn. Guatemalans often serve the soup with a side of rice and warm corn tortillas, sometimes including chilies and chili sauce, as well.

Place the chicken in a large pot and add the water or stock. Add the quartered onion with the salt and simmer very gently over a medium heat until the chicken pieces are cooked through, about 7–10 minutes for the breasts and 15–18 minutes for the legs and thighs. The meat should separate from the end of the leg bone when cooked, a thermometer will read 74°C (165°F) when inserted into the thickest part of the thigh or breast and the juices of the chicken will run clear.

When the chicken is cooked, remove from the pot and leave until cool enough to handle, then remove the chicken skin and discard. Using your hands, shred all the meat and discard the bones. Set the meat aside.

Meanwhile, roast the dried chilies in a dry frying pan over a medium heat for 2–4 minutes until fragrant. The chilies should be roasted and fragrant, not blackened. When roasted, place the chilies in a large bowl. Roast the pepitas in the same pan over a medium–high heat for 3 minutes, stirring frequently, until golden. Add to the bowl with the chilies and repeat with the sesame seeds, coriander seeds, peppercorns and cloves. Char the halved onion and tomatoes in the dry frying pan over a high heat for 3–5 minutes until blackened and soft, then add to the other ingredients. Place all the toasted ingredients, together with the oregano, cinnamon and water in a blender and process for 4–5 minutes until completely puréed. Set aside.

Strain the broth through a fine-mesh sieve, then pour back into the pot with the sliced onion, garlic, squash and potatoes and simmer gently for 3–4 minutes. Add the puréed ingredients and stir in the chicken. Simmer gently for an additional 3–4 minutes. Season with salt and serve.

Pollo en Jocon

Serves 4–6

2 corn tortillas
670 g (1½ lb) fresh tomatillos, husked
1 × 1.35 kg (3 lb) chicken, quartered
1.9 liters (64 fl oz/8 cups) water or
    Chicken Stock (page 237)
2 tablespoons salt
55 g (2 oz/½ cup) pepitas (pumpkin
    seeds), toasted
40 g (1½ oz/¼ cup) sesame seeds,
    lightly toasted
80 g (2¾ oz) cilantro (coriander),
    roughly chopped
2 teaspoons ground cumin
3 tablespoons rendered chicken fat
    or vegetable oil
1 white onion, cut into 1 cm (½ in) cubes
2 green bell peppers (capsicum), seeded and
    cut into 1 cm (½ in) cubes
4 large garlic cloves, finely chopped
4 jalapeño chilies, seeded and cut into
    1 cm (½ in) cubes

To garnish
12 corn tortillas, warmed
2 avocados, sliced

Guatemala's chicken and tomatillo stew is a tangy and soulful dish popular with the Mayan population. The tomatillos make a bright green sauce, and the tortillas and seeds create a rich thickness. Serve with sliced avocado and corn tortillas, and a side of steamed rice.

Submerge the 2 corn tortillas in a bowl of warm water for 30 minutes, or until tender and soggy. Remove from the water and reserve.

Place the tomatillos in a small pot, cover with water and bring to a simmer. Cook for 15–20 minutes until very tender. Strain the tomatillos and reserve.

Place the chicken and water or stock in a large pot with the salt. Weigh down the chicken under a few small plates to keep it submerged and simmer gently over a medium heat until the chicken pieces are cooked, about 7–10 minutes for the breasts and 15–18 minutes for the legs and thighs. The meat should separate from the end of the leg bone when cooked, a thermometer will read 74°C (165°F) when inserted into the thickest part of the thigh or breast and the juices of the chicken will run clear.

When the chicken is cooked, remove from the pot and leave until cool enough to handle, then remove the chicken skin and discard. Using your hands, shred all the meat and discard the bones. Set the meat aside and reserve the broth.

Meanwhile, place the pepitas and sesame seeds in a food processor and process until finely ground. Set aside in a bowl.

Add the reserved tortillas, tomatillos, cilantro, cumin and 240 ml (8 fl oz/1 cup) of the reserved broth to the food processor and process until well combined. Add more broth as needed to fully purée all the ingredients to a smooth consistency. Set aside.

Wipe out the pot, then add the chicken fat or oil and melt over a medium heat. Add the onion, bell pepper, garlic and jalapeños and cook slowly for 4–5 minutes, stirring constantly, until the vegetables are soft. If the bottom of the pan begins to darken, add 2 tablespoons water and stir with a wooden spoon, gently scraping any bits stuck on the bottom of the pot.

When tender, place the vegetables in the food processor with another 240 ml (8 fl oz/1 cup) of the reserved broth and process until smooth.

Place the ground seeds, tomatillo mixture, puréed vegetables and remaining broth back into the pot and bring to a simmer over a medium–high heat. Cook for 15 minutes, or until it is reduced by one-third. Add the reserved chicken and stir to combine. Season with salt and freshly ground black pepper and serve with the garnishes.

Caldo de Pollo

Serves 6

1 × 1.35 kg (3 lb) chicken, quartered
1.9 liters (64 fl oz/8 cups) water or
    Chicken Stock (page 237)
4 garlic cloves, sliced
1 large yellow onion, cut into 2 cm
    (¾ in) cubes
½ teaspoon black peppercorns
3 bay leaves
2 large carrots, cut into 2.5 cm (1 in) rounds
8 small yellow potatoes, peeled and halved
2 güisquil (chayote squash), cut into
    2 cm (¾ in) cubes
2 small güicoy or any summer squash,
    such as zucchini (courgette), cut into
    2.5 cm (1 in) half-moons
4 roma or plum tomatoes, roughly chopped
2 ears fresh corn, cut into 5 cm
    (2 in) round pieces
20 g (¾ oz) cilantro (coriander),
    roughly chopped
20 g (¾ oz) mint, roughly chopped

To serve
2 limes, cut into wedges
steamed white rice
corn tortillas

This classic Guatemalan chicken soup is commonly served with most of the vegetables alongside the broth. Often eaten on Sundays, when the whole family comes together for lunch, caldo de pollo is enjoyed with rice and tortillas for a complete meal. A great addition to the recipe is a couple of fresh bay leaves, if available.

Place the chicken in a large pot and add the water or stock, garlic, onion, peppercorns and bay leaves and bring to a gentle simmer over a medium heat. Simmer very gently until the chicken pieces are cooked through, about 7–10 minutes for the breasts and 15–18 minutes for the legs and thighs. The meat should separate from the end of the leg bone when cooked, a thermometer will read 74°C (165°F) when inserted into the thickest part of the thigh or breast and the juices of the chicken will run clear.

When the chicken is cooked, remove from the pot and leave until cool enough to handle, then remove the chicken skin and discard. Using your hands, shred all the meat and discard the bones. Set the meat aside.

Meanwhile, add the carrots, potatoes, squashes, tomato and corn to the broth in the pot and simmer gently for 6–10 minutes until the vegetables are cooked. Add the chicken to the pot, stir in the herbs and season with salt. Serve with lime wedges, steamed white rice and corn tortillas.

Poulet Creole

Serves 4

3 garlic cloves
½–1 scotch bonnet chili
½ green bell pepper (capsicum), seeded and
    roughly chopped
1 × 1.35 kg (3 lb) chicken, cut into 8 pieces
3 tablespoons rendered chicken fat
    or canola (rapeseed) oil
½ red bell pepper (capsicum), seeded
    and thinly sliced
4 spring (green) onions, roughly
    chopped into 2.5 cm (1 in) lengths
6 parsley sprigs, roughly chopped
1 large yellow onion, halved and thinly sliced
2 tablespoons tomato paste
950 ml (32½ fl oz/4 cups) water or
    Chicken Stock (page 237)
1 tablespoon cider vinegar

Unapologetically fierce with heat, this is an everyday meal in Haiti. Sauces may vary a bit, but this dish is always made by marinating chicken with garlic, scotch bonnet chili and green bell pepper (capsicum) prior to braising. The chili, known for its intense heat, permeates throughout the meat, giving the chicken depth of flavor. This dish is usually served with or over steamed white rice. If a lighter heat is preferred, use less than a whole chili in the marinade.

Place the garlic, chili and green bell pepper in a food processor and process to a rough paste. Rub the marinade over the chicken and refrigerate overnight.

Heat the chicken fat or oil in a pot over a medium heat. Add the red bell pepper, spring onions, parsley and onion and stir to combine. Cook over a medium heat for 3–4 minutes until the vegetables are tender. Add the tomato paste and stir to coat the vegetables, then add the chicken pieces and marinade, together with the water or stock and stir to combine. Simmer gently until the chicken pieces are cooked through, about 7–10 minutes for the breasts and 15–18 minutes for the legs and thighs. The meat should separate from the end of the leg bone when cooked, a thermometer will read 74°C (165°F) when inserted into the thickest part of the thigh or breast and the juices of the chicken will run clear.

Remove the chicken breasts when they are cooked, then return them to the pot when the thighs/legs are cooked. This will keep the light meat from overcooking. Stir in the vinegar and season with salt and freshly ground black pepper to serve.

Sancocho

Serves 4–6

2 tablespoons rendered chicken fat
    or vegetable oil
1 yellow onion, cut into 1 cm
    (½ in) cubes
3 garlic cloves, crushed
1 tablespoon dried oregano
1 × 1.35 kg (3 lb) chicken, quartered
1.9 liters (64 fl oz/8 cups) water or
    Chicken Stock (page 237)
1 tablespoon salt
1.35 kg (3 lb) starchy vegetables, such
    as yams, yucca, cassava, green plantains
2 ears fresh corn, cut into 5 cm
    (2 in) rounds
80 g (2¾ oz) culantro or cilantro
    (coriander), roughly chopped

Panamanian sancocho is a chicken soup, as opposed to the Puerto Rican sancocho, which uses beef. The color and flavor can vary from light brown to bright green to yellow and orange based on the use of peppers, tomato and herbs. Just like every regional or national chicken soup, every recipe is a little different, depending on the area and cook's preference. In Panama City, the soup is usually light brown due to the variety of root vegetables. Sancochos that are heavy in culantro (see page 50) have a bright, fresh flavor and a green hue. Yellow or orange versions include a lot of squash (pumpkin) or yams. Panamanian dishes are rarely spicy; however, sancocho chorrerano (made in the town of La Chorrera, outside Panama City) is an exception, made of only chicken, onions, garlic, chili peppers, oregano and ñame (yam). The version made in Chiriquí Province, which borders Costa Rica, is called sancocho chiricano and is served with a variety of vegetable garnishes.

Heat the chicken fat or oil in a large pot over a medium–high heat. Add the onion, garlic and oregano and cook for 3–4 minutes until the onion becomes tender and translucent. If the onion starts to brown, reduce the heat.

Place the chicken in the pot and add the water or stock and bring to a gentle simmer. Stir in the salt. Simmer gently until the chicken pieces are cooked, about 7–10 minutes for the breasts and 15–18 minutes for the legs and thighs. The meat should separate from the end of the leg bone when cooked, a thermometer will read 74°C (165°F) when inserted into the thickest part of the thigh or breast and the juices of the chicken will run clear.

When the chicken is cooked, remove from the pot and leave until cool enough to handle, then remove the chicken skin and discard. Using your hands, shred all the meat into large chunks and discard the bones. Set the meat aside.

Add the vegetables and corn to the pot and cook gently for 5 minutes, or until the vegetables are tender. Stir in the culantro and add the chicken. Season with salt and freshly ground black pepper and serve.

Aguadito de Pollo

Serves 4

4 × boneless, skinless chicken thighs
(approx. 280 g/10 oz)
150 g (5½ oz/¾ cup) white long-grain rice
1450 ml (49 fl oz/6 cups) water or
Chicken Stock (page 237)
1 tablespoon salt
3 yellow potatoes, peeled and cut into
1 cm (½ in) cubes
2 tablespoons vegetable oil
1 small red bell pepper (capsicum), seeded
and cut into 5 mm (¼ in) cubes
1 ear fresh corn, kernels cut off the cob
½ yellow onion
80 g (2¾ oz) culantro or cilantro (coriander)
3 garlic cloves
240 ml (8 fl oz/1 cup) cold water
50 g (1¾ oz/⅓ cup) frozen peas
1 lime

Aguadito de pollo is flavorful and textural. Variations of this soup feature different types of meat, and there is even a vegetable option. Culantro is a star in this herbal soup, and the amount added is up to the cook. Sometimes, spinach is chopped with the culantro to add green color without the pungency of culantro. Cilantro (coriander) can be substituted for culantro in this soup; some versions also include yucca in addition to potatoes. Steamed white rice is a traditional accompaniment.

Place the chicken, rice, and water or stock in a large pot with the salt and simmer gently over a medium heat for 15 minutes, or until the chicken pieces are cooked through and the juices of the chicken run clear. Halfway through cooking, add the potatoes.

Meanwhile, heat the oil in a small pan over a medium–high heat. Add the bell pepper and corn and sauté for 3–5 minutes until tender. Season with salt, then add to the soup.

When the chicken is cooked, remove from the pot and leave until cool enough to handle. Using two forks, shred the meat and return to the soup.

Place the onion, culantro and garlic in a blender with the water and process until completely puréed.

Add the peas to the soup and cook for 1 minute, then add the purée. Season the soup with salt, then squeeze the lime juice into the soup, adding as much tangy flavor as possible without it becoming sour. If the puréed onions taste too strong, let the broth simmer for a few more minutes before serving.

Chupe de Pollo con Chipotle

Serves 6

2 tablespoons rendered chicken fat
or vegetable oil
3 chipotle chilies in adobo sauce
1 large yellow onion, cut into 1 cm
(½ in) cubes
2 large carrots, cut into 2.5 cm (1 in) pieces
2 celery ribs (stalks), cut into 2.5 cm
(1 in) pieces
1 teaspoon ground cumin
1 teaspoon dried oregano
½ teaspoon dried thyme
6 garlic cloves, halved
1.9 liters (64 fl oz/8 cups) water
or Chicken Stock (page 237)
900 g (2 lb) red potatoes, peeled and
cut into 1 cm (½ in) pieces
700 g (1 lb 9 oz) canned white or
golden hominy, rinsed and drained

Some claim that there are 200 soups enjoyed in Peru. Soups are eaten for breakfast, lunch and dinner. This one is popular throughout the country, except for the coast, where there is a seafood variation – chupe de camarones (with prawns). Spicy with chilies, rich with cream and hearty with chicken, potatoes and hominy, one of my taste testers claimed this soup tasted like the best enchiladas ever.

Heat the chicken fat or oil in large pot over a medium heat. Add the chili, onion, carrots, celery, cumin, oregano, thyme and garlic and cook for 5–6 minutes, stirring occasionally, until the onions are tender and translucent. Stir in the water or stock, then bring to the boil. Reduce the heat to a simmer and cook for 4–6 minutes until the carrots are tender.

Using an immersion blender, or process in batches in a blender, purée the entire contents of the pot, then pour back into the pot and add the potatoes and hominy.

670 g (1½ lb) boneless, skinless chicken
   breasts, cut into bite-sized pieces
120 ml (4 fl oz/½ cup) whipping (thickened)
   cream
2 roma or plum tomatoes, cut into
   1 cm (½ in) cubes
40 g (1½ oz) cilantro (coriander),
   roughly chopped
60 ml (2 fl oz/¼ cup) lime juice
lime wedges, to serve

Season lightly with salt and cook at a very gentle simmer for 4–5 minutes until the potatoes are cooked. Add the chicken, stir and cook for a further 2–3 minutes until the chicken is cooked through. Add the cream, tomatoes, cilantro and lime juice and stir to combine. Season with salt and serve with lime wedges.

Asopao de Pollo

Serves 4–6

Packed with umami, this soup has all the ingredients of paella in soup format and is popular throughout the Caribbean. Savory chicken and rice are rich and satisfying, and salty olives and capers create a zingy tang making your taste buds ask for bite after bite. Garnishes vary, often including parmesan cheese, roasted red bell peppers (capsicum), asparagus spears and corn on the cob, cut into 5 cm (2 in) lengths.

1 × 1.35 kg (3 lb) chicken, quartered
2.4 liters (81 fl oz/10 cups) water
   or Chicken Stock (page 237)
2 tablespoons salt
3 tablespoons olive oil
8 garlic cloves, very finely chopped
1 large yellow onion, very finely chopped
225 g (8 oz) ham, very finely chopped
1 green bell pepper (capsicum), seeded and
   very finely chopped
1 tablespoon achiote paste
1 tablespoon tomato paste
2 tablespoons dried oregano
2 tablespoons cider vinegar
2 bay leaves
2 yautias (taro root) or small yellow
   potatoes, cut into 1 cm (½ in) pieces
2 carrots, cut into 1 cm (½ in) rounds
200 g (7 oz/1 cup) white long-grain rice
2 tablespoons capers
170 g (6 oz/1 cup) small green olives
   stuffed with red bell peppers
155 g (5½ oz/1 cup) frozen peas

Place the chicken and water or stock in a large pot with the salt. Weigh down the chicken under a few small plates to keep it submerged and simmer gently over a medium heat until the chicken pieces are cooked through, about 7–10 minutes for the breasts and 15–18 minutes for the legs and thighs. The meat should separate from the end of the leg bone when cooked through, a thermometer will read 74°C (165°F) when inserted into the thickest part of the thigh or breast and the juices of the chicken will run clear.

When the chicken is cooked, remove from the pot and leave until cool enough to handle, then remove the chicken skin and discard. Using your hands, shred all the meat and discard the bones. Set the meat aside. Strain the broth and reserve.

Wipe out the pot, then place over a low–medium heat. Add the olive oil, garlic, onion, ham and bell pepper and cook very slowly for 20 minutes until the vegetables are tender, but not browned. Add the achiote paste, tomato paste, oregano, vinegar and bay leaves and stir to combine. Add the yautias or potato, carrots, rice, capers and olives, then stir and cook for another minute. Add the reserved broth. Bring to a gentle simmer and cook for 10 minutes until the soup has slightly thickened and the rice is tender. Add the peas and reserved chicken, season with salt and freshly ground black pepper and serve.

Caldo de Pollo con Mofongo

Serves 4–6

Mofongo is to the Puerto Ricans what matzo balls are to the Eastern European Jews. It can easily be argued that mofongo is one of the top favorite foods of Puerto Rican cuisine. Fideos can absorb broth, so add water or stock to balance brothiness as needed.

2 tablespoons rendered chicken fat
   or vegetable oil
1 yellow onion, cut into 5 mm (¼ in) cubes
2 celery ribs (stalks), cut into 5 mm (¼ in) cubes
1 large carrot, cut into 5 mm (¼ in) cubes
1 × 1.35 kg (3 lb) chicken, quartered
1.9 liters (64 fl oz/8 cups) water
   or Chicken Stock (page 237)
2 potatoes, such as yukon gold, peeled
   and cut into 1 cm (½ in) cubes
200 g (7 oz/1½ cups) fideos or angel hair
   pasta, broken into 5 cm (2 in) lengths
10 g (¼ oz/½ cup) cilantro (coriander),
   leaves and stems chopped

Heat the chicken fat or oil in a large pot over a medium–high heat. Add the onion, celery and carrot and cook for 3–4 minutes until the onion becomes tender and translucent. If the onion starts to brown, reduce the heat.

Place the chicken in the pot and add the water or stock and simmer gently over a medium heat until the chicken pieces are cooked through, about 7–10 minutes for the breasts and 15–18 minutes for the legs and thighs. The meat should separate from the end of the leg bone when cooked, a thermometer will read 74°C (165°F) when inserted into the thickest part of the thigh or breast and the juices of the chicken will run clear.

Mofongo
60 ml (2 fl oz/¼ cup) vegetable oil
2 large green plantains, peeled and cut
    into 5 cm (2 in) rounds
2 × thick-cut bacon slices (rashers), approx.
    100 g (3½ oz), cooked until crispy
    and fat reserved
1 teaspoon ground black pepper
1 teaspoon dried oregano
2 teaspoons ground cumin
1 teaspoon garlic powder

Meanwhile, make the mofongo. Heat a large pan over a medium–high heat. Add the oil and plantain slices and sear on both sides for 2–3 minutes until the plantains are tender. Place the cooked plantains in a bowl and mash with the remaining ingredients and 2 tablespoons of the rendered bacon fat. Season with salt and roll into 8–12 balls. Set aside.

When the chicken is cooked, remove from the pot and leave until cool enough to handle, then remove the chicken skin and discard. Using your hands, shred all the meat and discard the bones. Set the meat aside.

Add the potatoes to the pot and simmer gently over a low–medium heat for 3–4 minutes, then add the fideos or pasta and chicken meat and cook for a further 5–8 minutes until the potatoes and fideos are tender. Season and stir in the cilantro.

Ladle the soup into serving bowls and place a few mofongo in the broth to serve.

93

Saoto

Serves 4

2 × whole chicken legs (approx. 670 g/1½ lb),
    legs and thighs connected
950 ml (32½ fl oz/4 cups) water
    or Chicken Stock (page 237)
5 cm (2 in) piece galangal root, peeled
    and sliced into 1 cm (½ in) rounds
4 garlic cloves, finely chopped
1 yellow onion, quartered
1 lemongrass stalk, outer leaves
    removed, bottom 10 cm (4 in)
    only, cut into thirds
1 Indonesian bay leaf or fresh bay leaf
5 whole allspice berries
1 teaspoon freshly ground black pepper
1 habanero or scotch bonnet pepper
240 ml (8 fl oz/1 cup) vegetable oil
50–100 g (1¾–3½ oz) bean thread
    vermicelli (glass or cellophane noodles)
6 large Hard-boiled Eggs (page 33)
300 g (10½ oz) bean sprouts
120 g (4½ oz/2 cups) shredded
    green cabbage
1 celery rib (stalk), thinly sliced into half
    moons

In 1863, after the abolition of slavery in Suriname, Javanese people arrived as contract workers. They brought this soup with them and it has been a staple ever since. It can be enjoyed as an appetizer or starter, or with a side of steamed rice as a main dish. The garnishes are a lengthy list, and optional. Variations will be served with any number of toppings. Since Suriname is a melting pot of many ethnicities, there are many ways to vary the ingredients in this soup. It's sometimes called Blauwgrond soup, referring to the neighborhood where it is often sold as a late night after-party or movie snack or meal.

Place the chicken, water or stock, galangal root, garlic, onion, lemongrass, bay leaf, allspice and black pepper in a large pot over a medium–high heat. Bring to the boil, then immediately reduce the heat to a very low simmer and simmer gently for 20 minutes, or until the chicken is cooked through, a thermometer reads 74°C (165°F) when inserted into the thickest part of the thigh or breast and the juices of the chicken run clear.

Add the whole habanero or scotch bonnet pepper to the soup and cook for a few minutes until tender. Remove and use to make sambal condiment (see below).

Meanwhile, heat the vegetable oil in a large pot over a high heat until shimmering or until it reads 180°C (350°F) on a thermometer. Working in batches, carefully add the noodles to the hot oil and deep-fry, stirring and flipping until puffed and crisp, then remove and drain on a plate lined with paper towel. Season with salt and set aside.

When the chicken is cooked, remove from the pot and leave until cool enough to handle, then remove the chicken skin and discard. Using your hands, shred all the meat and discard the bones. Add the meat to the soup. Season with salt and freshly ground black pepper.

Serve the soup with garnishes of a boiled egg, bean sprouts, cabbage, vermicelli, celery and sambal.

Serves 4

1 habanero or scotch bonnet pepper
1 garlic clove
1 tablespoon superfine (caster) sugar
75 ml (2½ fl oz) soy sauce

Sambal (Spicy Soy Sauce)

Boil the whole pepper for a short time in the soup (see above), then remove the chili from the broth and finely chop it with the garlic before adding the sugar and soy sauce. Store in an airtight container in the refrigerator for up to 1 week.

THE AMERICAS

Trinidad Chicken Soup

Serves 4–6

2 tablespoons rendered chicken
    fat or vegetable oil
1 yellow onion, cut into 1 cm (½ in) cubes
3 large garlic cloves, thinly sliced
3 bay leaves
3 thick thyme sprigs
½ teaspoon freshly ground black pepper
1 habanero pepper, finely chopped
250 g (9 oz/1 cup) whole canned
    tomatoes, puréed
1.9 liters (64 fl oz/8 cups) Chicken
    Stock (page 237)
1 × 1.35 kg (3 lb) whole chicken, quartered
1 tablespoon salt
4 yellow potatoes, peeled and cut into
    1 cm (½ in) cubes
2 green plantains, peeled and cut into
    1 cm (½ in) slices
225 g (8 oz) sweet potato, peeled and
    cut into 1 cm (½ in) cubes
225 g (8 oz) calabaza or butternut squash
    (pumpkin), peeled, seeded and cut into
    1 cm (½ in) cubes
6 parsley sprigs, chopped, to garnish

If you are lucky enough to be in Trinidad, you can buy a piping hot cup of this soup from a street vendor. Take care when chopping spicy peppers: wear gloves and wash your hands really well with warm soap and water afterwards. The heat of the habanero is very strong and the oils can do some damage to your eyes, nose and other body parts that may not enjoy the heat. Variations of this soup also include corn, cassava, carrots, coconut milk, wheat vermicelli noodles, dumplings or a knob of butter added at the end of cooking.

Heat the chicken fat or oil in a pot over a medium heat. Add the onion, garlic, bay leaves, thyme, the black pepper and the habanero pepper and cook for 3–5 minutes, stirring frequently until the ingredients are cooked through and the onions are translucent. Add the tomatoes, stock, chicken and the salt, then simmer gently over a medium heat until the chicken pieces are cooked through, about 7–10 minutes for the breasts and 15–18 minutes for the legs and thighs. The meat should separate from the end of the leg bone when cooked, a thermometer will read 74°C (165°F) when inserted into the thickest part of the thigh or breast and the juices of the chicken will run clear.

    When the chicken is cooked, remove from the pot and leave until cool enough to handle, then remove the chicken skin and discard. Using your hands, shred all the meat and discard the bones. Set the meat aside.

    Add the potatoes, plantains, sweet potato and squash to the soup and cook gently for 3–4 minutes until tender. Add the chicken, then season with salt and garnish with parsley.

Asia

NORTH, EAST +
SOUTHEAST ASIA

*Cambodia, China, Indonesia, Japan, Korea, Myanmar,
Philippines, Russia, Taiwan, Thailand, Vietnam*

Asia, the world's largest and most populous continent, is home to a great variety of produce and cooking methods. Common ingredients include ginger, soy, sesame, rice, garlic and chilies. In the case of rice, the variety used differs from region to region. Noodles, like rice, are an important part of Asian cuisine. While rice noodles are predominant in Southeast Asia, wheat noodles are common in China. Each country uses locally available foods, and cooking styles and dishes have also been influenced by migration over the centuries.

Russian cuisine includes salted or preserved fish and meats, fresh white cheeses, cultured dairy products and hearty soups. Vegetables that can be held over the cold winter, such as beets, cabbage, onions and potatoes, are staples in Russian cooking.

East Asia is the most populous area of the world and includes China, Japan, Korea and Mongolia. Long-grain rice, a wide variety of noodles, mung beans, soybeans and seafood are among the food staples.

Vietnam, Laos, Cambodia, Thailand, Myanmar, the Philippines, Malaysia and Indonesia are part of Southeast Asia. The dishes of this region feature highly aromatic ingredients, such as galangal, ginger, citrus, cilantro (coriander) and basil. The predominant rice is jasmine, which has a lovely fragrance when cooking. Fermented fish sauce is a staple in much of Southeast Asian cooking, adding depth of flavor.

Chicken soups in each region reflect the ingredients of that particular place. North Asian soups are made with root vegetables, East Asian chicken soups are simple and come garnished with greens and, sometimes, fermented vegetables (Yào Shàn Jī Tāng, pages 104 and 105), while the soups of Southeast Asia are fragrant with herbs, ginger, galangal and garlic, often with a deep richness from coconut milk (Ohn-No Khao Swè, page 125).

Sgnor Jruk Sach Moan

Serves 4

1 × 1.35 kg (3 lb) chicken, quartered
1.9 liters (64 fl oz/8 cups) water
   or Chicken Stock (page 237)
3 teaspoons uncooked broken jasmine rice
1 lemongrass stalk, cut into 3 pieces
   and slightly smashed
4 kaffir lime leaves
5 garlic cloves, smashed
1 yellow onion, thinly sliced
2 tablespoons salt
2–3 tablespoons fish sauce, or more
   to taste
1 teaspoon granulated sugar
3 limes, reserve 2 to cut into wedges
   to serve

To serve
4 spring (green) onions, thinly sliced
55 g (2 oz) Thai basil,
   roughly chopped
40 g (1½ oz) culantro or cilantro
   (coriander), roughly chopped
Chili Fish Sauce (see opposite)

Khmer cuisine is the dominant cooking style in Cambodia. The flavors are clean, bright and simple. Many Cambodians choose a vegetarian diet due to their Buddhist beliefs, but there are people who eat meat daily. This soup makes a regular appearance; it is inexpensive and can feed many people. The chicken can be substituted with fish, and vegetables may vary. Some variations include tomatoes, celery, pineapple and fried garlic. Serve with steamed broken jasmine rice.

Place the chicken, water or stock, rice, lemongrass, lime leaves, garlic and onion in a large pot with the salt. Weigh down the chicken under a few small plates to keep it submerged and simmer gently over a medium heat until the chicken pieces are cooked through, about 7–10 minutes for the breasts and 15–18 minutes for the legs and thighs. The meat should separate from the end of the leg bone when cooked, a thermometer will read 74°C (165°F) when inserted into the thickest part of the thigh or breast and the juices of the chicken will run clear.

   When the chicken is cooked, remove from the pot and leave until cool enough to handle, then remove the chicken skin and discard. Using your hands, shred all the meat and discard the bones. Add the meat to the pot.

   Season the soup with fish sauce, sugar, the juice of 1 lime and salt. Serve with spring onions, basil, culantro, lime wedges and chili fish sauce (see opposite).

Serves 4

3 tablespoons fish sauce
5 tablespoons sambal oelek
1 teaspoon granulated sugar
1 Thai (bird's eye) chili, thinly sliced

Chili Fish Sauce

Mix all the ingredients together in a bowl and set aside until ready to use. Store in an airtight container in the refrigerator for up to 1 week.

Yào Shàn Jī Tāng #1

Serves 4

24 dried jujube fruit (red dates)
2 pieces dried snow fungus
32 dried lotus seeds
1 × 1.35 kg (3 lb) chicken, quartered
1.9 liters (64 fl oz/8 cups) water
  or Chicken Stock (page 237)
24 straw mushrooms, quartered
1 ginseng tail (ginseng root)
2 teaspoons ground white pepper
1 tablespoon salt
3 spring (green) onions, cut into thin rings

Clean, with a herbal broth, this restorative chicken soup embodies the healing properties of ancient Chinese medicinal cooking. The ingredients are easy to find and straightforward to work with. Serve as a starter, or with a side of steamed rice for a light meal.

Rinse the jujube fruit, snow fungus and lotus seeds in cold water, then place in a large bowl or container filled with warm water and leave to soak for 20 minutes. Strain and place in a pot. Add the chicken, water or stock, straw mushrooms, ginseng tail, white pepper and salt and bring to a simmer over a high heat. Cook until the chicken pieces are cooked through, about 7–10 minutes for the breasts and 15–18 minutes for the legs and thighs. The meat should separate from the end of the leg bone when cooked, a thermometer will read 74°C (165°F) when inserted into the thickest part of the thigh or breast and the juices of the chicken will run clear.

When the chicken is cooked, remove from the pot and leave until cool enough to handle, then remove the chicken skin and discard. Using your hands, shred all the meat and discard the bones. Add the meat to the soup. Alternatively, cut the chicken into smaller portions and serve on the bone. Break up the snow fungus, then season with salt and stir in the spring onions.

Yào Shàn Jī Tāng #2

China

Serves 4

55 g (2 oz/½ cup) dried jujube fruit
    (red dates)
55 g (2 oz/½ cup) dried longan fruit
55 g (2 oz/2 whole) dried snow fungus
55 g (2 oz) wood ear mushrooms
1 × 670 g (1½ lb) black chicken, Silkie
    or Vikon variety, feet removed and
    carcass quartered
225 g (8 oz) ginger, peeled and cut into
    5 mm (¼ in) slices
950 ml (32½ fl oz/4 cups) shaoxing
    (Chinese cooking rice wine)
1.9 liters (64 fl oz/8 cups) water or
    Chicken Stock (page 237)
710 g (1 lb 9 oz) chicken bones
1 tablespoon salt
30 g (1 oz/¼ cup) goji berries
70 g (2½ oz/½ cup) raw peanuts, shelled,
    to garnish

This recipe yields a rich and aromatic broth with bold ginger flavors and embodies the healing properties of medicinal Chinese cuisine. Each berry, root and mushroom contributes to the holistic healing of body and spirit. In Chinese cuisine, chicken is cooked for long periods, which extracts an abundance of chicken flavor into the broth and makes the meat very tender. Ingredients may vary depending on family or region, but the tradition of using food to heal is strong across the country.

Rinse the jujube fruit, longan fruit, snow fungus and wood ear mushrooms in cold water, then place in a large bowl or container filled with warm water and leave to soak for 20 minutes. Strain and reserve.

Place the chicken in a large pot and cover with water. Bring to the boil over a high heat, then reduce the heat to a simmer and cook for 5 minutes. Drain.

Place the ginger, rice wine, water or stock, chicken, chicken bones and salt in the pot and bring to a simmer over a high heat. Cook for 1 hour, or until the chicken is cooked through and very tender.

When the chicken is cooked, remove from the pot and leave until cool enough to handle. Strain the broth and return to the pot. Cut the chicken into smaller portions to serve on the bone, before returning the meat back to the soup. Break up the snow fungus and add all the drained soaked ingredients together with the goji berries to the soup. Season with salt and garnish with peanuts.

Xiǎo Bái Cài Jī Tāng

China

Serves 4

3 tablespoons vegetable oil
4 cm (1½ inch) piece ginger, peeled
   and very finely chopped
5 garlic cloves, very finely chopped
120 ml (4 fl oz/½ cup) shaoxing (Chinese cooking rice wine)
1450 ml (49 fl oz/6 cups) water or Chicken Stock (page 237)
1 × 1.35 kg (3 lb) chicken, quartered
1 tablespoon salt
1 teaspoon ground white pepper
2 small baby bok choy heads, leaves separated
4 spring (green) onions, thinly sliced
40 g (1½ oz) cilantro (coriander), roughly chopped
2 tablespoons unseasoned rice vinegar

Cantonese seasonings of ginger, garlic and spring onions create a simple and aromatic broth, complementing the flavor and texture of the more neutral chicken. Steamed white rice, cooked wheat noodles, fried or poached eggs or cubes of tofu are optional additions to create a heartier meal. A drizzle of chili oil or toasted sesame oil provides additional flavor, too.

Heat the oil in a large heavy-bottomed pot over a medium–high heat. Add the ginger and garlic and cook for 2–4 minutes until the raw smell of garlic has dissipated, but the garlic is not brown. Add the cooking wine and cook for a further 2–4 minutes until the smell of the alcohol has dissipated. Add the water or stock, chicken, salt and white pepper. Weigh down the chicken under a few small plates to keep it submerged and simmer gently over a medium heat until the chicken pieces are cooked through, about 7–10 minutes for the breasts and 15–18 minutes for the legs and thighs. The meat should separate from the end of the leg bone when cooked, a thermometer will read 74°C (165°F) when inserted into the thickest part of the thigh or breast and the juices of the chicken will run clear.

   When the chicken is cooked, skin and shred the meat. Add the bok choy leaves to the broth and cook for 3 minutes until wilted. Stir in the chicken meat, spring onions, cilantro and vinegar. Season with salt and adjust the pepper to taste.

Rén Shēn Hēi Jī Tāng

China

Serves 4

1 × 670 g (1½ lb) black chicken, Silkie or Vikon variety,
   feet removed and carcass quartered
2.9 liters (97½ fl oz/12 cups) water or Chicken Stock (page 237)
30 g (1 oz) ginseng root
30 g (1 oz) huai shan (dried Chinese yam)
10 dried jujube fruit (red dates)
4 dried honey dates
2 tablespoons salt
20 g (¾ oz) goji berries
2 teaspoons yu zhu (yuzu) juice

This is a variation of Chinese herbal chicken soup. It was created for nourishment and healing, and adaptations are seen throughout the country.

Place the chicken in a large pot and cover with water. Bring to the boil over a high heat, then reduce the heat to a simmer and cook for 5 minutes. Strain and add the chicken back to the pot with the water or stock, ginseng, dried yam, jujube fruit, dates and salt. Bring to a simmer over a high heat and cook for 1 hour, or until the chicken is cooked through and very tender.

   Add the goji berries and yu zhu juice and cook for another 10 minutes. When the chicken is cooked, remove from the pot and leave to cool. Cut the chicken into smaller portions to serve on the bone, then add back to the soup. Season with salt and serve.

Hǎi Nán Jī (Hainanese Chicken)

Serves 4

Broth
1 × 1.35 kg (3 lb) chicken, quartered
15 cm (6 in) piece ginger, peeled and
    cut into 5 mm (¼ in) slices
5 whole spring (green) onions, cut into
    2.5 cm (1 in) sections
1 teaspoon toasted sesame oil

Rice
400 g (14 oz/2 cups) white long-grain rice
2 tablespoons rendered chicken fat
    or vegetable oil
3 garlic cloves, very finely chopped
2.5 cm (1 in) piece ginger, peeled and
    very finely chopped
½ teaspoon toasted sesame oil
kosher salt or sea salt

Chili sauce
1 tablespoon fresh lime juice
60 ml (2 fl oz/¼ cup) reserved chicken
    poaching broth
2 teaspoons granulated sugar
60 ml (2 fl oz/¼ cup) sriracha chili sauce
4 garlic cloves
2.5 cm (1 in) piece ginger, peeled and
    thinly sliced
½ teaspoon salt

To serve
dark soy sauce
1 cucumber, thinly sliced
cilantro (coriander) sprigs or
    spring (green) onions, thinly sliced

Hainanese chicken rice is a dish of poached chicken and seasoned rice, served with the poaching broth, chili sauce, dark soy sauce, cilantro (coriander) and spring onions. The dish was adapted from the Hainanese dish Wenchang chicken and was popularized in other countries by immigrants from Hainan province. It is considered one of the national dishes of Singapore, and is also seen throughout Southeast Asia, particularly Malaysia (nasi ayam) and Thailand (khao man gai) where it is a culinary staple. Sometimes I brine the chicken for this dish; it is not necessary, but adds a wonderful saltiness to the meat. For tenderest results, cook the chicken gently and very slowly. Keep the skin on when cooking – the fat is good in the broth and keeps the meat moist.

For the broth, lightly season the chicken carcass with salt inside and outside, then stuff the chicken with ginger slices and spring onions. Place the chicken in a pot that just fits it snugly and fill with cold water to 2.5 cm (1 in) above the chicken. Bring to the boil over a high heat, then immediately reduce the heat to low to barely keep a simmer and cook for 20–30 minutes until the breasts and thickest part of the thighs register 74°C (165°F) on a thermometer and the juices of the chicken run clear.

When the chicken is cooked, remove the pot from the heat. Immediately lift the chicken out of the pot and into a bath of ice water to cool for 3–4 minutes. Discard the ginger and spring onion. This essential step creates the lovely and traditional firm texture of the chicken skin and will also stop the cooking process, keeping the meat soft and tender. Once the skin is chilled, remove the chicken from the water, rub the skin with sesame oil and carve the chicken. Reserve the poaching broth.

To make the rice, soak it in a large bowl of cool water for 15 minutes, then drain. Heat the chicken fat or oil in a saucepan over a medium–high heat. When hot, add the garlic and ginger and fry for 2–4 minutes until tender, but not golden. Reduce the heat if necessary. Add the drained rice and stir to coat, then cook for 2 minutes. Add the sesame oil and mix well. In the same pan, add 475 ml (16 fl oz/2 cups) of the reserved poaching broth and some salt and bring to the boil. Immediately reduce the heat to low, cover with a lid and cook for 15 minutes. Remove from the heat and leave, covered, for another 5–10 minutes.

To make the chili sauce, blend all the ingredients in a blender until smooth and bright red.

There should be 1.45–1.7 liters (49–57 fl oz/6–7 cups) of the reserved poaching broth left over to serve as soup. Just before serving, heat up the soup until piping hot and taste and season with salt as necessary.

Serve the chicken and rice with the chili sauce, soy sauce, cucumber slices and a bowl of hot broth garnished with cilantro or spring onions.

Laksa

Serves 4

3 dried red chilies

4 red Thai (bird's eye) chilies

5 cm (2 in) piece ginger, peeled and thinly sliced

4 garlic cloves

3 shallots

3 lemongrass stalks, outer leaves removed, bottom 10 cm (4 in) only, cut into thirds

1 tablespoon ground coriander

2 teaspoons curry powder

1 teaspoon ground cumin

120 ml (4 fl oz/½ cup) vegetable oil

4 teaspoons Thai shrimp paste

225 g (8 oz) fresh wide rice noodles

800 ml (27 fl oz) canned coconut milk

750 ml (25½ fl oz/3 cups) water or Chicken Stock (page 237)

2 teaspoons palm sugar (jaggery) or light brown sugar

2 × whole chicken legs (approx. 670 g/1½ lb), leg and thigh attached, skin on

fish sauce, to taste

4 large Soft-boiled Eggs (page 115), halved

2 Persian cucumbers, cut into matchsticks

115 g (4 oz) bean sprouts

¼ bunch mint, leaves only

2 limes, cut into wedges

sambal oelek, to taste

Versions of this fragrant laksa paste (curry) are seen in Malaysia, Singapore, Indonesia and Southern Thailand. It is believed to have originated as a blend of Chinese ingredients and Southeast Asian cooking practices. Chinese wheat noodles can replace rice noodles, and seafood can be used to replace chicken. Laksa paste is a bit labor-intensive to make, and some ingredients may take an extra trip out, but it is worth it. Laksa paste can be made a week ahead, stored airtight in the refrigerator, or can be frozen in ice-cube trays for up to two months.

Place the chilies, ginger, garlic, shallot, lemongrass, coriander, curry powder, cumin, 60 ml (2 fl oz) vegetable oil and the shrimp paste in a blender and process until very fine. Set aside.

Place the noodles in a bowl and cover with cold water, then place a plate on top of the noodles to keep them fully submerged. Soak for 15 minutes, then strain and set aside.

Heat a large pot over a high heat and add the remaining oil. Add the curry paste mixture and cook for 45 seconds, stirring and smearing the paste into the oil, until aromatic. Slowly whisk in the coconut milk, water or stock and palm sugar, then add the chicken legs and bring to a simmer. Cook for 30 minutes, turning the chicken occasionally, until tender and the broth is very flavorful. The meat should separate from the end of the leg bone when cooked and a thermometer will read 74°C (165°F) when inserted into the thickest part of the leg. Season to taste with fish sauce and salt. Add the noodles and cook for another 1–2 minutes until tender.

Serve garnished with cooked eggs, cucumbers, bean sprouts, mint, lime wedges and sambal oelek.

Keihan

Serves 4

Mushrooms
4 dried shiitake mushrooms
120 ml (4 fl oz/½ cup) boiling water
2 tablespoons sake
1 tablespoon soy sauce
1 tablespoon mirin
1 teaspoon granulated sugar

Soup
450 g (1 lb) boneless, skinless chicken
    breasts, or chicken tenders
950 ml (32½ fl oz/4 cups) Chicken
    Stock (page 237)
2 tablespoons sake
½ teaspoon salt
2 tablespoons soy sauce

Rice
400 g (14 oz/2 cups) white
    medium-grain rice

Egg crepes
3 large eggs
½ teaspoon cornstarch (cornflour)
1 teaspoon sake
½ teaspoon granulated sugar
⅛ teaspoon salt

To garnish
1 teaspoon dried orange peel
20 g (¾ oz/¼ cup) spring onion, chopped
30 g (1 oz) very finely chopped takuan
    (pickled daikon radish) or green
    papaya pickles (may substitute with
    your favorite pickles)
1 handful shredded nori (seaweed)

This chicken soup is a bit of a project. It hails from the Amami Islands, the southern islands of Japan, and dates back as far as the Edo period (1603–1868). The soup is still widely enjoyed, and for good reason. Not only is it tasty, and rich in umami flavors, its garnishes are unique and special, especially the thin egg crepe cut into fettuccini-like strips – a treat in itself.

Soak the shiitake mushrooms for 30–60 minutes in a heatproof bowl filled with the boiling water to reconstitute. Strain and reserve the liquid. Trim the stems from the mushrooms and discard. Slice the mushrooms into thin strips and place in a pan with the soaking liquid, sake, soy sauce, mirin and sugar. Cook over a low heat for 2–3 minutes until the liquid has mostly evaporated. Leave to cool.

For the soup, place the chicken breasts in a saucepan with the stock, sake, salt and soy sauce. Bring to the boil, skimming off any scum that rises to the surface, then reduce the heat to low and cook for 10 minutes, or until the chicken is cooked through. Remove from the heat and leave to cool.

To make the rice, soak it in a bowl of cold water for 15 minutes, then drain and rinse until the water runs clear. Place the rice in a large pot with 475 ml (16 fl oz/ 2 cups) cold water, then cover and place over a high heat. When the water boils, reduce the heat to the lowest setting, cover and cook very gently for 10–12 minutes until the water has been absorbed and the rice is tender. Remove from the heat and leave, covered, for 10 minutes.

For the crepes, place the eggs, cornstarch, sake, sugar and salt in a blender and process until combined.

Preheat an 18 cm (7 in) nonstick frying pan over a medium heat. Ladle in one-quarter of the egg mixture and make an 18 cm (7 in) egg crepe. Remove and repeat with the remaining egg mixture. Stack the crepes on a plate to cool, with baking paper between each crepe. When they are cool, remove the paper and thinly slice the stack into 5 mm (¼ in) ribbons.

When the chicken is cool to the touch, remove from the soup and, using your hands, shred the meat, then set aside. Do not discard the soup.

When the rice is cooked, fluff it up using a fork and divide among four serving bowls. Top with the shredded chicken, sliced mushrooms and shredded egg crepes.

Reheat the reserved chicken broth and pour over the rice and toppings. Garnish with orange peel, spring onion, pickles and nori.

Shio Chicken Ramen

Serves 4

Stock
1 large yellow onion, halved
5 cm (2 in) piece ginger, peeled and
   cut into 5 mm (¼ in) pieces
1 garlic head, cut in half lengthways
1 × 1.35 kg (3 lb) chicken, quartered
1.9 liters (64 fl oz/8 cups) water or
   Chicken Stock (page 237)
1 tablespoon salt

Dashi
1 (10 × 10 cm/4 × 4 in) piece kombu
950 ml (32½ fl oz/4 cups) water
20 g (¾ oz/1½ cups) dried katsuobushi
   (bonito flakes)

Tare
2 tablespoons sake
1 tablespoon mirin
½ teaspoon granulated sugar
2 teaspoons toasted sesame oil
½ teaspoon soy sauce
2 tablespoons salt

Ramen and toppings
450 g (1 lb) fresh or dried ramen noodles
2 toasted nori sheets, quartered
2 large Soft-boiled Eggs, halved
   (see opposite)
Marinated Spring Onions
   (see opposite)
chili oil

Shio, meaning salt, is the oldest form of ramen seasoning. This soup is made with dashi, a seaweed-based stock with bonito. Dashi is best used the same day, but it may be kept in the refrigerator for up to three days and can be frozen for up to two months. Source good, fresh ramen noodles at a local Asian grocery – they will be much higher quality and make for a better soup. If you are new to Japanese cooking, this is a great recipe for a weekend project.

For the chicken stock, place the vegetables, chicken, water or stock and salt in a large pot. Place a few small plates on top of the chicken and vegetables to keep them submerged and simmer gently over a medium heat until the chicken pieces are cooked through, about 7–10 minutes for the breasts and 15–18 minutes for the legs and thighs. The meat should separate from the end of the leg bone when cooked, a thermometer will read 74°C (165°F) when inserted into the thickest part of the thigh or breast and the juices of the chicken will run clear.

When the chicken is cooked, remove from the pot and leave until cool enough to handle, then remove the chicken skin and discard. Using your hands, shred all the meat and discard the bones. Set the meat aside.

Strain the stock through a fine-mesh sieve into a large airtight container. The stock can be stored for 2–3 days in the refrigerator, or for up to 3 months in the freezer.

For the dashi, combine the kombu with the water in a pot over a low–medium heat. The water should be approaching a boil after about 20 minutes. When the water comes to the boil, immediately turn off the heat and remove the kombu. Add the dried bonito flakes and wait for 20–30 minutes until the flakes have absorbed water and sink to the bottom of the pot.

Strain the broth through a fine-mesh sieve, but do not squeeze the excess liquid from the bonito flakes, as this will make the dashi cloudy and bitter. The dashi can be stored in a large airtight container for 2–3 days in the refrigerator, or for up to 3 months in the freezer.

For the tare, combine all the ingredients in a small bowl with the salt and mix thoroughly. Set aside.

Combine the stock, dashi and tare in a large pot, making sure all the tare ingredients dissolve in the soup. Keep warm on the stove until ready to serve.

To assemble the ramen, bring a large pot of seasoned water to the boil. Add the noodles and boil until just tender. Place each portion in a ramen bowl. Ladle the warm broth over to cover the noodles, making sure the soup comes to right above the noodles, then top each bowl with two quarters of the toasted nori, half an egg and the marinated spring onions. Drizzle with chili oil and serve immediately.

Marinated Spring Onions

Serves 4

about 30 spring (green) onions, finely chopped diagonally, rinsed thoroughly in cold water and dried
3 tablespoons toasted sesame oil
1½ teaspoons sea salt
¾ teaspoon soy sauce
¾ teaspoon granulated sugar
¾ teaspoon freshly ground black pepper

Thoroughly mix all the ingredients together in a bowl. Set aside until ready to use.

Soft-boiled Eggs

Makes 2 eggs

2 large eggs, cold

Bring a pot of water to the boil, then carefully add the eggs, one at a time, and gently boil for 7 minutes. Drain the eggs and transfer to a bowl of ice-cold water to stop them cooking. Leave to cool, then peel and set aside.

Tori Paitan Ramen

Japan

Serves 4–6

900 g (2 lb) chicken bones (wings, backs and necks with
    some meat attached)
450 g (1 lb) chicken feet
2.4 liters (81 fl oz/10 cups) water
2 × 30 cm (12 in) pieces kombu
2 negi (Japanese leeks) or leeks, cut into 2.5 cm (1 in) thick slices
1 garlic head, cut in half along the equator
10 cm (4 in) piece ginger, peeled and sliced
1 tablespoon kosher salt or sea salt
120 ml (4 fl oz/½ cup) vegetable oil
175 g (6 oz) fresh shiitake mushrooms, trimmed and quartered
6 Asian shallots, thinly sliced
450 g (1 lb) fresh or dried ramen noodles
2 large Soft-boiled Eggs (page 115)
20 spring (green) onions, green parts only, thinly sliced
2 tablespoons toasted white and black sesame seeds
12 pieces toasted nori, about 10 × 15 cm (4 × 6 in)
soy sauce
toasted sesame oil

Due to the lack of marrow in chicken bones (as compared to pork bones), a chicken broth will never have the same qualities as a pork-style ramen. Because chicken wingtips and feet have a high ratio of cartilage and skin to meat and bone, they are perfect for getting a rich, sticky broth.

Place the chicken bones and feet, water, kombu, negi or leeks, garlic, ginger and salt in a pot and simmer over a low–medium heat for 6–8 hours. Alternatively, cook in a pressure cooker on high for 2 hours. Strain the broth, pressing out all the liquid from the meat and bones, and reserve.

Heat 2 tablespoons of the vegetable oil in a pan over a medium–high heat. Add the mushrooms and cook until tender and golden. Season with salt. Set aside. Add the remaining oil to the pan and heat over a low–medium heat. Add the shallots and cook for 10 minutes until golden. Strain and set aside.

Rewarm the broth and season with salt.

Bring a pot of seasoned water to the boil. Add the noodles and boil for 1–2 minutes until just tender. Place a portion of noodles in 4–6 ramen bowls. Ladle the broth over, making sure it comes to above the noodles, then top with an egg, spring onions, mushrooms, shallots, sesame seeds and nori. Drizzle with soy and sesame oil to taste.

White Stew

Japan

Serves 4–6

1 tablespoon vegetable oil
55 g (2 oz) thick-cut bacon, cut into matchsticks
1 small onion, cut into 5 mm (¼ in) cubes
2 garlic cloves, thinly sliced
12 button mushrooms, halved
1 bay leaf
60 ml (2 fl oz/¼ cup) white wine
2 tablespoons all-purpose (plain) flour
750 ml (25½ fl oz/3 cups) Chicken Stock (page 237)
1 tablespoon salt
1 yellow potato, such as yukon gold, peeled and cut into
    1 cm (½ in) cubes
280 g (10 oz) boneless, skinless chicken breasts, cut into
    2.5 cm (1 in) cubes
140 g (5 oz) broccoli, cut into florets
120 ml (4 fl oz/½ cup) half and half or light (single) cream
30 g (1 oz) butter

Dairy was not a big part of the Japanese diet until after World War II, when Westerners began traveling to the country with frequency. As a result of this influence, dairy was added to a number of dishes. This soup is a balance of East/West flavors, and it is so popular and such a part of Japanese culture now that convenience 'mix packets' can be bought at the supermarket to make it. White stew is a light chowder; the combination of bacon, mushrooms and potato creates lovely umami notes. The dairy can be substituted with soy milk.

Heat the oil in a large pot over a medium–high heat. Add the bacon, onion, garlic, mushrooms and bay leaf and cook for 3–4 minutes until the onions begin to become translucent. Add the white wine, then stir in the flour, making sure there are no lumps. Add the stock and salt and bring to a gentle simmer. Add the potatoes and cook for 3–4 minutes, then add the chicken and broccoli. Cook very gently for 3–4 minutes until the chicken is cooked and the potatoes are tender.

Stir in the half and half or cream, then season with salt and freshly ground black pepper and ladle into serving bowls. Top each bowl with a small pat (½ tablespoon) of butter, which will melt into the soup, and serve.

Dak Kalguksu

Serves 4

1 × 1.35 kg (3 lb) chicken, quartered
1 yellow onion, half cut into quarters,
   the other half cut into thin half-moons
15 garlic cloves, thinly sliced
7.5 cm (3 in) piece ginger, peeled and
   thinly sliced
3 spring (green) onions, white parts cut into
   2.5 cm (1 in) pieces, green parts cut into
   thin rounds
1.9 liters (64 fl oz/8 cups) water
   or Chicken Stock (page 237)
1 zucchini (courgette), julienned
1 teaspoon salt
1 tablespoon vegetable oil
1 teaspoon toasted sesame oil
7.5 cm (3 in) square dried kombu
2 tablespoons soy sauce
Fresh Noodles (see below)
Yangneomjang Sauce (see below/opposite)

Fresh noodles
420 g (15 oz/3 cups) all-purpose (plain)
   flour, plus extra for dusting
¾ teaspoon salt
1 tablespoon vegetable oil
240 ml (8 fl oz/1 cup) water, plus extra
   as needed

Yangnyeomjang sauce
3 tablespoons soy sauce
1 teaspoon toasted sesame oil
1½ teaspoons gochugaru (Korean
   red pepper flakes)
1 teaspoon white sesame seeds
1 garlic clove
3 spring (green) onions, finely chopped

Dak (chicken) kalguksu is made with a rich chicken broth and shredded chicken with noodles. Kalguksu means 'knife noodles', and refers to a noodle soup that is traditionally made with hand-cut noodles. It is a favorite in Korea, especially in the summer months – Koreans believe hot soup has cooling properties. Cook the noodles in a separate pot so the soup does not get starchy and cloudy. Variations include julienned or sliced vegetables such as onion, zucchini (courgette), carrot or potato. Dak kalguksu is often served with kimchi.

Place the chicken in a large pot with the onion, 14 cloves of sliced garlic, ginger, spring onion whites and the water or stock. Bring to the boil over a medium–high heat, skimming any foam off the top, then reduce the heat to low–medium and simmer very gently. Place a few small plates on top of the chicken to keep it submerged, then cook, uncovered, for 20–30 minutes until a thermometer registers 74°C (165°F) when inserted into the thickest part of the thigh and breast and the juices of the chicken run clear.

Meanwhile, make the noodles and sauce (see below and opposite).

Place the julienned zucchini in a small bowl with the salt and leave for about 15 minutes, then, using your hands, squeeze out the excess water from the zucchini. Heat a sauté or frying pan over a medium–high heat and add the vegetable oil. Add the zucchini and cook for 2–3 minutes, stirring, until tender. Set aside.

When the chicken is cooked, remove from the pot and leave until cool enough to handle, then remove the chicken skin and discard. Using your hands, shred all the meat and discard the bones. Place the meat in a bowl and combine with the remaining sliced garlic, the sesame oil and the salt and freshly ground black pepper.

Strain the broth through a fine-mesh sieve, rinse the pot and pour the broth back into the pot. Add the dried kombu, onion slices and soy sauce and bring to a gentle simmer over a low–medium heat for 5 minutes. Season with salt and pepper to taste. Remove the kombu and warm the soup over a medium heat, just to keep warm.

Meanwhile, bring a large pot of salted water to the boil. Add the noodles, stir and cook for 1–2 minutes until tender.

Remove the noodles with a strainer and divide the noodles, zucchini and chicken among four large soup bowls. Ladle the hot broth over the top and garnish with the yangnyeomjang sauce and thinly sliced spring onion greens.

Fresh Noodles

Mix the flour, salt and oil together in a large bowl. Add 175 ml (6 fl oz/¾ cup) water and stir by hand. Add the remaining water, a little at a time, until the dough comes together. If more water is needed, add 1 tablespoon water at a time until the dough is firm and cohesive.

Knead the dough with the heel of your hand on a generously floured work surface for 7–8 minutes until it is fairly smooth. The dough should feel slightly stiff.

You can adjust the dough by kneading in a little more flour or more water (just enough to wet your hands). Wrap in plastic wrap and leave to rest in the refrigerator for 1 hour. After resting, the dough should feel soft and smooth.

Line a baking tray with baking paper, then dust it with flour and set aside. Using a sharp knife, cut the dough into four pieces. Keep the dough covered with plastic wrap or a tea towel. Working with one piece at a time, flatten it on a floured work surface and roll it out into a thin sheet, about 30 × 35 cm (12 × 14 in). The rectangle does not need to be perfect. Don't incorporate too much additional flour into the noodle dough or the noodles will become tough.

Cut the dough into strips about 5 mm (¼ in) wide with a sharp knife and dust with flour to keep the noodle strands separate. Place on the prepared baking tray until ready to use. The noodles can be refrigerated on the baking tray and covered with an additional piece of baking paper, then wrapped in plastic wrap. Use the noodles within 24 hours. They can also be frozen on a baking tray, then stored airtight in the freezer and cooked directly from frozen.

Yangnyeomjang Sauce

Place all the ingredients in a small bowl and stir to combine. Use immediately, or store in an airtight container in the refrigerator for up to 1 week.

Dakjuk

Dakjuk is Korean chicken and rice porridge. Everyone has a preference on how thick or thin they like their porridge, but no one way is correct. Traditionally, this soup is made with water, but I cook mine with rich stock because it is nutritious and delicious. For a thinner soup style, use 200 g (7 oz/1 cup) rice; for a thicker porridge style, use 300 g (10½ oz/1½ cups) rice. Traditional variations are to omit the egg in the soup and add a poached egg on top before serving, seasoning with chili sauce or serving with kimchi.

Serves 4–6

4 large eggs
6 spring (green) onions, thinly
    sliced into rounds
250 g (9 oz/1¼ cups) jasmine rice, soaked
    in a bowl of cold water for 1 hour
10 garlic cloves, thinly sliced

Broth
1 × 1.35 kg (3 lb) chicken
5 garlic cloves, cut in half
3.3 liters (112 fl oz/14 cups) water
    or Chicken Stock (page 237)
1 tablespoon salt

For the broth, place the chicken and garlic in a large pot. The chicken should fit in the pot snugly with the garlic. Add the water or stock and the salt and bring to the boil. Immediately reduce the heat to low–medium and simmer very gently. Place a few small plates on top of the chicken to keep it submerged, then cook, uncovered, for 20–30 minutes until a thermometer registers 74°C (165°F) when inserted into the thickest part of the thigh and breast and the juices of the chicken run clear.

Meanwhile, beat the eggs in a bowl until combined. Stir in the spring onions and set aside.

When the chicken is cooked, strain the liquid and reserve the broth. Leave until the chicken is cool enough to handle, then remove the chicken skin and discard. Shred all the meat from the carcass and discard the bones. Set the meat aside.

Rinse and dry the pot. Rinse the rice, then add the garlic, rice and broth to the pot and bring to the boil over a medium–high heat. Reduce the heat to a very gentle simmer and cook for 60–90 minutes, stirring occasionally, until the rice is tender and has absorbed all the broth. Add more broth or water as needed to keep the soup at a porridge consistency. Season with salt and add the chicken meat. Turn off the heat and drizzle in the beaten eggs and spring onions. Wait for 10 seconds, then gently stir a couple of times to incorporate the egg. Ladle into bowls and garnish with the sauce and seasoning.

Salt and Pepper Seasoning

Serves 4

2 tablespoons salt
½ teaspoon ground black pepper

Mix the salt and pepper together in a small bowl. Use to sprinkle on top of the dish for seasoning. This is very popular in Korean cuisine.

Soy, Chili and Sesame Sauce

Serves 4–6

60 ml (2 fl oz/¼ cup) soy sauce
2 tablespoons unseasoned rice wine vinegar
2 tablespoons very finely sliced spring
    (green) onion
2 teaspoons granulated sugar
2 teaspoons white sesame seeds, toasted
2 teaspoons gochugaru (Korean chili flakes)

Mix all ingredients in a small bowl. Drizzle as preferred on Dakjuk.

Yeong Gye Baeksuk

Serves 4

1 × 1.35 kg (3 lb) chicken
10 garlic cloves, halved
1 yellow onion, quartered with root
    end holding quarters together
1.9 liters (64 fl oz/8 cups) water
    or Chicken Stock (page 237)
1 tablespoon salt
4 spring (green) onions, sliced
    into thin rings

Yeong gye baeksuk is soup made with young chicken only. The broth is clear and the soup is served simply, with cooked onion, shreds of chicken and broth. The soup is said to have healing properties for those with ailments, including allergies and exhaustion. It is usually served with kimchi and dried roasted seaweed. Variations of this soup include dak baeksuk, soup made with adult chicken without any additional herbal ingredients, and Samgyetang, soup made with young chicken, ginseng, dates and sweet rice stuffing (page 122).

Place the chicken, garlic and onion in a large pot. The chicken should fit in the pot snugly with the garlic and onion. Add the water or stock and salt and bring to the boil. Immediately reduce the heat to low–medium and simmer very gently. Place a few small plates on top of the chicken to keep it submerged, then cook, uncovered, for 20–30 minutes until a thermometer registers 74°C (165°F) when inserted into the thickest part of the thigh and breast and the juices of the chicken run clear.

When the chicken is cooked, strain the liquid to remove any solids and reserve the broth. Leave the chicken to cool enough to handle, then remove the chicken skin and discard. Using your hands, shred all the meat from the carcass and discard the bones. Add the meat back to the soup.

Ladle the broth, chicken and ¼ wedge of cooked onion into serving bowls and garnish with spring onions, sauce and salt and pepper seasoning (see opposite). Serve with jasmine rice in the soup or on the side. The chicken can also be served on the side and dipped into the sauce.

Serves 4

3 tablespoons soy sauce
3 teaspoons rice wine vinegar

Soy and Vinegar Sauce

Mix the soy sauce and vinegar together in a small bowl and use to season the soup.

Samgyetang

Serves 4

4 Cornish hens, about 670 g (1½ lb)
   each, giblets or innards removed and
   set aside for another use
200 g (7 oz/1 cup) glutinous rice or
   sweet rice, rinsed and soaked in
   cold water for 2 hours
4 fresh ginseng roots
8 dried jujube fruit (red dates)
32 garlic cloves
2.9 liters (97½ fl oz/12 cups) water
   or Chicken stock (page 237)
4 spring (green) onions, white parts
   cut into 2.5 cm (1 in) lengths, green
   parts cut into thin rings
5 cm (2 in) piece ginger, peeled and
   very thinly sliced
1 tablespoon salt
Sesame Dipping Sauce (see below), to serve
Sweet and Sour Soy Dipping Sauce
   (see below), to serve

This soup is served as a summer dish in Korea, eaten as a way to retain energy and to balance the body's heat in the intense humidity of the season. Koreans have a saying: Fight fire with fire. So, they designate the three hottest days of the year as sambok. The dates vary each year, but they usually fall in July and August. First is chobok (beginning), ten days later is jungbok (middle), and twenty days after that is malbok (last). During this time, samgyetang restaurants will have lines forming out the door, while inside they are packed with diners eating hot, steamy, ginseng-infused soup, with sweat running down their foreheads. Samgyetang is made at home, too. Serve with kimchi.

Put the hens on a chopping board, pat dry with paper towel and remove any extra fat around the body cavities with a knife or kitchen scissors.

Drain the soaked rice water. Stuff each hen with rice, 1 ginseng, 2 jujube fruit and 8 garlic cloves. Place the hens in a large heavy-bottomed pot. They should fit comfortably next to one another. Add any leftover rice, then pour in the water or stock, spring onion whites, ginger and salt. Cover with a lid and simmer gently over a medium heat for 45 minutes, ladling some of the broth over the hens occasionally to keep them moist.

Season with salt and garnish with spring onion greens. Serve with dipping sauces.

Serves 4

3 tablespoons soy sauce
2 tablespoons distilled white vinegar
1 teaspoon honey
½ yellow onion, very finely chopped
1 jalapeño chili, finely chopped

Sweet and Sour Soy Dipping Sauce

Combine the soy sauce, vinegar and honey together in a small bowl. Mix well with a spoon, then add the onion and jalapeño. Set aside.

Serves 4

2 teaspoons salt
1 teaspoon white sesame seeds, toasted
½ teaspoon ground black pepper
2 tablespoons toasted sesame oil

Sesame Dipping Sauce

Combine the salt, sesame seeds, ground black pepper and sesame oil in a small bowl and mix well. Set aside.

Ohn-No Khao Swè

Serves 4–6

2 yellow onions, ½ cut into 2 cm
    (¾ in) cubes and remaining 3 halves cut
    into thin half-moons
5 cm (2 in) piece ginger, peeled and
    roughly chopped
2 tablespoons chickpea flour
2 garlic cloves, thinly sliced
750 ml (25½ fl oz/3 cups) water or
    Chicken Stock (page 237)
450 g (1 lb) chicken thighs, bone-in with
    skin attached, hacked into 1 cm
    (½ in) chunks
2 tablespoons vegetable oil
1 teaspoon ground turmeric
2 teaspoons paprika
400 ml (13½ fl oz) canned coconut milk
1 teaspoon cayenne pepper
fish sauce, to taste
450 g (1 lb) fresh or dried Chinese-style
    wheat noodles

To garnish
lime wedges
cilantro (coriander) leaves
sliced shallots or red onions
Hard-boiled Eggs (page 33), cut into
    slices or halves
roasted chili powder
Fried Rice Noodles (see below)
fish sauce, to taste

Burma is home to a great number of cultures and ingredients; Burmese borrow what they love from those who have moved to their country. In this soup, wheat noodles reflect China's influence (rice noodles are more traditional to Southeast Asian countries). Ohn-no khao swè, like Hainanese chicken rice (page 108), was a catalyst for culinary innovation in neighboring countries. Thailand's Chiang Mai is famous for its khao soi, Malaysians favor laksa, and India's khow suey is a riff on ohn-no khao swè. To note, many brands of canned coconut milk are much thicker than what is used in Southeast Asia. For a more authentic broth and a lighter consistency, blend half canned coconut milk and half water.

Place the cubed onion, ginger, chickpea flour, garlic and water or stock into a blender and purée until very smooth. Set aside.

Lay the chicken pieces out on a plate and sprinkle lightly with salt and freshly ground black pepper, then set aside.

Heat a large pot over a medium–high heat and add the oil. When the oil is hot, toss in the chicken and stir-fry for 5–7 minutes until lightly browned. Some of the fat will render from the chicken skin. Add the sliced onions and cook slowly for 5–7 minutes, allowing the onions to caramelize. When the onions are just about golden, add the turmeric and paprika and stir to combine. Add the puréed onion mixture and the remaining water or stock and stir well. Bring to the boil, then reduce the heat to low and simmer gently, uncovered, for 20–25 minutes until the chicken is tender. Add the coconut milk, cayenne and fish sauce, then season to taste with more salt, if needed.

Bring a large pot of water to a simmer. Add the wheat noodles and cook (for 3–4 minutes for fresh and 6–8 minutes for dry) until tender. Drain the noodles and divide among 4 large soup bowls. Ladle the soup over the noodles and garnish with your preferred toppings.

Serves 4–6

750 ml (25½fl oz/3 cups) vegetable oil
50–100 g (1¾–3½ oz) vermicelli rice noodles

Fried Rice Noodles

Heat a 5 cm (2 in) depth of vegetable oil in a small frying pan over a medium–high heat. When the oil is hot, gently lay the dried rice noodles in the hot oil and when the noodles puff up, use a slotted spoon to remove them onto a plate lined with paper towel to drain. Set aside for the garnish.

Tinolang Manok

Chicken Tinola

Serves 4–6

2 tablespoons rendered chicken
  fat or vegetable oil
1 large yellow onion, very finely chopped
6 garlic cloves, thinly sliced
10 cm (4 in) piece ginger, peeled and
  sliced into very thin coins
4 bay leaves
1 × 1.35 kg (3 lb) chicken, quartered
1.9 liters (64 fl oz/8 cups) water
  or Chicken Stock (page 237)
60–70 ml (2–2¼ fl oz/¼ cup) fish sauce
670 g (1½ lb/4 cups) unripened green
  papaya (about ½ large papaya), peeled
  and cubed
1 bok choy head, leaves and stalks
  cut into 2.5 cm (1 in) pieces

The green papaya in this lovely, restorative soup is evocative of the Philippines – and is definitely not something you see every day in a soup. It has a vegetal flavor, but it is a fruit. (Do be careful not to overcook the papaya, or its texture will become mushy.) The ginger, fish sauce and bok choy all play up the Asian profile and make this soup light, crisp, clean, aromatic and refreshing. Tinola is traditionally served with steamed jasmine rice, and the bok choy is often replaced with fresh malunggay (horseradish tree) leaves or ampalaya (bitter melon). Amp up the heat with the addition of fresh sliced chili, such as jalapeño, serrano or something similar.

Heat the chicken fat or oil in a large pot over a medium heat. Add the onion, garlic, ginger and bay leaves and cook for 3–4 minutes until the onion becomes translucent. Add the chicken, water or stock and fish sauce and simmer gently over a medium heat until the chicken pieces are cooked through, about 7–10 minutes for the breasts and 15–18 minutes for the legs and thighs. The meat should separate from the end of the leg bone when cooked, a thermometer will read 74°C (165°F) when inserted into the thickest part of the thigh or breast and the juices of the chicken will run clear.

When the chicken is cooked, remove from the pot and leave until cool enough to handle, then remove the chicken skin and discard. Using your hands, shred all the meat and discard the bones. Set the meat aside.

Meanwhile, add the papaya to the pot and simmer gently for 5 minutes, or until just tender. Add the bok choy and chicken, then season with salt and freshly ground black pepper and serve.

Pancit Molo

Serves 4–6

120 ml (4 fl oz/½ cup) vegetable oil
15 garlic cloves, finely sliced
225 g (8 oz) small peeled and
    deveined prawns
4 spring (green) onions, thinly sliced

Broth
1 × 1.35 kg (3 lb) chicken
2 garlic cloves
2.4 liters (81 fl oz/10 cups) water
    or Chicken Stock (page 237)
1 tablespoon salt
60–70 ml (2–2¼ fl oz/¼ cup) fish sauce

Dumplings
450 g (1 lb) ground (minced) pork
¼ large yellow onion, finely diced
½ teaspoon toasted sesame oil
1 large egg, whisked with a fork and
    divided in half
2 teaspoons salt
24 wonton wrappers

See image on page 127.

The Spanish colonized the Philippines from 1521 to 1898 and the Chinese set up trade posts in Filipino coastal towns as early as the Sung Dynasty (960–1127 AD). Pancit molo resembles Chinese wonton soup, but with an addition of ingredients and flavors that meld the Filipino, Chinese and Spanish cuisines. The name pancit molo refers to the famous Filipino town Molo. Wontons were first included in the seaport village, adding a Chinese element to the soup. Spanish fried garlic was included as a garnish and Filipino fish sauce added roundness and umami. The traditional components are Chinese wontons (a mixture of ground/minced pork wrapped in wonton wrapper), shredded chicken meat and prawns. Pancit (or pansit) is the Filipino word for noodles. Although there are no traditional noodles in this soup, it earns the name from the wonton wrappers.

To make the broth, place the chicken and garlic in a large pot. The chicken should fit in the pot snugly with the garlic. Add the water or stock and salt and bring to the boil. Immediately reduce the heat to low–medium and simmer very gently. Place a few small plates on top of the chicken to keep it submerged, then cook, uncovered, for 20–30 minutes until a thermometer registers 74°C (165°F) when inserted into the thickest part of the thigh and breast and the juices of the chicken run clear.

Meanwhile, caramelize the garlic. Warm the vegetable oil in a small frying pan over a medium heat. Add the sliced garlic, reduce the heat to low and cook gently for 10–15 minutes until the garlic is caramelized. Strain immediately and reserve the garlic for the garnish.

To make the dumplings, line a baking tray with baking paper. Combine the pork, onion, sesame oil, ½ egg and salt in a bowl. Place 1 tablespoon of the pork mixture in the center of a wonton wrapper and, using your index finger, moisten two adjacent sides of the wrapper with the remaining whisked egg. Fold the wonton into a triangle, squeezing out any air pockets, then moisten one of the long ends with egg and bring the two long ends together, similar to a tortellini. Place the dumplings on the lined tray and repeat until the filling is used up. The filling should make about 24 dumplings.

When the chicken is cooked, strain the liquid to remove any solids and reserve the broth. Leave the chicken until cool enough to handle, then remove the chicken skin and discard. Using your hands, shred all the meat from the carcass and discard the bones. Set the meat aside.

Rinse and dry the pot, then pour the broth back into the pot. Add the fish sauce and season with salt. Bring to a gentle simmer, then add the wontons and cook for 2 minutes. Add the prawns, spring onion and chicken meat and cook for 1 minute, or just until the prawns are barely cooked. Garnish with the caramelized garlic.

Arroz Caldo

Serves 4–6

175 ml (6 fl oz/¾ cup) vegetable oil
22 garlic cloves, thinly sliced
1 yellow onion, cut into thin half-moons
5 cm (2 in) piece ginger, peeled and thinly
  sliced then cut into matchsticks
250 g (9 oz/1¼ cups) jasmine rice
1 tablespoon salt
2 tablespoons fish sauce
6 spring (green) onions, sliced to garnish
3 large Hard-boiled Eggs (page 33), halved,
  to serve
2 calamansi or limes, to serve

Broth
1 × 1.35 kg (3 lb) chicken
5 garlic cloves, halved
3.3 liters (112 fl oz/14 cups) water
  or Chicken Stock (page 237), plus extra
  if required
1 tablespoon salt

This is the Filipino interpretation of congee, the thick rice porridge popular in many Asian cultures. Chicken and rice are simmered in a ginger-based broth until the grains have disintegrated into porridge-like consistency. Fried garlic bits, a Spanish contribution, chopped spring onions and calamansi juice offer additional layers of gentle, complex flavor. Arroz caldo is most commonly served as a midday merienda, or snack, but as it often includes meat, eggs or seafood, it is substantial enough as a meal on its own. Arroz caldo is usually made with uncooked rice, but leftover steamed rice can be substituted to reduce the cooking time. Serve with chili oil and fish sauce.

To make the broth, place the chicken and garlic in a large pot. The chicken should fit in the pot snugly with the garlic. Add the water or stock and salt and bring to the boil. Immediately reduce the heat to low–medium and simmer very gently. Place a few small plates on top of the chicken to keep it submerged, then cook, uncovered, for 20–30 minutes until a thermometer registers 74°C (165°F) when inserted into the thickest part of the thigh and breast and the juices of the chicken run clear.

Meanwhile, caramelize the garlic. Warm 120 ml (4 fl oz/½ cup) of the vegetable oil in a small frying pan over a medium heat. Add two-thirds of the sliced garlic, reduce the heat to low and cook gently for 10–15 minutes until the garlic is caramelized. Strain immediately and reserve the garlic for the garnish.

When the chicken is cooked, strain the liquid to remove any solids and reserve the broth. Leave the chicken until cool enough to handle, then remove the chicken skin and discard. Using your hands, shred all the meat from the carcass and discard the bones. Set the meat aside.

Rinse and dry the pot. Heat the remaining oil in the pot over a medium–high heat. Add the onion, ginger and remaining sliced garlic and sauté, stirring frequently, for 5 minutes until the onions are translucent. Stir in the rice, then add the strained broth and season with the salt. Add enough water or stock to the broth to make 2.9 liters (97½ fl oz/12 cups) in total. Bring to the boil, then reduce the heat to a very gentle simmer and cook, stirring occasionally, for 60–90 minutes until the rice is tender and has absorbed all the broth. Add more stock or water as needed to keep the soup at a porridge consistency. Season the soup with salt, add the reserved chicken and stir in the fish sauce.

Garnish the soup with spring onion slices, the reserved crispy garlic and ½ hard-boiled egg. Serve with calamansi or limes to squeeze over the soup.

ASIA

Russskij Kurinij Sup s Kljotskami

Russia

Serves 4

1 × 1.35 kg (3 lb) chicken
2 carrots, cut into 2.5 cm (1 in) pieces
1 yellow onion, roughly chopped
3 garlic cloves, halved
2 bay leaves
1.9 liters (64 fl oz/8 cups) water
   or Chicken Stock (page 237)
1 tablespoon salt
3 yellow potatoes, such as yukon gold,
   peeled and cut into bite-sized pieces
2 bay leaves
15 g (½ oz) dill, chopped

Dumplings
280 g (10 oz/2 cups) all-purpose (plain)
   flour, plus extra for dusting
½ teaspoon salt
¼ teaspoon granulated sugar
2 large eggs
1 tablespoon sour cream
90 g (3 oz) butter, melted

Not so different from chicken and dumplings in the Southern United States, this rib-sticky dish is the frugal attempt, like many chicken soups, to fill the belly with inexpensive doughy dumplings. The one-up this recipe offers is the classic Russian sour cream smetana, used in many dishes with abandon. These dumplings are rich and decadent and simple to make.

Place the chicken, carrots, onion, garlic and bay leaves in a large pot. The chicken should fit in the pot snugly with the vegetables. Add the water or stock and salt and bring to the boil. Immediately reduce the heat to low–medium and simmer very gently. Place a few small plates on top of the chicken to keep it submerged, then cook, uncovered, for 20–30 minutes until a thermometer registers 74°C (165°F) when inserted into the thickest part of the thigh and breast and the juices of the chicken run clear.

Meanwhile, make the dumplings. Sift the flour, salt and sugar into a bowl. Using a fork, stir the eggs and the sour cream into the flour mixture. The dough will look shaggy and dry. Pour in the melted butter and stir, then knead using your hands until the butter is well incorporated and the dough is cohesive. The dough should be very soft but not sticky.

Transfer the dough to a lightly floured chopping board and divide into two pieces. Roll each piece into a long slim log, about 2.5 cm (1 in) in diameter, then cut each log into 1 cm (½ in) slices. The dumplings will expand when cooking, so make sure to keep the slices small and uniform. Ideally, they should be bite-sized.

When the chicken is cooked, strain the broth to remove any solids and pour back into the pot. Leave the chicken until cool enough to handle, then remove the chicken skin and discard. Using your hands, shred all the meat from the carcass and discard the bones. Set the meat aside.

Bring the soup to a gentle simmer, add the potato and bay leaves. Cook for 3 minutes, then add the dumplings, cover with a lid and cook at a gentle simmer for 5–7 minutes until the dumplings are tender. Add the chicken, season with salt and pepper and stir in the dill.

Russkij Kurinij Sup s Lapshoj

My heritage is Russian and Polish and this is the style of chicken soup I grew up with. It was the broth for matzo ball soup, usually strained, and the cure-all ('Jewish penicillin') when my family was sick. The thickness of the noodles can vary depending on how they are rolled; the thicker the noodle, the more dense and chewy the texture. Thinner noodles have a more delicate texture, thicker are more rustic. Noodles plump up as they cook, and noodles will absorb the broth. Cook the noodles on the side and add to each bowl to keep the soup from losing its brothy base.

Serves 4–6

2 tablespoons rendered chicken fat
    or vegetable oil
2 large carrots, cut into 1 cm (½ in) cubes
1 yellow onion, cut into 1 cm (½ in) cubes
2 celery ribs (stalks), cut into 1 cm
    (½ in) cubes
3 potatoes, peeled and cut into 1 cm
    (½ in) cubes
¼ bunch parsley, roughly chopped

Broth
1 × 1.35 kg (3 lb) chicken
2 carrots, cut into 2.5 cm (1 in) pieces
1 yellow onion, roughly chopped
3 garlic cloves, halved
2 bay leaves
1.9 liters (64 fl oz/8 cups) water
    or Chicken Stock (page 237)
1 tablespoon salt

Noodles
280 g (10 oz/2 cups) all-purpose (plain)
    flour, plus extra for dusting
2 teaspoons salt
2 large eggs

See image on page 130.

To make the broth, place the chicken, carrots, onion, garlic and bay leaves in a large pot. The chicken should fit in the pot snugly with the vegetables. Add the water or stock and salt and bring to the boil. Immediately reduce the heat to low–medium and simmer very gently. Place a few small plates on top of the chicken to keep it submerged, then cook, uncovered, for 20–30 minutes until a thermometer registers 74°C (165°F) when inserted into the thickest part of the thigh and breast and the juices of the chicken run clear.

Meanwhile, make the noodles. Place the flour, salt and eggs in a bowl and, using a fork, stir to combine. The dough will look shaggy and dry. Add 4 tablespoons water and knead with your hands for 10 minutes, or until the dough is cohesive. Add 1–2 tablespoons water if needed to reach a soft, pliable dough that is not sticky. Wrap the dough in plastic wrap and leave to rest at room temperature for 30 minutes.

When the chicken is cooked, strain the liquid to remove any solids and reserve the broth. Leave the chicken until cool enough to handle, then remove the chicken skin and discard. Using your hands, shred all the meat from the carcass and discard the bones. Set the meat aside.

Line a baking tray with baking paper and lightly flour it. Divide the noodle dough into four pieces. Using a pasta roller or rolling pin, roll the dough into sheets 5 mm (¼ in) thick, then cut the dough into 10 cm (4 in) long and 1 cm (½ in) wide noodles. If the dough is moist, dredge it through flour before rolling so the dough does not stick to the surface or roller. Do not knead more flour into the dough. Place the cut noodles on the prepared baking tray. Don't overlap the noodles or they may stick together. Leave to dry at room temperature for 30 minutes, or freeze on the baking tray for longer storage. Store frozen in an airtight container until ready to use and cook from frozen. Frozen noodles will need an extra 2–3 minutes to cook.

Rinse and dry the pot, then add the chicken fat and heat over a medium–high heat until melted. Add the carrot, onion and celery and cook, stirring frequently, for 3–4 minutes until the vegetables begin to soften. Season with salt, then, when the vegetables are tender, add the potatoes and broth and bring to a gentle simmer. Cook for another 5 minutes, or until the potatoes are tender.

Bring a pot of salted water to a simmer. Add the noodles and cook for 2–3 minutes until tender. Thicker noodles will be tender and chewy.

Add the cooked noodles and reserved chicken to the soup, then season with salt and freshly ground black pepper and stir in the parsley.

Sup s Pelmenjami

Russia

Pelmeni are to Russians what tortellini are to Italians. They are small dumplings filled with meat and served in soup, or filled with cheese or potato and tossed in butter. When making pelmeni, it is very important to roll the dough as thinly as possible for the tenderest dumplings. The broth is light and clear, with the regional flavorings of dill and caraway and soft-boiled eggs to garnish.

Serves 4

1 × 1.35 kg (3 lb) chicken
2 carrots, cut into 2.5 cm (1 in) pieces
1 yellow onion, roughly chopped
3 garlic cloves, halved
2 bay leaves
1.9 liters (64 fl oz/8 cups) water
    or Chicken Stock (page 237)
1 tablespoon salt
225 g (8 oz) ground (minced) skinless
    chicken thighs
1 egg yolk
30 g (1 oz) dill, finely chopped
½ teaspoon ground caraway
½ teaspoon ground coriander
¼ teaspoon black pepper
1 teaspoon salt
2 large Soft-boiled Eggs (page 115),
    halved, to garnish

Pelmeni

280 g (10 oz/2 cups) all-purpose (plain)
    flour, plus extra for dusting
2 teaspoons salt
2 large eggs
60 ml (2 fl oz/¼ cup) water, plus extra
    as needed

See image on page 130.

For the pelmeni, mix the flour and salt in a bowl. Using a fork, stir in the eggs and the water. Once the dough starts to form, knead in the bowl or on a work surface until it is a cohesive ball. Add 1 teaspoon extra water at a time until the dough is soft, but not sticky. Wrap in plastic wrap and refrigerate for 45 minutes.

Place the chicken, carrots, onion, garlic and bay leaves in a pot. The chicken should fit in the pot snugly with the vegetables. Add the water or stock and salt and bring to the boil. Immediately reduce the heat to low–medium and simmer very gently. Place a few small plates on top of the chicken to keep it submerged, then cook, uncovered, for 20–30 minutes until a thermometer registers 74°C (165°F) when inserted into the thickest part of the thigh and breast and the juices of the chicken run clear.

When the chicken is cooked, strain the liquid to remove any solids and pour back into the pot. Leave the chicken until cool enough to handle, then remove the chicken skin and discard. Using your hands, shred all the meat from the carcass and discard the bones. Add the meat back to the pot. Season the soup with salt and freshly ground black pepper and bring to a gentle simmer.

Meanwhile, mix the ground chicken with the egg yolk, 1½ teaspoons finely chopped dill, the caraway, coriander, pepper and salt in a bowl. Cover and refrigerate until ready to use.

Lightly flour a baking tray. Roll out the dough on a lightly floured work surface or use a pasta roller to create a 46 cm (18 in) circle, about 3 mm (⅛ in) thick, or thinner if you can. Using a 6 cm (2½ in) cutter, cut out 32 circles, rerolling scraps as needed. Place 1 teaspoon of the chicken filling in the center of each circle of dough, brush the edges with water and fold in half to form a half-moon, sealing the edges. Take the two points of each half-moon and bring them together to form a tortellini-like dumpling. Place the completed dumplings on the prepared baking tray and refrigerate until ready to use.

Bring a large pot of generously salted water to the boil. Add the dumplings and cook for 2–3 minutes until they float to the surface and are cooked through. Using a slotted spoon, remove the dumplings from the water and transfer to four serving bowls. Ladle the broth and some pieces of chicken over the dumplings and garnish each with chopped dill and half an egg.

The dumplings can be frozen in a single layer on a floured baking tray. When frozen, transfer to an airtight container and keep frozen for up to 1 month. To cook frozen pelmeni, cook directly from frozen. the dumplings will take an extra 1–2 minutes to float in boiling water. Cook for 1–2 minutes after the dumplings float and proceed with the rest of the recipe for serving.

Ma You Ji Tang

Serves 4–6

3 tablespoons black sesame oil
    or toasted sesame oil
10 cm (4 in) piece ginger, peeled and
    sliced lengthways, then whacked with
    a chef's knife or cleaver
1 × 1.35 kg (3 lb) chicken, quartered
750 ml (25½ fl oz) Taiwanese rice wine
950 ml (32½ fl oz/4 cups) water
1 garlic head, sliced in half at the equator
4 spring (green) onions, white parts cut into
    2.5 cm (1 in) pieces, green parts julienned
8 black peppercorns
30 g (1 oz) rock sugar

The base of this recipe was sent to me by an acquaintance whose parents grew up in Taiwan. She was raised in the US eating variations of this soup; each time it was served, the seasonings were different. Sometimes the soup was seasoned with soy sauce or served with a dab of chili paste. If cooked noodles were in the refrigerator, they were added. Similarly, cooked rice, spinach or bok choy. Soft-boiled eggs were also a favorite addition, as well as shiitake mushrooms and fresh shaved serrano chilies. The flavor punches were pickles, salty condiments and hot sauce.

Place a large pot over a medium–high heat and add the sesame oil. Add the ginger and chicken pieces and brown the chicken on all sides for 5–7 minutes. Reduce the heat to medium, add the wine, water, garlic, spring onion whites, black peppercorns and rock sugar and season with salt. Bring to a simmer, cover the pot partially with a lid and simmer gently until the chicken pieces are cooked through, about 7–10 minutes for the breasts and 15–18 minutes for the legs and thighs. The meat should separate from the end of the leg bone when cooked, a thermometer will read 74°C (165°F) when inserted into the thickest part of the thigh or breast and the juices of the chicken will run clear.

   When the chicken is cooked, remove from the pot and leave the chicken until cool enough to handle, then remove the chicken skin and discard. Using your hands, tear the meat into large chunks and add back to the pot. Season with salt, if necessary, garnish with the julienned spring onions and serve.

Oo Ji Tang

Serves 4

3 salted turnip stalks or Chinese salted
mustard greens
1 × 670 g (1½ lb) black chicken, Silkie
    or Vikon variety, feet removed and
    carcass quartered
3 tablespoons vegetable oil
4 garlic cloves, thinly sliced
5 cm (2 in) piece ginger, peeled and
    cut into thin rounds
115 g (4 oz) shiitake mushrooms,
    stemmed and caps quartered
1.9 liters (64 fl oz/8 cups) water or
    Chicken Stock (page 237)

Silkie chicken is so named for the breed's silky soft plumage. The chickens have black skin and black bones, blue earlobes and five toes on each foot; hence the nickname black-boned chicken. The meat is grayish black and is typically used for soups. It is not uncommon to find Silkie chickens at Asian supermarkets around the globe; typically frozen. Although there are just a few ingredients in this soup, each ingredient brings its purpose, creating a complex, warm broth.

Rinse the salted turnips in cold water, then place in a container filled with fresh water and leave to soak for 1 hour, changing the water 3 times during soaking. Drain the turnips, slice into thin pieces and reserve.

   Fill a large heavy-bottomed pot with water and place over a high heat. When the water simmers, add the chicken and blanch for 2–3 minutes. Remove the chicken from the pot and drain the water. Set the chicken aside.

Wipe out the pot and place over a medium–high heat. Add the oil, garlic, ginger and mushrooms and cook, stirring constantly, making sure not to burn the garlic. Reduce the heat if necessary. Add the chicken and water or stock, then weigh down the chicken under a few small plates to keep it submerged and bring to a gentle simmer over a medium heat until the chicken pieces are cooked through, about 7–10 minutes for the breasts and 15–18 minutes for the legs and thighs. The meat should separate from the end of the leg bone when cooked, a thermometer will read 74°C (165°F) when inserted into the thickest part of the thigh or breast and the juices of the chicken will run clear.

When the chicken is cooked, remove from the pot and leave until cool enough to handle, then remove the chicken skin and discard. Using your hands, shred the meat and add back to the soup. Alternatively, cut the chicken into smaller portions and serve on the bone. Season the soup with salt and ground white pepper and serve.

Khao Tom Gai

Serves 4

90 ml (3 fl oz/⅓ cup) vegetable oil
24 garlic cloves, thinly sliced
7.5 cm (3 in) piece ginger, peeled and
  cut into very thin strips
250 g (9 oz/1 cup) Khao Tom Buey
  (see below), or leftover steamed
  jasmine rice
950 ml (32½ fl oz/4 cups) water
  or Chicken Stock (page 237)
2 tablespoons salt
40 ml (1¼ fl oz) soy sauce
20 ml (¾ fl oz) fish sauce
280 g (10 oz) chopped, ground (minced)
  or very finely chopped chicken breast
  or thigh
4 large eggs
4 spring (green) onions, thinly sliced
½ bunch cilantro (coriander),
  roughly chopped

Similar to tom kha gai, this soup features rice in the soup, rather than on the side. This is a rice porridge, one of many styles in Asia, and is a typical breakfast dish. The thickness of the soup varies according to preference. Some versions include prawns or pork and will have similar names (gai means chicken in Thai). For a tidier presentation, poach the eggs in a separate pot and add when ready to serve. This soup is always made with cooked rice or rice porridge, and typically the type of rice is broken jasmine (see page 12). Fish sauce, lemongrass, kaffir lime and Thai (bird's eye) chilies are common additions.

Heat the oil in a pot over a medium–high heat and stir in the garlic and ginger. Stir constantly until golden, then remove three-quarters of the garlic-ginger mixture and set aside for the garnish.

Stir in the khao tom buey and water or stock and season with the salt, soy sauce and fish sauce. Cook over a medium–high heat for 3–5 minutes until thickened. Add the chicken, stir and gently crack the eggs into the soup to poach for 1 minute, or until the egg is set. Alternatively, you can stir the eggs into the soup.

Ladle the hot rice soup into four bowls and spoon a poached egg into each, if poaching. Top with the fried garlic and ginger mixture, spring onions, cilantro and ground white pepper to serve.

Serves 4

200 g (7 oz/1 cup) broken jasmine rice
  or jasmine rice
1450 ml (49 fl oz/6 cups) water or
  Chicken Stock (page 237)

Khao Tom Buey (Plain Rice Porridge)

Bring the rice and water or stock to a simmer over a medium–high heat, stirring frequently for 20–30 minutes until the liquid is absorbed and the rice is the consistency of porridge. Use as directed in the recipe.

Khao Soi

Serves 4

Soup
1–2 Thai (bird's eye) chili, more or
    less to taste
2 small Asian shallots, quartered
4 garlic cloves
1 lemongrass stalk, outer leaves
    removed, bottom 10 cm (4 in)
    only, cut into thirds
1 teaspoon kaffir lime zest,
    or 2 whole kaffir lime leaves
2.5 cm (1 in) piece fresh turmeric,
    cut into thirds or 1 tablespoon
    ground turmeric
2.5 cm (1 in) piece ginger, peeled
80 g (2¾ oz) cilantro (coriander) stalks,
    5 cm (2 in) cut from the very base
    of the stalks, leaves and thin stems
    reserved for another use
1 teaspoon whole coriander seeds
6 Thai black cardamom pods or 1 green
    cardamom pod, inner seeds only
1½ tablespoons Thai shrimp paste
240 ml (8 fl oz/1 cup) vegetable oil, plus
    120 ml (4 fl oz/½ cup) extra if using to
    process curry ingredients in a blender
450 g (1 lb) fresh Chinese-style egg noodles
800 ml (27 fl oz) canned coconut milk,
    do not shake tins
750 ml (25½ fl oz/3 cups) water or
    Chicken Stock (page 237)
2 tablespoons palm sugar (jaggery) or soft
    brown sugar
4 × whole chicken legs (approx. 1.35 kg/3 lb),
    leg and thigh attached
fish sauce, to taste

To garnish
4 Asian shallots, thinly sliced
2 limes, cut into wedges
85 g (3 oz/½ cup) pickled Chinese
    mustard leaves and stems

See image on page 138.

With origins in Chiang Mai, Northern Thailand, khao soi is related to the Burmese Ohn-no Khao Swè (page 125). The name khao soi refers to the traditional noodles used for this dish. After steaming large sheets of dough, the noodles were cut with scissors into their final size and shape. It is rare to see these traditional noodles used, but some places in Laos and Thailand still practice the original recipe. The curry is fragrant and rich from coconut milk, and the pickled mustard greens give it a good, clean pungency.

Place the chili, shallots, garlic, lemongrass, lime zest, turmeric, ginger, cilantro stalks, coriander seeds and cardamom in a large mortar and pound with a pestle for 10 minutes to a fine paste, then add the shrimp paste. Alternatively, place all the ingredients in a blender with the 120 ml (4 fl oz/½ cup) vegetable oil and process until very fine. Set aside. The ingredients will only become a fine enough paste in a very powerful blender.

Separate out one-quarter of the noodles (enough noodles to make a crispy fried-noodle topping for 4 bowls) and set the remaining noodles aside. Heat 240 ml (8 fl oz/1 cup) vegetable oil in a large pot over a high heat until shimmering (the temperature should read 180°C (350°F) on a thermometer). Working in batches, carefully add the noodles to the hot oil and deep-fry, stirring and flipping until golden brown and crisp. Season with salt and set aside.

Discard all but 1 tablespoon of the oil from the pot. Using a spoon, skim 2 tablespoons of creamy fat off the top of the coconut milk and add to the pot. Cook over a high heat, stirring constantly, for 2 minutes, or until the coconut milk breaks and the oil begins to lightly smoke. Add the curry paste mixture and cook for 45 seconds, stirring and smearing the paste into the oil, until aromatic.

Slowly whisk in the coconut milk, followed by water or stock and palm sugar. Add the chicken legs and bring to a simmer. Cook for 30 minutes, turning the chicken occasionally, until the chicken is tender and the broth is very flavorful. Season to taste with fish sauce and salt.

Bring a separate pot of salted water to the boil. Add the remaining uncooked noodles and cook for 1 minute until tender. Drain the noodles and add to the soup. Divide the soup among 4 bowls and garnish with fried noodles, sliced shallots, lime wedges and pickled mustard greens on the side.

Tom Kha Gai

Thailand

Serves 4–6

3 lemongrass stalks, tough leaves
  removed and inner layers cut into
  2.5 cm (1 in) strips
5 cm (2 in) piece galangal or ginger, peeled
  and cut into very thin rounds
6 kaffir lime leaves
1450 ml (49 fl oz/6 cups) fresh coconut milk
  or 950 ml (32½ fl oz/4 cups) canned
  coconut milk and 475 ml (16 fl oz/2 cups)
  water
1 large white onion, cut into 1 cm (½ in)
  wedges without the core
2 roma or plum tomatoes, cut into
  8 wedges each
5 Thai (bird's eye) chilies, cut from end/tip
  to stem but not in half
225 g (8 oz) oyster mushrooms, torn
  into smaller pieces
450 g (1 lb) boneless, skinless chicken
  breast, cut into bite-sized pieces
3 tablespoons fish sauce
60 ml (2 fl oz/¼ cup) lime juice
80 g (2¾ oz) cilantro (coriander),
  roughly chopped

Tom kha gai is one of Thailand's most popular soups. The name directly translates to chicken galangal soup, galangal being the brightly flavored rhizome, similar to ginger, that flavors it. The best tom kha gai is cooked gently, allowing the perfume-like flavors to develop and the chicken to remain tender. Traditionally, this soup is served with steamed jasmine rice.

Place the lemongrass in a pot with the galangal, lime leaves and coconut milk and place over a medium heat. Stir well to incorporate, then only stir gently in one direction so as not to agitate the broth too much. The key is not to boil the coconut milk or it may curdle. Keep the heat low enough to barely hit a simmer the entire time the soup is cooking.

Add the onion, tomatoes, chilies, mushrooms, chicken and fish sauce and stir very gently to incorporate. Cook slowly for 5–7 minutes until the chicken is cooked through and the mushrooms and onions are tender. Add lime juice and cilantro and season with salt and serve.

ASIA

Phở Gà

Serves 4

5 cm (2 in) piece ginger, peeled
6 Asian shallots or 2 European shallots
1 × 1.35 kg (3 lb) chicken, quartered
2.9 liters (97½ fl oz/12 cups) water
  or Chicken Stock (page 237)
1 tablespoon coriander seeds, toasted
15 g (½ oz) rock sugar
670 g (1½ lb) fresh rice noodles
40 g (1½ oz/¼ cup) white or yellow
  onion, thinly sliced
30 g (1 oz/¼ cup) spring (green) onions,
  sliced
20 g (¾ oz/¼ cup) cilantro (coriander),
  roughly chopped
80 g (2¾ oz) Vietnamese coriander (rau ram)
180 g (6½ oz/2 cups) mung bean sprouts
1 red chili pepper or jalapeño chili,
  thinly sliced
2 limes, cut into wedges

Beef phở is most commonly associated with Vietnamese noodle soup, but there are variations of phở with pork, chicken and even seafood. This chicken version features a light broth, rice noodles, tender poached chicken and fragrant herbs. Chicken phở is less complex than its rich beef counterpart, but that is exactly what it is about. The broth is cooked for much less time, and the flavors that develop are cleaner and brighter. Serve garnishes on the side and add a little at a time as you eat your soup. Sometimes, Chinese crullers are served alongside.

Preheat the oven to 180°C (350°F). Place the ginger and shallots in a small roasting pan and roast for 30 minutes, or until the shallots are tender. Remove from the oven and leave to cool. When cool, peel the shallots and cut the ginger into thin slices. Set aside.

Place the chicken in a large pot and add enough water to cover the chicken. Bring to a simmer and cook for 3–4 minutes, then strain the water and place the chicken back in the pot. Add the water or stock, ginger, shallots and coriander seeds and bring to a gentle simmer over a medium heat. Simmer until the chicken pieces are cooked, about 7–10 minutes for the breasts and 15–18 minutes for the legs and thighs. The meat should separate from the end of the leg bone when cooked, a thermometer will read 74°C (165°F) when inserted into the thickest part of the thigh or breast and the juices of the chicken will run clear.

When the chicken is cooked, remove from the pot and leave to cool. Put the pot back over a low heat, partially cover with the lid and continue cooking very gently for 1 hour. After 1 hour, stir in the rock sugar until it has dissolved. Season with salt.

When the chicken is cool, remove all the meat in large chunks and discard the skin and bones. Set the meat aside.

Soak the noodles in a large bowl of room temperature water for 30 minutes, then drain. Bring a large pot of water to the boil, add the noodles and cook for 1–2 minutes until tender. Drain the noodles and rinse off the excess starch under cool water, then divide among four bowls. Slice the chicken and add to the bowls.

Pour the hot broth over the noodles and chicken and serve garnished with sliced onion, spring onions, cilantro, Vietnamese coriander, bean sprouts, chili and lime wedges.

SOUTH + WEST ASIA + THE MIDDLE EAST

Afghanistan, Armenia, Bhutan, Georgia, India, Iran, Iraq, Israel, Lebanon, Nepal, Pakistan, Palestine, Sri Lanka, Turkey

Many borders of this region have been redrawn over time, causing the blending of food cultures and ingredients. Most countries boast rich and complex spices, a result of the Silk Road winding through Central, South and West Asia, introducing foreign flavors that soon became thought of as local and, as a result, heavily influenced dishes and cuisines. Basmati rice is the common variety of rice in the region, while potatoes are a popular starch in soups and other dishes.

Breads and flatbreads are an important part of every meal; every country has its own favorite and style. Traditional ingredients include sumac, bulgur, chickpeas, mint, parsley, sesame seeds, honey, olives and olive oil. Georgians are said to have been the first to make wine; now there are several countries in this region producing very good-quality wines, which are exported to countries all over the world.

Afghanistan and Pakistan share a very similar soup, Yakhni (page 144 and page 175). Both have similar ingredients and a similar cooking method, yet a different way of serving the dish. Sri Lanka's Kanjee (page 179) is reminiscent of Southeast Asian cuisine, reflecting the influence from its neighbors further east. The use of spices makes this region's chicken soups fragrant and rich, yet clean and hearty.

Yakhni

Serves 4

90 ml (3 fl oz/⅓ cup) olive oil
1 large yellow onion, cut into 1 cm
   (½ in) cubes
2 roma or plum tomatoes, cut into
   1 cm (½ in) cubes
1.9 liters (64 fl oz/8 cups) water
   or Chicken Stock (page 237)
150 g (5½ oz/1 cup) yellow or red lentils
   or 200 g (7 oz/1 cup) basmati rice
900 g (2 lb) skinless chicken breast, bone in
2 large carrots, cut into 5 cm (2 in) pieces
2 large russet potatoes, peeled and cut
   into 4 cm (1½ in) half-moons
80 g (2¾ oz) cilantro (coriander), leaves
   and stems roughly chopped, plus sprigs
   to garnish
1 tablespoon ground turmeric
1 tablespoon ground coriander
1 teaspoon cayenne pepper
1 tablespoon ground cardamom
55 g (2 oz) fresh spinach
1 lemon, to serve

My friend Asya Ghafarshad's parents immigrated to the US from Afghanistan in the 1960s. Asya was born in the US and her mom tells her stories of growing up in Afghanistan wearing miniskirts and smoking cigarettes. Her parents own an iconic restaurant in Claremont, California, the town where I went to high school and college. It is called Walter's and serves delicious continental cuisine, as well as Afghan favorites. This is her father's chicken soup. Asya likes to cook the chicken breasts on the bone to make the broth, then shred the cooked chicken and add it back to the soup just as it is nearly done. She does not peel the carrots and the vegetables are cut into larger chunks, just the way her dad made the soup.

Heat the oil in a large pot over a medium–high heat. Add the onion and cook for 3–4 minutes until it begins to become translucent. Add the tomatoes and cook for 3 minutes until the tomatoes release their juices. Add the remaining ingredients, then bring to the boil. Immediately reduce the heat to a gentle simmer and cook for 20 minutes, or until the vegetables are tender, the soup has thickened and the chicken is cooked – a thermometer will read 74°C (165°F) when inserted into the thickest part of the breast and the juices of the chicken will run clear.

   When the chicken is cooked, remove from the pot and leave until cool enough to handle. Using your hands, shred all the meat and discard the bones. Add the meat back to the soup and season with salt and freshly ground black pepper. Squeeze the lemon juice into the soup, adding as much tangy flavor as possible without it becoming sour, and garnish with cilantro sprigs.

Spas

Serves 4

1 × 1.35 kg (3 lb) chicken, quartered
1.9 liters (64 fl oz/8 cups) water or
    Chicken stock (page 237)
2 tablespoons salt
75 g (2¾ oz/½ cup) dried wheat
    berries, rinsed
2 tablespoons rendered chicken fat
    or olive oil
1 yellow onion, cut into 1 cm (½ in) dice
4 garlic cloves, very finely chopped
20 g (¾ oz) parsley, roughly chopped
3 celery ribs (stalks) with greens, sliced
    into thin half-moons
1 carrot, cut into 5 mm (¼ in) rounds
2 zucchini (courgettes), cut into 1 cm
    (½ in) dice
240 ml (8 fl oz/1 cup) plain yogurt
2 large eggs
2 tablespoons roughly chopped basil
    or 2 teaspoons dried
2 tablespoons roughly chopped oregano
    or 2 teaspoons dried
2 tablespoons roughly chopped mint
    or 2 teaspoons dried
1 lemon

Yogurt bound with egg is used to thicken spas, adding a tangy richness to this bright, clean, nourishing and satisfying soup. Basmati rice, bulgur or barley can replace wheat berries, although wheat berries are most commonly used. Vegetable garnishes may vary depending on growing season. Sometimes, spas is made with water or vegetable stock, sometimes with chicken stock, and other times, chicken meat is added to the soup. It is traditionally served with warm pita or lavash and pickled vegetables.

Place the chicken and water or stock in a large pot with the salt. Weigh down the chicken under a few small plates to keep it submerged and simmer gently over a medium heat until the chicken pieces are cooked through, about 7–10 minutes for the breasts and 15–18 minutes for the legs and thighs. The meat should separate from the end of the leg bone when cooked, a thermometer will read 74°C (165°F) when inserted into the thickest part of the thigh or breast and the juices of the chicken will run clear.

When the chicken is cooked, remove from the pot and leave until cool enough to handle, then remove the chicken skin and discard. Using your hands, shred all the meat and discard the bones. Set the meat aside and reserve the broth.

To cook the wheat berries, place them in a saucepan and add enough water to cover the grains by about 5 cm (2 in). Bring to the boil, then immediately reduce the heat to a slow simmer, cover with a lid and cook for 40–45 minutes until the grains are chewy. Drain and set aside.

Wipe out the pot, then add the chicken fat or oil and heat over a medium heat. Add the onion, garlic, parsley, celery and carrot and cook slowly for 5–7 minutes, stirring constantly, until the vegetables are soft.

Add the reserved broth and bring to a gentle simmer. Add the zucchini and cook for 2 minutes, or until the zucchini is tender.

Place the yogurt and eggs in a bowl and whisk until very well combined. Add a spoonful of the hot broth to the egg mixture and stir until combined. Repeat with more hot broth until the eggs have heated up. This will help the egg to incorporate into the soup smoothly. When the eggs have enough warm broth to warm up, turn off the heat and add the egg mixture to the soup, stirring constantly. Add the wheat berries, reserved chicken and herbs and stir to combine. Squeeze the lemon juice into the soup, adding as much tangy flavor as possible without it becoming sour. Season with salt and freshly ground black pepper and serve.

Jasha Maroo

Serves 4–6

1 × 1.35 kg (3 lb) chicken, quartered
1.9 liters (64 fl oz/8 cups) water or
   Chicken Stock (page 237)
2 tablespoons salt
3 tablespoons chicken fat or vegetable oil
4 garlic cloves, sliced
2 yellow onions, cut into 1 cm (½ in) cubes
2.5 cm (1 in) piece ginger, peeled and
   very finely chopped
1 leek, white parts only, sliced into thin
   half-moons
2 roma or plum tomatoes, cut into
   1 cm (½ in) cubes
4 red or green Thai (bird's eye) chilies,
   slit down the middle
80 g (2¾ oz) cilantro (coriander),
   roughly chopped

Simple in its ingredients, but strong and rich in flavor, this rustic soup is typically accompanied by red rice. It is sweet with onions, leeks and tomatoes, fiery from chilies, bright with ginger, and herbal from cilantro (coriander). It will warm you on a cold day and cool you off on a hot day.

Place the chicken and water or stock in a large pot with the salt. Weigh down the chicken under a few small plates to keep it submerged and simmer gently over a medium heat until the chicken pieces are cooked through, about 7–10 minutes for the breasts and 15–18 minutes for the legs and thighs. The meat should separate from the end of the leg bone when cooked, a thermometer will read 74°C (165°F) when inserted into the thickest part of the thigh or breast and the juices of the chicken will run clear.

When the chicken is cooked, remove from the pot and leave until cool enough to handle, then remove the chicken skin and discard. Cut the chicken into large chunks on the bone (leg, thigh, halve breasts) and reserve to serve larger pieces of chicken in the broth. Alternatively, shred all the meat and discard the bones. Set the meat aside.

Reserve the broth and wipe out the pot, then add the chicken fat or oil and heat over a medium heat. Add the garlic, onion, ginger and leek and cook slowly, stirring constantly for 3–4 minutes until the vegetables are soft. Add the tomato and chilies, then add the reserved stock and bring to a very gentle simmer. Add the reserved chicken and stir to combine. Season with salt and freshly ground black pepper, then stir in the cilantro.

Chikhirtma

Georgia

Serves 4

1 × 1.35 kg (3 lb) chicken, quartered
1.9 liters (64 fl oz/8 cups) water or
    Chicken Stock (page 237)
2 tablespoons salt
85 g (3 oz) butter
3 yellow onions, cut into 5 mm (¼ in) cubes
2 tablespoons all-purpose (plain) flour
¼ teaspoon ground cinnamon
80 g (2¾ oz) cilantro (coriander), leaves
    and tender stems roughly chopped
6 large egg yolks
2 tablespoons lemon juice

To garnish
6 mint sprigs, leaves and tender stems
    roughly chopped
6 dill sprigs, leaves and tender stems
    roughly chopped
6 parsley sprigs, leaves and tender stems
    roughly chopped
6 basil sprigs, leaves and tender stems
    roughly chopped
Adjika (page 152)

This soup is made for families as a comfort meal, to heal the sick, and to cure a hangover. The creaminess is warming on a cold day, and the herbs add a bright note to this otherwise rich soup. Some versions of chikhirtma include potatoes, asparagus, corn or peas, and the Adjika (page 152) adds bold heat.

Place the chicken and water or stock in a large pot with the salt. Weigh down the chicken under a few small plates to keep it submerged and simmer gently over a medium heat until the chicken pieces are cooked through, about 7–10 minutes for the breasts and 15–18 minutes for the legs and thighs. The meat should separate from the end of the leg bone when cooked, a thermometer will read 74°C (165°F) when inserted into the thickest part of the thigh or breast and the juices of the chicken will run clear.

When the chicken is cooked, remove from the pot and leave until cool enough to handle, then remove the chicken skin and discard. Using your hands, shred all the meat and discard the bones. Set the meat aside and reserve the broth.

Wipe out the pot, then add the butter and melt over a medium heat. Add the onions and cook slowly, stirring constantly for 6 minutes, or until the onions are soft and slightly golden. Add the flour, cinnamon and cilantro and cook for a further 2–3 minutes. Add the reserved broth, then bring to a gentle simmer, stirring constantly, for about 10 minutes, or until the broth thickens.

Place the egg yolks and lemon juice in a bowl and whisk until well combined. Add a spoonful of the hot broth to the yolk mixture and stir until combined. Repeat with more hot broth until the yolks have heated up. This will help the yolks to incorporate into the soup smoothly. When the yolks have enough warm broth to warm up, turn off the heat and add the yolk mixture to the soup, stirring constantly. Stir in the reserved chicken, then season with salt and freshly ground black pepper. Garnish with the herbs and adjika, added to taste.

151

ASIA

Adjika

Makes 540 g (1 lb 3 oz)

1 tablespoon cilantro (coriander) stems
2 hot red chilies
8 garlic cloves
1½ sweet red peppers
100 g (3½ oz) walnuts
1 teaspoon coriander seeds
1 teaspoon anise seeds
1 teaspoon dried red hot chilies
1 tablespoon khmeli suneli (Georgian
  spice blend)
1 teaspoon fennel seeds
1 teaspoon dried basil
1 teaspoon dried oregano
1 teaspoon dried thyme
1 tablespoon white wine vinegar

Adjika (ahh-jah-kah) is the super spicy condiment that graces every Georgian table. Varieties include dry and wet, depending on whether dried or fresh chilies are used, and green and red, depending on the color chili used. Every home has their favorite blend of spices and balance of how much of each ingredient is used. Always taste a little before adding to your dish, as most are hot, hot, hot!

Preheat the oven to 180°C (350°F).

Purée the cilantro, chilies, garlic and red peppers in a food processor until finely combined. Place the puréed ingredients in a small pan over a medium heat and cook, stirring frequently, for 3 minutes until the raw smell of garlic has dissipated.

Place the walnuts, in a single layer, on a baking tray and toast in the oven, stirring them occasionally to prevent them burning, until fragrant, then leave to cool. When cool, crush them into a fine powder using a knife or food processor.

Repeat the toasting process with the coriander seeds, anise seeds and dried chilies, watching carefully so they do not burn. Once they are toasted and fragrant, let them cool completely. Combine the remaining dried herbs/spices with the toasted spices and transfer to a spice grinder or mortar and pestle to grind into a fine blend.

Add the spice mix and walnuts to the cooked purée, season with salt and vinegar and stir to combine. Store in an airtight container in the refrigerator for up to 1 month.

Qartuli Katmis da Bostneulis Supi

Georgia

Serves 4–6

1 × 1.35 kg (3 lb) chicken, quartered
1.9 liters (64 fl oz/8 cups) water or
    Chicken Stock (page 237)
2 tablespoons salt
1 yellow onion, cut into 5 mm (¼ in) cubes
2 large russet potatoes, peeled and cut into
    1 cm (½ in) cubes
2 large carrots, cut into 5 mm (¼ in) cubes
4 garlic cloves, halved
3 tablespoons butter
30 g (1 oz) parsley, finely chopped
10 g (¼ oz) dill, finely chopped
2 celery ribs (stalks), very finely diced
Adjika (see opposite)

This simple soup's distinction comes with the addition of dill and Adjika (see opposite). The dill, or any combination of tender herbs, adds bright and herbal notes, while the Adjika adds heat. Adjika is a table staple in Georgia, like a bottle of hot chili sauce in Mexican cuisine. It can be a paste or a dry mix and is used for everything from seasoning meat to adding heat at the table. The vegetables are cooked in the broth and not sautéed prior, lending a very fresh and tender quality.

Place the chicken and water or stock in a large pot with the salt. Weigh down the chicken under a few small plates to keep it submerged and simmer gently over a medium heat until the chicken pieces are cooked through, about 7–10 minutes for the breasts and 15–18 minutes for the legs and thighs. The meat should separate from the end of the leg bone when cooked, a thermometer will read 74°C (165°F) when inserted into the thickest part of the thigh or breast and the juices of the chicken will run clear.

When the chicken is cooked, remove from the pot and leave until cool enough to handle, then remove the chicken skin and discard. Using your hands, shred all the meat and discard the bones. Set the meat aside.

In the same pot with the broth, add the onion, potato, carrots, 2 garlic cloves and butter and bring to a gentle simmer. Cook for 8 minutes, or until the vegetables are tender.

Very finely chop the remaining garlic and add to the soup. Stir in the reserved chicken and add the parsley, dill and celery. Season the soup with salt and adjika.

ASIA

Chikan Rasam

Serves 4

1½ tablespoons coriander seeds
2 tablespoons cumin seeds
1 tablespoon black peppercorns
3 tablespoons ghee or vegetable oil
1 yellow onion, sliced thinly into half-moons
8 garlic cloves, roughly smashed
5 cm (2 in) piece ginger, peeled and
    finely chopped
1–2 dried red chilies, torn into pieces
2 sprigs curry leaves
4 tablespoons tamarind paste
1450 ml (49 fl oz/6 cups) Chicken Stock
    (page 237)
450 g (1 lb) boneless, skinless chicken thighs,
    cut into 2.5 cm (1 in) pieces

Chikan rasam, or South Indian spicy chicken soup, is an aromatic soup of fragrant spices enhanced with the souring properties of tamarind. Some recipes substitute lemon, but tamarind is more common. Chickan rasam is garnished with cilantro (coriander) and mint and is served with steamed basmati rice on cold wintery nights.

Toast the spices in a small sauté or frying pan over a medium–high heat, stirring frequently, for 2–4 minutes until fragrant. Watch them carefully so they don't burn. Leave to cool. When cool, grind the spices finely in a spice or coffee grinder and set aside.

Melt the ghee or vegetable oil in a large pot over a medium–high heat. Add the onion, garlic and ginger and cook uncovered, stirring frequently, for 4–5 minutes until the onion starts to become golden. Add the spices, chilies (1–2 depending on the type of chili) and the curry leaves and stir to combine. Cook for 2 minutes, then add the tamarind paste and stock and stir. Add the chicken and season with salt. Simmer gently over a medium heat for about 20 minutes. The broth will reduce and the flavors will become rich and spicy. Using two forks, gently pull the chicken into smaller pieces, then season with salt.

Kongu Nadu

Serves 4–6

1 × 1.35 kg (3 lb) chicken, quartered
1.9 liters (64 fl oz/8 cups) water or
    Chicken Stock (page 237)
2 tablespoons salt
3 tablespoons chicken fat or vegetable oil
1 large yellow onion
1 tablespoon black peppercorns
2 teaspoons cumin seeds
30 g (1 oz/⅓ cup) coriander seeds
2 teaspoons fennel seeds
4 cloves
¼ cinnamon stick
2 Thai (bird's eye) chilies, stemmed
15 fresh curry leaves and 1 stalk
1 teaspoon poppy seeds
35 g (1¼ oz/½ cup) unsweetened
    grated coconut

Kongu Nadu is a region in southern India and is said to grow the best turmeric. Traditionally, the people in this area were vegetarians and sustained themselves mostly on a variety of locally cultivated grains and beans. This brothy chicken soup features turmeric, aromatic spices and herbs. It is usually served with basmati rice, idli, naan or dosa.

Place the chicken and water or stock in a large pot with the salt. Weigh down the chicken under a few small plates to keep it submerged and simmer gently over a medium heat until the chicken pieces are cooked, about 7–10 minutes for the breasts and 15–18 minutes for the legs and thighs. The meat should separate from the end of the leg bone when cooked, a thermometer will read 74°C (165°F) when inserted into the thickest part of the thigh or breast and the juices of the chicken will run clear.

When the chicken is cooked, remove from the pot and leave until cool enough to handle, then remove the chicken skin and discard. Using your hands, shred all the meat and discard the bones. Set the meat aside. Strain the broth and reserve.

1 tablespoon toasted sesame oil
5 cm (2 in) piece ginger, peeled and sliced
4 garlic cloves
½ teaspoon ground turmeric
1 tomato, cut into 1 cm (½ in) cubes
475 ml (16 fl oz/2 cups) cool water
1 bunch cilantro (coriander), leaves roughly
   chopped and stems finely chopped

Place the chicken fat or oil, onion, peppercorns, cumin, coriander, fennel, cloves and cinnamon in a large sauté or frying pan over a high heat and stir constantly while the spices toast. Make sure the heat warms and toasts the spices, but does not char or burn them. Leave to cool.

Place the cooled mixture, the chilies, curry leaves and stalk, poppy seeds, coconut, sesame oil, ginger, garlic, turmeric and tomato in a high-powered blender with the cool water and process until a smooth paste forms.

Wipe out the pot, then place over a medium–high heat and add the purée. Cook slowly, stirring constantly for 3–5 minutes until the mixture becomes slightly darker. Add the reserved broth and cook at a gentle simmer for 10 minutes.

Add the reserved shredded chicken, if not saving for another use, to the soup and stir to combine. Season with salt, then stir in the cilantro and serve.

155

Ghormeh Sabzi

Serves 4

115 g (4 oz) dried kidney beans
2 tablespoons salt
1 × 1.35 kg (3 lb) chicken, quartered
2.4 liters (81 fl oz/10 cups) water or
    Chicken Stock (page 237)
3 tablespoons vegetable oil
1 yellow onion, cut into 1 cm (½ in) cubes
1 leek, cut into thin half-moons
9 spring (green) onions, cut into 1 cm
    (½ in) pieces
2 tablespoons ground turmeric
2 teaspoons cumin seeds, ground
1½ tablespoons fenugreek seeds, ground
1 bunch parsley, roughly chopped
1 bunch cilantro (coriander),
    roughly chopped
8 black Persian dried limes, each pierced
    several times with a fork

Every Persian will insist this is a stew, not a soup. And that's fine. It still deserves a place in this canon as it is a warm dish with a broth and is a unique contribution from a country with spectacular cuisine. Persians have a knack for elevating bright and herbal flavors ahead of rich or cloying textures, and this dish gets its liveliness from the dried lime. It is rich in greens (leek, cilantro/coriander, parsley), and nutritious. Sometimes, ghormeh sabzi is made with lamb instead of chicken, and it is typically served with basmati rice and pita.

Place the dried kidney beans in a bowl and cover with cool water, to at least 5 cm (2 in) above the beans. Cover and leave to soak overnight at room temperature. The next day, drain the beans and place in a pot. Fill with water, covering the beans by 7.5 cm (3 in) and cook over a medium heat for 20–30 minutes until tender. Season the beans with salt and leave to cool in the cooking water.

Place the chicken and water or stock in a large pot with the salt. Weigh down the chicken under a few small plates to keep it submerged and simmer gently over a medium heat until the chicken pieces are cooked, about 7–10 minutes for the breasts and 15–18 minutes for the legs and thighs. The meat should separate from the end of the leg bone when cooked, a thermometer will read 74°C (165°F) when inserted into the thickest part of the thigh or breast and the juices of the chicken will run clear.

When the chicken is cooked, remove from the pot and leave until cool enough to handle, then remove the chicken skin and discard. Using your hands, shred all the meat and discard the bones. Set the meat aside. Strain the broth and reserve.

Wipe out the pot, then place over a medium heat. Add the oil, then add the onion, leek and spring onions and sauté for 2–4 minutes until the vegetables are tender, but not browned. Add the spices, stir and cook for 1 minute. Add the parsley, cilantro, dried limes and reserved broth, then stir and bring to a gentle simmer. Cook for 10–15 minutes until the herbs are tender and the stew has thickened. Gently squeeze the dried limes to release their inner liquid and pulp, then discard the limes.

Drain the kidney beans and add to the stew with the reserved chicken. Cook for 1 minute, just to warm the chicken, then season with salt and freshly ground black pepper and serve.

Ash-e-jow

Serves 6

670 g (1½ lb) chicken thighs, bone in
    and skin on
1450 ml (49 fl oz/6 cups) water or Chicken
    Stock (page 237), plus extra as needed
1 tablespoon salt
240 ml (8 fl oz/1 cup) vegetable oil
2 large yellow onions, sliced into thin
    half-moons
1½ teaspoons ground turmeric
85 g (3 oz/½ cup) pearl barley
85 g (3 oz/½ cup) brown or green lentils
100 g (3½ oz/½ cup) basmati rice
2 carrots, cut into 5 mm (¼ in) cubes
    or grated
2 garlic cloves, thinly sliced
2 bay leaves

To garnish
240 ml (8 fl oz/1 cup) kashk or sour cream
1 bunch cilantro (coriander), leaves and
    stems, finely chopped
1 lime, cut into wedges

See image on page 158.

Like kitchari from India, this is a thick porridge-like soup filled with chicken, hearty grains and beans. Variations include barley, lentils, basmati rice, chickpeas, kidney beans and white beans. As with all porridge-like soups, there is no correct consistency; some prefer a thicker soup, while others favor a brothier version. Varying chicken cuts (breasts, thighs, legs) are all appropriate (to read about substitution see pages 15–6). Persians love their herbs, and often add parsley, dill or spinach.

Place the chicken in a pot. The chicken should fit in the pot snugly. Add the water or stock and the salt and bring to the boil. Immediately reduce the heat to a very gentle simmer and simmer, uncovered, for 20–30 minutes until the chicken is cooked and very tender, a thermometer reads 74°C (165°F) when inserted into the thickest part of the thighs and the juices of the chicken run clear.

Meanwhile, caramelize the onions. Heat the oil in a small frying pan over a medium heat. Add the sliced onions, reduce the heat to low and cook gently for 20–30 minutes until the onions are very deeply caramelized. Strain immediately and reserve the onions for the garnish.

When the chicken is cooked, strain the liquid to remove any solids and reserve the broth. Leave the chicken until cool enough to handle, then remove the chicken skin and discard. Using your hands, shred all the meat and discard the bones. Set the meat aside.

Rinse out the pot from making the broth, then add the turmeric, barley, lentils, rice, carrots, garlic, bay leaves and reserved broth and bring to a simmer, stirring occasionally, for 40–60 minutes until the soup becomes a loose porridge and the grains are tender. Add more water or stock if needed to achieve the desired texture. Add the chicken meat to warm through, then season liberally with salt and serve with the garnishes and caramelized onion.

Morgh Zaferani

Iran

Serves 4

1 × 1.35 kg (3 lb) chicken, quartered
1.9 liters (64 fl oz/8 cups) water or
    Chicken Stock (page 237)
2 tablespoons salt
3 carrots, cut into 1 cm (½ in) cubes
2 yellow potatoes, cut into 1 cm
    (½ in) cubes
pinch of saffron threads
85 g (3 oz) vermicelli noodles (or angel
    hair pasta), broken into quarter lengths
    (7.5 cm/3 in pieces)
1 lemon
2 tablespoons roughly chopped parsley
2 tablespoons barberries

A cupful of morgh zaferani is often served at special occasions and elegant dinner parties. The golden hue of this soup also reminds many Persians of their childhood, when their mothers or grandmothers served this soup to cure illness. The soup sometimes contains pieces of chicken; more often Persian cooks will reserve the chicken meat for another dish. Serve with lemon to squeeze into the soup, and garnish with barberries.

Place the chicken and water or stock in a large pot with the salt. Weigh down the chicken under a few small plates to keep it submerged and simmer gently over a medium heat until the chicken pieces are cooked through, about 7–10 minutes for the breasts and 15–18 minutes for the legs and thighs. The meat should separate from the end of the leg bone when cooked, a thermometer will read 74°C (165°F) when inserted into the thickest part of the thigh or breast and the juices of the chicken will run clear.

When the chicken is cooked, remove from the pot and leave until cool enough to handle, then remove the chicken skin and discard. Using your hands, shred all the meat and discard the bones. Set the meat aside.

Strain the broth and pour back into the pot. Add the carrots, potatoes and saffron. Make sure to finely crumble the saffron as it is added to the broth and cook slowly, stirring constantly, for 5–7 minutes until the vegetables are soft. Add the noodles and cook for 2–3 minutes until al dente.

Add the reserved shredded chicken, if not saving for another use, to the soup and stir to combine. Squeeze in the lemon juice, adding as much tangy flavor as possible without it becoming sour, then season with salt. Stir in the parsley and barberries and serve.

Soup-e morgh #1

Serves 4–6

1 × 1.35 kg (3 lb) chicken, quartered
1.9 liters (64 fl oz/8 cups) water or
   Chicken Stock (page 237)
1 yellow onion, quartered
4 garlic cloves, halved
1 large carrot, cut into 1 cm (½ in) rounds
2 celery ribs (stalks), cut into 4 cm
   (1½ in) batons
1 turnip, cut into 6 pieces
1 large russet potato, peeled and cut into
   6 large pieces
5 cm (2 in) piece ginger, peeled
2.5 cm (1 in) piece fresh turmeric, peeled
3 bay leaves
1 cinnamon stick
3 Persian black or yellow dried limes,
   pierced 4 times with a fork
2 tablespoons salt
¼ bunch cilantro (coriander),
   roughly chopped
1 fresh lime

This is a simple soup, clean and delicious. Turmeric and ginger are especially aromatic and also have health benefits. Lime and cilantro (coriander) liven up the soup post cooking – do make sure to include these ingredients. If fresh turmeric is difficult to find, substitute ½ teaspoon ground turmeric instead.

Place all the ingredients, except the cilantro (coriander) and fresh lime, in a large pot with the salt. Weigh down the chicken under a few small plates to keep it submerged and simmer gently over a medium heat until the chicken pieces are cooked through, about 7–10 minutes for the breasts and 15–18 minutes for the legs and thighs. The meat should separate from the end of the leg bone when done, a thermometer will read 74°C (165°F) when inserted into the thickest part of the thigh or breast and the juices of the chicken will run clear.

When the chicken is cooked, remove from the pot and leave until cool enough to handle, then remove the chicken skin and discard. Using your hands, shred all the meat and discard the bones. Add the meat to the soup. Gently squeeze the dried limes to release their inner liquid and pulp, then discard the limes.

Stir in the chopped cilantro, then season the soup with lime juice and salt and freshly ground black pepper.

Soup-e morgh #2

Serves 4

1 × 1.35 kg (3 lb) chicken, quartered
1.9 liters (64 fl oz/8 cups) water or
    Chicken Stock (page 237)
2 tablespoons salt
3 tablespoons chicken fat or vegetable oil
1 leek, cut into 5 mm (¼ in) cubes
2 carrots, cut into 1 cm (½ in) rounds
2 garlic cloves, very finely chopped
½ teaspoon ground turmeric
1 bay leaf
½ cinnamon stick
1 teaspoon cumin seeds
2 Persian black or yellow dried limes,
    pierced with a fork several times
Reshteh (see below), or 115 g (4 oz) dried
    reshteh noodles or angel hair pasta
1 lime
½ bunch cilantro (coriander),
    roughly chopped

One of the brilliant things about Persian cooking is the way richer foods still manage to be light and bright. Bring in fresh herbs and acidic citrus and you will find yourself with a lively, clean broth. If you can make the noodles (reshteh) from scratch, it is well worth it.

Place the chicken and water or stock in a large pot with the salt. Weigh down the chicken under some small plates to keep it submerged and simmer over a medium heat until the chicken is cooked, about 7–10 minutes for the breasts and 15–18 minutes for the legs and thighs. The meat should separate from the end of the leg bone when cooked, a thermometer will read 74°C (165°F) when inserted into the thickest part of the thigh and the juices of the chicken will run clear.

When the chicken is cooked, remove from the pot and leave until cool enough to handle, then remove the chicken skin and discard. Using your hands, shred all the meat and discard the bones. Set the meat aside. Strain the broth and reserve.

Wipe out the pot, then place over a medium heat and add the fat or oil. Add the vegetables and sauté for 3–5 minutes until tender, but not browned. Add the spices and dried limes and cook for 1 minute. Add the broth and bring to a gentle simmer.

If using dried reshteh noodles, cook them according to the package directions before adding to the soup with the chicken. If using fresh, add the noodles and chicken to the soup and cook for 1 minute, or until the noodles are tender. Using a fork, press the dried lime against the side of the pot to release the juices, then discard the lime. Squeeze in the lime juice, adding as much tangy flavor as possible without it becoming sour, then stir in the cilantro and season.

Serves 4

150 g (5½ oz/1 cup) '00' pasta flour
½ teaspoon salt
150 ml (5 fl oz/⅔ cup) water

Reshteh

Place the flour in a bowl and make a well in the middle. Add the salt and the water to the well, then, using a fork, stir until a dough comes together. If needed, add 1 tablespoon water at a time until a firm dough comes together, but is not sticky. Knead for 3–5 minutes until the dough is smooth. Cover and leave the dough to rest for 30 minutes.

Roll the noodles using either a pasta roller or by hand. If by hand, roll the dough out on a lightly floured work surface until the dough is 2 mm (¹⁄₁₆ in) thick. Use as much flour as needed to prevent the dough from sticking to the work surface, but don't add any more water.

Using a knife, cut the dough into very thin strands, like spaghetti. Toss with flour to keep them from sticking. Lay the noodles on a floured tea towel (dish towel) and leave to dry for 2 hours prior to cooking. If not using immediately, refrigerate until ready to use, or freeze if not using the same day for up to 1 month and cook from frozen.

Kubbeh Hamusta

Serves 4–6

Filling
450 g (1 lb) boneless, skinless chicken
 breast or thighs
1.9 liters (64 fl oz/8 cups) water or
 Chicken Stock (page 237)
2 tablespoons salt
3 tablespoons chicken fat or vegetable oil
1 yellow onion, cut into 5 mm (¼ in) cubes
2 garlic cloves, very finely chopped
2 teaspoons Baharat (page 169)
½ bunch parsley, finely chopped

Kubbeh
740 g (1 lb 10 oz/2 cups) semolina
240 ml (8 fl oz/1 cup) water
2 teaspoons vegetable oil
2 teaspoons salt

Soup
220 g (8 oz/ 1 cup) dried chickpeas
3 tablespoons chicken fat or vegetable oil
1 large onion, very finely chopped
3 large celery ribs (stalks), chopped into
 small pieces
½ tablespoon ground turmeric
3 zucchini (courgettes), cut into 2.5cm
 (1 in) rounds

Kubbeh, kibbeh or kobeba are all common names for dumplings in soup or dumplings that have been fried, depending on where you are from. Iraqis call them kubbeh while Egyptians call them kobeba. No matter the cooking method, the dumplings will be made of dough, semolina, rice or bulgur, or a combination of these, and are filled with some type of meat, or vegetables and legumes. The type of semolina used in the Middle East is more like farina, what Americans see as cream of wheat or farina wheat cereal in the supermarket. The type of semolina used for pasta will not yield tender dumplings in this application. The jewel-like beet soup broth is called marak kubbeh adom, red kubbeh soup. This version is kubbeh hamusta. Hamusta means vinegary, akin to a bright lemony flavor. There are many ways to make the dumplings; the goal is a highly seasoned interior surrounded by a tender poached doughy exterior. Form the dumpling dough as thin as possible for the tenderest bite. For those who grew up on kubbeh soup, there may be nothing quite as comforting as a piping hot bowl.

For the soup, place the dried chickpeas in a bowl and cover with cool water, to at least 5 cm (2 in) above the chickpeas. Cover and leave to soak overnight at room temperature. The next day, drain the chickpeas and simmer in a large pot of water for 20 minutes, or until tender. When the chickpeas are tender, season with salt and leave to cool in the cooking water.

For the filling, place the chicken and water or stock in a large pot with the salt. Weigh down the chicken under a few small plates to keep it submerged and simmer gently over a medium heat until the chicken pieces are cooked, about 7–10 minutes for the breasts and 15–18 minutes for the legs and thighs. A thermometer will read 74°C (165°F) when inserted into the thickest part of the thigh or breast and the juices of the chicken will run clear.

When the chicken is cooked, remove from the pot and leave until cool enough to handle. Using your hands, shred all the meat and discard the bones. Set the meat aside. Strain the broth and reserve.

Heat the chicken fat or oil in the same pot over a medium heat. Add the onion, garlic and baharat and cook slowly, stirring constantly for 4–5 minutes until the vegetables are soft. If the bottom of the pan begins to darken, add 2 tablespoons water and gently stir with a wooden spoon to remove any bits stuck on the bottom of the pot. Add the chicken and parsley and season well with salt and freshly ground black pepper.

Pulse the chicken mixture in a food processor, or chop by hand, so that pieces are very small (minced), but are not a paste.

For the soup, heat the chicken fat or oil in a clean pot over a medium heat. Add the onion and celery and cook gently for 3–4 minutes until the vegetables are tender. Stir in the turmeric, then add the reserved stock and simmer gently.

Meanwhile, combine the semolina, water, oil and salt in a small bowl until it comes together into a slightly sticky dough. If it is wet, add a little more semolina. Leave for 15 minutes to allow the water to absorb.

Using damp hands, take a ping-pong-sized amount of dough from the bowl and flatten the dough on the palm of your hand in the general shape of a circle. Place 1 teaspoon of the meat mixture in the center, pinch up the edges and roll into a ball. Keep the dough as thin as possible, as this will help make a tender dumpling. Repeat with all the remaining balls.

Gently place the balls in the soup, as many as will fit without crowding, and simmer gently for 30 minutes. Add the chickpeas and zucchini and simmer for another 2–3 minutes. Season with salt.

Gundi

Serves 6

Meatballs
2 tablespoons rendered chicken fat
    or vegetable oil
1 yellow onion, cut into 5 mm (¼ in) cubes
2 teaspoons cumin seeds
2 teaspoons coriander seeds
2 teaspoons caraway seeds
450 g (1 lb) ground (minced) chicken thighs
110 g (4 oz/1 cup) chickpea flour
2 teaspoons ground turmeric
1½ teaspoons baking soda (bicarbonate
    of soda)
1 tablespoon salt
2–3 tablespoons cool water

Soup
2 tablespoons rendered chicken fat
    or vegetable oil
2 yellow onions, cut into 1 cm (½ in) cubes
3 carrots, cut into 1 cm (½ in) cubes
4 garlic cloves, crushed
2 bay leaves
1.9 liters (64 fl oz/8 cups) Chicken Stock
    (page 237)
1 tablespoon salt

At first bite of this wonderful soup, the flavors of gundi are reminiscent of falafel. All of the rich, warm spices we are familiar with, in a rustic and simple broth. Gundi is to Iranian Jews what the matzo ball is to Eastern European Jews. Sometimes made with chickpeas, this recipe uses chickpea flour. Some versions include small potatoes cut in half and poached in the broth. Although the recipe hails from Iran, most Persian Jews live in Israel now and Israel is where the soup lives on.

For the meatballs, melt the chicken fat in a large sauté or frying pan over a high heat. Add the onions and gently cook for 3–6 minutes until tender and caramelized. Leave to cool completely.

Combine the cumin, coriander and caraway in a small sauté or frying pan and cook over a high heat for 2–4 minutes until the seeds become fragrant and just begin to pop. Remove from the heat immediately so that they do not burn. Leave to cool completely, then grind to a powder in a spice grinder or spice mill. Set aside.

Mix the cooled onions, spices, chicken, chickpea flour, turmeric, baking soda and salt together in a bowl. Add 1 tablespoon cool water at a time, until the mixture comes together. Form the mixture into small balls, about 2.5 cm (1 in), and place on a baking tray. Refrigerate for 1 hour.

For the soup, melt the chicken fat in a large pot over a medium–high heat. Add the onions, carrots, garlic and bay leaves, stir to combine and cook, stirring frequently, for 4–5 minutes until the vegetables become slightly tender and the onions are translucent. Add the stock and salt and bring to a simmer. Gently add the meatballs, partially cover with a lid and cook for 5–7 minutes until the meatballs are cooked through. Make sure to simmer gently to keep the meatballs from breaking apart. Season with salt and freshly ground black pepper and serve.

Hawaij l' Morok

Serves 4

3 tablespoons chicken fat or vegetable oil
3 carrots, cut into 1 cm (½ in) pieces
2 small onions, cut into 1 cm (½ in) cubes
2 celery ribs (stalks), cut into 1 cm
    (½ in) pieces
5 garlic cloves, lightly crushed
3 tablespoons Hawaij Spice (see below),
    or more to taste
1.9 liters (64 fl oz/8 cups) water or
    Chicken Stock (page 237)
½ bunch parsley, leaves and stems
    roughly chopped
½ bunch cilantro (coriander), leaves and
    stems roughly chopped
900 g (2 lb) boneless, skinless chicken thighs
6 small potatoes, peeled and cut into 2.5 cm
    (1 in) pieces

This is the Sabbath chicken stew for Yemenite Jews. Chicken is braised slowly in a rich and aromatic broth, with potatoes, carrots, celery and herbs. It is warm, aromatic and satisfying. As most Yemenite Jews live in Israel, this soup is now inextricably linked to the Jews of Israel and the diaspora.

Heat the chicken fat or oil in a large pot over a medium–high heat. Add the carrots, onions, celery and garlic and sauté for 3–6 minutes until the onions are translucent. Add the hawaij and stir to combine. Add the water or stock, parsley and cilantro and bring to a gentle simmer. Once the water begins to simmer, skim off the fat and other foamy impurities from the surface. Add the chicken and simmer over a medium heat for 30 minutes, or until the chicken is tender and easily shreds. Add the potatoes 10 minutes before the chicken is cooked. When the chicken is tender, season with salt to taste.

Serves 4

1½ tablespoons black peppercorns
1 tablespoon, plus 1 teaspoon
    cumin seeds
1 tablespoon green cardamom pods
1 tablespoon caraway seeds
1 tablespoon coriander seeds
2½ teaspoons celery seeds
1 teaspoon cloves
1¾ teaspoon ground cinnamon
20 g (¾ oz/3 tablespoons) ground turmeric
20 g (¾ oz) fine sea salt

Hawaij Spice Mix

There are two completely different hawaij spice mixtures, both hailing from Yemenite cuisine: one for soup and one for coffee. The soup mixture is also used in stews, curry-style dishes, rice and vegetable dishes, and even as a barbecue rub. Basically, it consists of cumin, black pepper, turmeric and cardamom. More elaborate versions may also contain cloves, caraway, nutmeg, saffron, coriander and ground dried onions.

Combine the black peppercorns, cumin, cardamom, caraway, coriander, celery seeds and cloves in a heavy-bottomed frying pan over a very low heat and toast for 10 minutes, or until fragrant and golden. Be very careful not to blacken or burn the spices. Remove from the heat and leave to cool completely. Grind the spices finely in a spice grinder, then add the remaining ingredients and sift through a fine-mesh sieve. Store the blend in an airtight container for up to 1 month.

Sephardi Matzo Ball Soup

Israel

Serves 6

2 tablespoons rendered chicken fat or olive oil
1 large onion, cut into 1 cm (½ in) cubes
2 carrots, cut into 1 cm (½ in) rounds
2 celery ribs (stalks), cut into 1 cm (½ in)
    half-moons
1 tablespoon ground cumin
1½ teaspoons ground turmeric
1.9 liters (64 fl oz/8 cups) water or
    Chicken Stock (page 237)
1 tablespoon salt
1 × 1.35 kg (3 lb) chicken, quartered
2 tablespoons dill, leaves and
    stems chopped
2 tablespoons cilantro (coriander),
    leaves and stems chopped
Skhug (see below)

Kneidlach

1 teaspoon salt
2 tablespoons rendered chicken fat or
    olive oil
2 large eggs
125 g (4½ oz/½ cup) matzo meal
2 tablespoons Chicken Stock (page 237)
1 teaspoon chopped parsley
1 tablespoon chopped cilantro (coriander)

Serves 6

2 tablespoons coriander seeds
2 tablespoons cumin seeds
8 cardamom pods
80 g (2¾ oz) cilantro (coriander) with stems,
    cut into quarter lengths
4 garlic cloves
2 large jalapeño chilies, cut into thirds
120 ml (4 fl oz/½ cup) olive oil
juice of 1 lemon

Kneidlach is the Yiddish word for matzah (or matzo) balls; and in Israel, food cultures get merged. Here is a classic mash-up of Ashkenazi matzo ball soup that has been combined with aromatic broth flavored with more typically Sephardic spices and garnished with Skhug (see below), a Yemenite herbed hot sauce.

To make the kneidlach, combine all ingredients together in a bowl and stir to make a thick batter. Cover with plastic wrap and refrigerate for 30 minutes.

Heat the chicken fat or olive oil in a large pot over a medium–high heat. Add the onion, carrot and celery and sauté for 3–4 minutes until tender. Add the cumin, turmeric and water or stock and season with the salt. Bring to a gentle simmer over a medium heat, then add the chicken and simmer very gently until the chicken pieces are cooked, about 7–10 minutes for the breasts and 15–18 minutes for the legs and thighs. The meat should separate from the end of the leg bone when cooked, a thermometer will read 74°C (165°F) when inserted into the thickest part of the thigh or breast and the juices of the chicken will run clear.

When the chicken is cooked, remove from the pot and leave until cool enough to handle, then remove the chicken skin and discard. Using your hands, shred all the meat and discard the bones. Set the meat aside.

Meanwhile, bring a large pot of salted water to a simmer and scoop golf-ball-sized portions of the kneidlach batter into the water. Simmer for 30 minutes, with the lid slightly ajar. Turn off the heat, cover and leave for 30 minutes.

Add the chicken meat to the pot, then stir in the chopped herbs and season with salt and freshly ground black pepper. Add the kneidlach to the soup and serve with the skhug.

Skhug

Place the spices in a frying pan over a medium–high heat and toast for 2–4 minutes until fragrant. Leave to cool, then grind the spices in a spice grinder or coffee grinder.

Place the cilantro, garlic and jalapeño in a food processor and pulse to process, scraping the sides of the bowl a few times with a spatula. Add the spices and olive oil and pulse once or twice. Scrape the contents into a small bowl and stir in the lemon juice. Season with salt. Store in an airtight container in the refrigerator for 1–2 weeks.

Shorbet Djaj w Riz

Serves 4

1 × 1.35 kg (3 lb) chicken, quartered
1450 ml (49 fl oz/6 cups) water or
   Chicken Stock (page 237)
2 tablespoons salt
3 tablespoons olive oil
1 yellow onion, cut into 5 mm (¼ in) cubes
2 celery ribs (stalks), cut into 5 mm
   (¼ in) cubes
60 g (2 oz/¼ cup) tomato paste
1 tablespoon Baharat (see opposite)
1 cinnamon stick
100 g (3½ oz/½ cup) basmati rice
40 g (1½ oz) parsley, roughly chopped,
   to garnish

This Lebanese soup is a simple everyday dish. It can be made richer by using tomato paste, or lighter by using a tomato purée (passata) or Tomato Sauce (page 239). The warm flavors of baharat are an instant burst of flavor. Baharat is a spice blend that is commonly used throughout many Middle Eastern countries and some parts of North Africa.

Place the chicken and water or stock in a large pot with the salt. Weigh down the chicken under a few small plates to keep it submerged and simmer gently over a medium heat until the chicken pieces are cooked through, about 7–10 minutes for the breasts and 15–18 minutes for the legs and thighs. The meat should separate from the end of the leg bone when cooked, a thermometer will read 74°C (165°F) when inserted into the thickest part of the thigh or breast and the juices of the chicken will run clear.

When the chicken is cooked, remove from the pot and leave until cool enough to handle, then remove the chicken skin and discard. Using your hands, shred all the meat and discard the bones. Set the meat aside. Strain the broth and reserve.

Wipe out the pot then place over a medium heat and add the olive oil, onion and celery and sauté for 2–4 minutes until the vegetables are tender, but not browned. Add the tomato paste, baharat and cinnamon, stir and cook for 1 minute. Add the reserved broth and rice, then stir and bring to a gentle simmer. Cook for 8–10 minutes until the rice is tender.

Add the reserved chicken and cook for 1 minute, just to warm the chicken. Season with salt and freshly ground black pepper and garnish with the chopped parsley.

Makes 50 g (1¾ oz/½ cup)

3 tablespoons black peppercorns
3 tablespoons cumin seeds
1½ tablespoons coriander seeds
1 tablespoon cloves
4 cardamom pods
1 tablespoon dried mint
1 teaspoon ground nutmeg
⅛ teaspoon ground cinnamon

Baharat

Place the peppercorns, cumin, coriander, cloves and cardamom in a small frying pan over a medium–high heat for 3–6 minutes, toasting slowly. Stir constantly, until the spices are toasty and fragrant. Make sure not to burn the spices. When toasted, leave to cool.

When cool, grind the spices in a spice grinder or spice mill, then stir in the mint, nutmeg and cinnamon. Store in an airtight container for up to 1 month.

Shorbet Djaj w Shaariyeh

Lebanon

Serves 4

3 tablespoons olive oil
1 × 1.35 kg (3 lb) chicken, quartered
1.9 liters (64 fl oz/8 cups) water or
    Chicken Stock (page 237)
1 yellow onion, quartered
1 carrot, cut into 5 cm (2 in) lengths
2 bay leaves
6 whole white peppercorns
1 tablespoon whole allspice berries
3 parsley sprigs
3 garlic cloves
1 large cinnamon stick
2 tablespoons salt
115 g (4 oz) vermicelli noodles, broken
    into 5 cm (2 in) lengths
1 lemon
20 g (¾ oz) parsley, roughly chopped,
    to garnish

Chicken soup in Lebanese cuisine is simply a chicken cooked in water and seasoned with cinnamon and lemon. Magic happens with simplicity when a few ingredients with the right balance come together. Here, the warm spices are gentle, but certainly present, never overwhelming the chicken or noodles. You can substitute the vermicelli with basmati rice; it will take 12–15 minutes to cook. Make sure to cook slowly or add a little water back to the broth as the longer cooking time for the rice can reduce the amount of liquid in the pot.

Heat a large heavy-bottomed pot over a medium–high heat with the olive oil. When the oil is hot, season the chicken with salt, add to the pot and brown the chicken on all sides. Add the water or stock with the onion, carrot, bay leaves, white peppercorns, allspice, parsley, garlic, cinnamon and 2 tablespoons salt. Weigh down the chicken under a few small plates to keep it submerged and simmer gently over a medium heat until the chicken pieces are cooked through, about 7–10 minutes for the breasts and 15–18 minutes for the legs and thighs. The meat should separate from the end of the leg bone when cooked, a thermometer will read 74°C (165°F) when inserted into the thickest part of the thigh or breast and the juices of the chicken will run clear.

    When the chicken is cooked, remove from the heat and strain the broth, discarding the vegetables and spices. Set the chicken aside. Pour the broth back into the pot and bring to a gentle simmer. Season with salt and freshly ground black pepper and add the vermicelli noodles. Cook for 3 minutes, or until the noodles are tender. Return the chicken to the pot, squeeze in a little lemon juice, adding as much tangy flavor as possible without it becoming sour, then garnish with the chopped parsley.

Thukpa

Serves 6

1 teaspoon ghee or butter
1.9 liters (64 fl oz/8 cups) Chicken Stock
  (page 237)
1 × 1.35 kg (3 lb) chicken, quartered
1 tablespoon salt
1 large carrot, cut into thin matchsticks
1 red bell pepper (capsicum), seeded and
  thinly sliced
90 g (3 oz/1 cup) mung bean sprouts
400 g (14 oz) fresh rice noodles
120 ml (4 fl oz/¼ cup) fresh lime juice
½ bunch cilantro (coriander),
  roughly chopped
Nepali Chili Sauce (see opposite)

Chili paste
1 small yellow onion, cut into 2 cm
  (¾ in) cubes
2 garlic cloves, halved
2.5 cm (1 in) piece ginger, peeled and halved
2 teaspoons cumin seeds
½ teaspoon ground turmeric
¼ teaspoon ground sichuan peppercorns
2 jalapeño chilies
20 g (¾ oz) cilantro (coriander), chopped
2 roma or plum tomatoes, cut into
  2 cm (¾ in) cubes

Thukpa is a Himalayan noodle soup, usually served with chicken, and sometimes yak or mutton, and finished with a handful of greens. It is popular in Nepal, Tibet and Bhutan, and some areas in India, such as Majnu-ka-tilla where refugee communities have been established. Thuk means heart, referring to a heart-warming dish, or a treasured dish to hold close to the heart. In Bhutan, the soup is usually made with buckwheat noodles; buckwheat grows well in colder climates with a shorter growing season. Traditionalists say that a New Year celebration is not complete without thukpa; others believe it is too good to save for occasions alone.

Place all the chili paste ingredients in a blender and process until combined and mostly processed. The mixture should be small cubes and not fully puréed.

For the soup, melt the ghee or butter in a pot over a medium heat. Add the chili paste and cook, stirring frequently, for 5–7 minutes until the ingredients are cooked through. Add the stock, chicken and salt and simmer gently over a medium heat until the chicken pieces are cooked through, about 7–10 minutes for the breasts and 15–18 minutes for the legs and thighs. The meat should separate from the end of the leg bone when cooked, a thermometer will read 74°C (165°F) when inserted into the thickest part of the thigh or breast and the juices of the chicken will run clear.

When the chicken is cooked, remove from the pot and leave until cool enough to handle, then remove the chicken skin and discard. Using your hands, shred all the meat and discard the bones. Set the meat aside.

Meanwhile, bring a separate pot of water to the boil. Add the carrot, red bell pepper and mung beans and cook gently for 2–3 minutes until the vegetables are tender. Remove the vegetables from the water and add to the soup.

Add the rice noodles to the boiling water and cook briefly for 2 minutes, or just until the noodles are tender. Drain the noodles and add them to the soup along with the chicken. Season with lime juice and salt and add the chopped cilantro. Serve immediately, adding Nepali Chili Sauce (see opposite) to taste.

Serves 6

2 habanero peppers (chilies),
   roughly chopped
1 red bell pepper (capsicum), seeded and
   cut into 1 cm (½ in) cubes
3 garlic cloves, roughly chopped
1 cm (½ in) piece ginger, peeled
120 ml (4 fl oz/½ cup) distilled white vinegar
¼ teaspoon kosher salt or sea salt

Nepali Chili Sauce

Combine all the ingredients in a small pot over a medium–high heat. Once the mixture is simmering, reduce the heat to low, cover with a lid and simmer for 7–10 minutes until the peppers are tender. Do not inhale the vapors, as they will sting your nose and eyes.

    Transfer the mixture to a blender and purée until smooth, then pour into a jar and leave uncovered to cool. Cover tightly with a lid and refrigerate for 3 days. Keep stored in the refrigerator for several weeks or months.

Yakhni

Serves 4

1 × 1.35 kg (3 lb) chicken, quartered
1.9 liters (64 fl oz/8 cups) water
   or Chicken Stock (page 237)
2 yellow onions, each cut into 6 pieces
1 garlic head, cut in half along the equator
5 cm (2 in) piece ginger, peeled
   and very finely chopped
2 carrots, cut into 5 cm (2 in) pieces
12 roma or plum tomatoes, quartered
2 bay leaves
10 cloves
2 teaspoons black peppercorns
1 cinnamon stick
2 teaspoons ground cumin
1 tablespoon coriander seeds
2 tablespoons salt
½ bunch cilantro (coriander),
   roughly chopped

Pakistan and Afghanistan are neighbors and have a long history: politically, historically, culinarily and more. It is no surprise that they share many dishes, similar, but with distinct tweaks. Afghan Yakhni (page 144) includes the vegetables in the soup, while the Pakistani version does not. In Pakistani yakhni, the vegetables can be discarded, or are eaten on the side or with another meal. This aromatic broth acts as a tea and is ideal for warming up in winter and healing flu or a cold.

Place the chicken, water or stock, onion, garlic, ginger, carrots, tomatoes, bay leaves, cloves, peppercorns, cinnamon, cumin, coriander seeds and salt in a large pot. Weigh down the chicken under a few small plates to keep it submerged and simmer gently over a medium heat until the chicken pieces are cooked through, about 7–10 minutes for the breasts and 15–18 minutes for the legs and thighs. The meat should separate from the end of the leg bone when cooked, a thermometer will read 74°C (165°F) when inserted into the thickest part of the thigh or breast and the juices of the chicken will run clear.

    When the chicken is cooked, remove from the pot and leave until cool enough to handle, then remove the chicken skin and discard. Using your hands, shred all the meat and discard the bones. Set the meat aside. Strain the broth and reserve.

    Wipe out the pot and pour in the strained broth. Add the chicken, then season with salt and stir in the cilantro.

Hanan's Mom's Palestinian Chicken Soup

Serves 4–6

60 ml (2 fl oz/¼ cup) chicken fat or olive oil
1 yellow onion, cut into 1 cm (½ in) cubes
2 celery ribs (stalks), cut into 1 cm
    (½ in) cubes
120 g (4½ oz) curly parsley, leaves and
    stems roughly chopped
80 g (2¾ oz) cilantro (coriander), leaves
    and stems roughly chopped
1.9 liters (64 fl oz/8 cups) water or
    Chicken Stock (page 237)
670 g (1½ lb) boneless, skinless chicken
    thighs, cut into 2.5 cm (1 in) pieces
100 g (3½ oz/½ cup) basmati rice

I met Hanan on an airplane coming home from Israel. She introduced herself as Christian Palestinian, 'the peaceful kind'. In turn, I introduced myself as 'Jewish American, the peaceful kind'. We chatted about all sorts of things. She now lives in San Jose and still loves to cook the food she grew up with. Not knowing my interest in chicken soup, she shared her mother's recipe. Her advice is that the soup should only have a small handful of rice because the broth is most important, especially when someone is sick.

Heat the chicken fat or oil in a pot over a medium–high heat. Add the onion and celery and cook, stirring frequently for 3–4 minutes until the onion is translucent and slightly golden. Add 80 g (2¾ oz) of the parsley and all the cilantro and stir to combine, then add the water or stock and bring to a simmer. Reduce the heat to a gentle simmer, add the chicken, stir and cook for 15 minutes. Add the rice, stir and cook for a further 10 minutes, or until the chicken and rice are tender. Season with salt and garnish with the remaining parsley.

Kanjee

Serves 2

400 g (14 oz/2 cups) broken jasmine rice
2 long branches curry leaves
1 Thai (bird's eye) green chili
3 roma or plum tomatoes, quartered
4 garlic cloves, halved
½ red onion, julienned
⅛ teaspoon ground fenugreek
1 teaspoon ground turmeric
½ teaspoon Sri Lankan chili powder
2 × whole chicken legs (approx. 670 g/1½ lb),
    leg and thigh attached, skin on
1.9 liters (64 fl oz/8 cups) water
800 ml (27 fl oz) canned coconut milk
1 tablespoon salt
2 tablespoons vegetable oil
2 (5 × 10 cm/2 × 4 in) pieces
    pandan leaves
4 cardamom pods, lightly crushed
1 cinnamon stick
3 cloves
½ teaspoon cumin seeds
½ teaspoon brown mustard seeds
½ teaspoon tamarind paste
30 g (1 oz/½ cup) unsweetened coconut
    flakes, toasted

I was urged to try this recipe by Rahmi, a high school classmate from Sri Lanka. I piled the ingredients in my Instant Pot and made a batch. I had a friend over for lunch and knew she would enjoy the flavors. We both ate two bowls and I divided the leftovers between us to enjoy later. Sri Lanka's kanjee can be made with chicken, seafood or vegetables, and is known for its intense flavors and comforting texture. The Sri Lankans I have spoken to suggest chicken is the unanimous favorite, while the dish evokes two memories: breaking fast during Ramadan and their grandmother making kanjee for them.

In an Instant Pot or pressure cooker, place the rice, 1 branch of the curry leaves, the green chili, tomatoes, garlic, ¼ red onion, the fenugreek, turmeric, chili powder, chicken, water and coconut milk and salt. Stir to combine, then cook for 20 minutes on high with slow release.

For the stovetop method, place the rice, curry leaves, green chili, tomatoes, garlic, ¼ red onion, fenugreek, turmeric, chili powder, chicken, water and coconut milk and salt in a large pot and stir to combine. Bring to a gentle simmer over a medium heat and cook for 1 hour until the rice had broken down and the porridge has thickened.

For either method, place a heavy-bottomed pan over a medium–high heat. Add the oil, pandan leaves, remaining curry leaves, cardamom, cinnamon, cloves, cumin, mustard seeds and remaining red onion and cook for 2–3 minutes until the spices begin to smell fragrant and the mustard seeds begin to pop. Don't let the spices burn. Immediately stir into the cooked kanjee with the tamarind paste. Remove and discard the chicken bones, then season with salt and pepper and top with coconut flakes.

Ekşili Tavuk Çorbası

Serves 4–6

2 egg yolks
2 tablespoons all-purpose (plain) flour
60 ml (2 fl oz/¼ cup) lemon juice
2 tablespoons rendered chicken fat
    or vegetable oil
2 large carrots, cut into 1 cm (½ in) cubes
1 onion, cut into 1 cm (½ in) cubes
large pinch of saffron threads
1 tablespoon pul biber, aleppo pepper
    or urfa pepper
900 g (2 lb) potatoes, such as yukon gold,
    peeled and cut into 1 cm (½ in) cubes

Broth
1 × 1.35 kg (3 lb) chicken
2 carrots, cut into 2.5 cm (1 in) pieces
1 yellow onion, cut into 1 cm (½ in) cubes
3 garlic cloves, halved
2 bay leaves
1.9 liters (64 fl oz/8 cups) water or
    Chicken Stock (page 237)
1 tablespoon salt

Lemon juice gives this soup its signature sourness, while pul biber, the Turkish red pepper, adds heat and a slight tang and, when combined with saffron, lends the broth a lovely amber color. The slurry of egg yolks, flour and lemon juice imbues a smooth, plush texture, boosting the protein and making it even cozier than your average chicken soup, with a surprising acidity. In Turkey, the vegetables can vary by season. Green beans are a common addition to this dish, which has roots in the Çorum, Gaziantep, Hatay and Kahramanmaraş provinces of Turkey.

To make the broth, place the chicken, carrots, onion, garlic and bay leaves in a pot. The chicken should fit in the pot snugly with the vegetables. Add the water or stock and salt and bring to the boil. Immediately reduce the heat to a very gentle simmer, place a couple of small plates on top of the chicken to keep it submerged and cook, uncovered, for 20–30 minutes until the chicken is cooked, a thermometer registers 74°C (165°F) when inserted into the thickest part of the thigh and breast and the juices of the chicken run clear.

Meanwhile, combine the egg yolks, flour and lemon juice in a blender or in a bowl and process or whisk until very smooth. Set aside.

When the chicken is cooked, strain the liquid to remove any solids and reserve the broth. Leave the chicken until it is cool enough to handle, then remove the chicken skin and discard. Using your hands, shred all the meat from the carcass and discard the bones. Set the meat aside.

Rinse and dry the pot, then place over a medium–high heat and add the chicken fat. Add the carrots, onion, saffron and pul biber and cook, stirring frequently, for 3–4 minutes until the vegetables begin to soften. Season with salt, then, when tender, add the potatoes, then the broth and bring to a gentle simmer. Cook for 5 minutes, or until the potatoes are tender. Add the reserved chicken and season again with salt.

Slowly drizzle and stir 475 ml (16 fl oz/2 cups) of the warm broth into the reserved egg mixture to warm it, then gently whisk the egg mixture into the soup and warm over a very low heat. Too high a heat will curdle the soup. Stir gently for 2–3 minutes until the soup has slightly thickened, then serve.

Terbiyeli Şehriyeli Tavuk Çorbası

Turkey

Serves 4

1.9 liters (64 fl oz/8 cups) water or
    Chicken Stock (page 237)
1 × 1.35 kg (3 lb) chicken, quartered
1 tablespoon salt
250 g (9 oz/1 cup) whole plain yogurt
1 large egg yolk
2 tablespoons all-purpose (plain) flour
3 teaspoons butter
3 small garlic cloves, thinly sliced
1 tablespoon aleppo pepper
⅛ teaspoon cayenne pepper
50 g (1¾ oz/¼ cup) basmati rice
225 g (8 oz/1¼ cups) canned
    chickpeas, drained
85 g (3 oz) vermicelli noodles, broken
    into quarter lengths
1 lemon
3 tablespoons mint, roughly chopped,
    to garnish

All the flavors you want to enjoy in Turkey are in this unique soup: yogurt, mint, noodles, chickpeas, lemon and Aleppo pepper. And although this soup contains egg yolk and butter as well, it's not quite as rich as you would think. Rather, it's clean and bright, with a velvety texture and lemony zip. It's the rice that really makes it substantial, and the mint adds aroma. The uncommon flavor combination feels celebratory as it awakens the palate. Anatolians often eat this soup for breakfast.

Place the water or stock, chicken and salt in a large pot. Weigh down the chicken under a few small plates to keep it submerged. Bring to the boil, then immediately reduce the heat to a very low simmer and simmer very gently for 20–30 minutes until the chicken is cooked through, a thermometer reads 74°C (165°F) when inserted into the thickest part of the thigh or breast and the juices of the chicken run clear. When the chicken is cooked, remove from the pot and leave until cool enough to handle.

Combine the yogurt, egg yolk and flour in a bowl and whisk until smooth. Set aside.

Place the butter, garlic, aleppo pepper and cayenne in a small frying pan and warm gently over a low heat for 2 minutes, or just until the garlic is no longer raw. Do not brown the butter. Set aside.

When the chicken is cool, remove the chicken skin and discard. Using your hands, shred all the meat from the carcass and discard the bones. Set the meat aside. Strain the broth and pour back into the pot. Add the rice and cook for 8–10 minutes until the rice is tender. Add the reserved chicken to the pot with the chickpeas and vermicelli and cook for 2 minutes, or until just tender.

Slowly drizzle and stir 475 ml (16 fl oz/2 cups) of the warm broth into the yogurt mixture to warm it, then gently whisk the yogurt mixture into the soup and warm over a very low heat. Too high a heat will curdle the soup. Stir gently for 2–3 minutes until the soup is slightly thickened. Season with salt and freshly ground black pepper and squeeze in lemon juice, adding as much tangy flavor as possible with it becoming sour. Ladle the soup into bowls and garnish with mint and a spoonful of the chili butter.

Şehriye Çorbası

Serves 4

30 g (1 oz) butter
360 g (12½ oz/1½ cups) fresh or canned
    diced tomatoes
950 ml (32½ fl oz/4 cups) water or
    Chicken Stock (page 237)
1 tablespoon salt
1 teaspoon freshly ground black pepper
2 × skinless chicken breasts (approx.
    280 g/10 oz), diced
85 g (3 oz/1 cup) dried vermicelli pasta,
    broken into quarter lengths
4 parsley sprigs, chopped
1 lemon, cut into 4 wedges

This is likely the most popular chicken soup in Turkey, probably because it is so easy and quick to make. It is a go-to recipe for chicken leftovers and a good, ready-made stock. This soup can be made with a half chicken; in this recipe, I use only the breasts, which cook faster than legs or thighs. The addition of lemon makes it refreshing, and vermicelli add some heartiness. The noodles will continue to absorb the broth if there are leftovers, so thin it out as needed. The tomatoes bring a touch of acidity and sweetness. Altogether, this soup ends up with a lot of body without being particularly heavy.

Melt the butter in a large pot over a medium heat. Add the tomatoes and cook gently for 5 minutes. Add the water or stock with the salt and 1 teaspoon pepper and bring to a gentle simmer over a low–medium heat. Add the chicken and vermicelli and cook for 3–4 minutes until the noodles are tender and the chicken is cooked through. Add the chopped parsley, season with salt and pepper and ladle into bowls. Serve with a lemon wedge and eat immediately.

Terbiyeli Pirinçli Tavuk Çorbası

Serves 4

1.9 liters (64 fl oz/8 cups) water or
    Chicken Stock (page 237)
2 × whole chicken legs (approx. 670 g/1½ lb),
    leg and thigh attached, skin on
1 yellow onion, cut into 2 cm (¾ in) cubes
2 carrots, cut into large pieces
3 parsley sprigs
3 bay leaves
1 teaspoon black peppercorns
1 tablespoon salt
100 g (3½ oz/½ cup) white long-grain rice
2 tablespoons olive oil
15 g (½ oz) butter
2 tablespoons tomato paste
1 tablespoon chili paste, such as harissa
1 tablespoon all-purpose (plain) flour
2 teaspoons dried mint
225 g (8 oz/1¼ cups) canned chickpeas,
    drained
1 lemon

Count on chickpeas for protein, chili paste for warmth and long-grain rice for heft in this soup. I like using thighs in this recipe because they can cook longer and remain tender and flavorful. The chili paste is the hallmark, even though some recipes omit it. (Chili paste can vary in intensity, so it is best to use to taste.) This is one of the most filling, satisfying and complex dishes in the Turkish soup lexicon.

Place the water or stock, chicken, onion, carrots, parsley, bay leaves, black peppercorns and salt in a large pot over a medium–high heat and simmer gently for 20 minutes, or until the chicken is cooked through and the meat separates from the end of the leg bone. Remove the chicken from the pot and strain the broth, discarding the vegetables. Pour the broth back into the pot, add the rice and simmer gently for 5–7 minutes, or until the rice is almost tender.

    When the chicken is cool, using your hands, shred the meat into small pieces and discard the bones. Set the meat aside.

    While the rice is cooking, combine the oil, butter, tomato paste, chili paste, flour and mint in a small pan and cook over a medium heat, stirring, for 1–2 minutes until combined and slightly darker in color. Scrape the mixture into the soup, then add the chicken and chickpeas. Return the soup to a gentle simmer and cook for another 3–4 minutes until the rice is tender. Season with lemon juice and salt and serve.

Europe

NORTHERN +
EASTERN EUROPE

Finland, Moldova, Norway, Romania, Ukraine

Northern European countries tend to have long, cold winters and shorter growing seasons. Ingredient availability therefore relies on foods that can be stored, whether canned or cellared, including cabbage, apples, celeriac, carrots and potatoes. Rice is atypical in this region. However, many soups are enriched with egg, boosting nutrition and calories for those long winter days and nights.

Thanks to pickling, smoking, drying and other preserving methods, Northern and Eastern Europeans are still able to enjoy variety in flavors, textures and ingredients year round. Ukrainian Temnyy Kuryachyy Sup (page 199) includes juice of pickles or capers, brightening up a soup that is packed with vegetables and herbs. While many chicken soups are thought of as a winter meal, Finland's Kesäkeitto (page 189) is full of fresh vegetables from the summer garden. Moldovan Bureachiță (page 192) is a lovely soup that borrows its main element from its Eastern neighbors. Russian pelmeni are the focal point and provide heartiness in this simple tomato soup.

The region is diverse, using much of what they have and are able to grow. However, they also benefit from borrowed ingredients, which have been influential to their collective cuisine.

Kesäkeitto

Finnish Chicken Summer Soup

Serves 4

1 × 1.35 kg (3 lb) chicken, quartered
1.9 liters (64 fl oz/8 cups) water or
    Chicken Stock (page 237)
2 tablespoons salt
500 g (1 lb 2 oz) spring (green) onions, sliced
    into thin rings
4 large carrots, cut into 5 mm (¼ in) rounds
45 g (1½ oz) butter
310 g (11 oz/2 cups) fresh peas
450 g (1 lb) fresh green beans, cut into
    2.5 cm (1 in) pieces
600 ml (20½ fl oz/2½ cups) heavy
    (double) cream
3 tablespoons cornstarch (cornflour)
1 bunch dill, roughly chopped, to garnish

This soup is designed to celebrate summer produce. Sometimes it is made with chicken, sometimes simply with chicken broth, and sometimes it is vegetarian, using vegetable stock. Occasionally, whey or milk is used to produce a lighter version. All manner of vegetables work well, depending on what is growing in the garden: broccoli, green beans, cauliflower, new potatoes, zucchini (courgette), carrot, onion, asparagus tips, kohlrabi, onion, turnips, fennel, radishes, okra, corn and peas. Always peas.

Place the chicken and water or stock in a large pot with the salt. Weigh down the chicken under a few small plates to keep it submerged and simmer gently over a medium heat until the chicken pieces are cooked through, about 7–10 minutes for the breasts and 15–18 minutes for the legs and thighs. The meat should separate from the end of the leg bone when cooked, a thermometer will read 74°C (165°F) when inserted into the thickest part of the thigh or breast and the juices of the chicken will run clear.

When the chicken is cooked, remove from the pot and leave until cool enough to handle, then remove the chicken skin and discard. Using your hands, shred all the meat and discard the bones. Set the meat aside.

Add the spring onions, carrots, butter, peas and green beans to the broth in the pot and cook slowly over a medium heat, stirring constantly for 3–4 minutes until the vegetables are tender.

Meanwhile, mix the cream and cornstarch together in a small bowl until smooth. Add to the soup and bring to a gentle simmer, stirring constantly, for 1–2 minutes until the broth thickens slightly. Stir in the reserved chicken, then season with salt and freshly ground black pepper. Garnish with chopped dill and serve.

Zeama

Serves 4

1 × 1.35 kg (3 lb) chicken, quartered
2.4 liters (81 fl oz/10 cups) water or
  Chicken Stock (page 237)
2 tablespoons salt
3 tablespoons rendered chicken fat
  or olive oil
1 yellow onion, cut into 5 mm (¼ in) cubes
2 large carrots, cut into 5 mm (¼ in) cubes
1 celery rib (stalk), including leaves, cut into
  5 mm (¼ in) cubes
2 thyme sprigs
1 roma or plum tomato, cut into 5 mm
  (¼ in) cubes
225 g (8 oz) Egg Noodles (see below)
7 g (¼ oz/¼ cup) finely chopped
  fresh parsley
2 g (⅙ oz/¼ cup) finely chopped dill
1 lemon

Moldova, nestled between Romania and Ukraine, serves a soup like most traditional chicken soups of Eastern Europe. The difference is the addition of fresh tomato, giving a soft sweetness to the broth. Noodles are added to the soup just before serving, and fresh herbs enliven the broth. Moldovans usually serve this soup with a traditional corn porridge called mămăligă, which is very similar to polenta.

Place the chicken and water or stock in a large pot with the salt. Weigh down the chicken under a few small plates to keep it submerged and simmer gently over a medium heat until the chicken pieces are cooked through, about 7–10 minutes for the breasts and 15–18 minutes for the legs and thighs. The meat should separate from the end of the leg bone when cooked, a thermometer will read 74°C (165°F) when inserted into the thickest part of the thigh or breast and the juices of the chicken will run clear.

When the chicken is cooked, remove from the pot and leave until cool enough to handle, then remove the chicken skin and discard. Using your hands, shred all the meat and discard the bones. Set the meat aside. Reserve the broth.

Wipe out the pot, then warm the chicken fat or oil over a medium heat. Add the onion, carrot, celery and thyme and cook for 4–5 minutes until the vegetables are tender. Add the tomato and cook slowly, stirring constantly for a further 2–3 minutes. Add the reserved broth and bring to a very gentle simmer.

Bring a separate pot of water to the boil, then add the noodles and cook for 2 minutes, or until al dente. Drain and add to the soup, with the reserved chicken and herbs. Stir to combine, then squeeze in enough lemon to add as much tangy flavor as possible without it becoming sour. Season with salt and freshly ground black pepper and serve.

Makes 225 g (8 oz)

140 g (5 oz/1 cup) all-purpose (plain)
  flour, plus extra for dusting
2 large eggs

Egg Noodles

Place the flour in a bowl. Make a well in the center of the flour and break the eggs into the well. Using a fork, stir until a dough comes together. If needed, add 1 tablespoon water at a time until a firm but not sticky dough comes together. Knead for 3–5 minutes until the dough is smooth. Cover with plastic wrap and leave to rest at room temperature for 30 minutes.

Roll the noodles using either a pasta roller or by hand. If by hand, roll out the dough on a lightly floured work surface until it is 2 mm (1/16 in) thick. Use as much flour as needed to prevent the dough from sticking to the work surface, but don't add any more water. Using a knife, cut the dough into very thin slivers, then toss in flour to keep the noodles from sticking to each other. Refrigerate on a floured tea towel (dish towel) until ready to use.

Sup s Kletzkami

Serves 4

1 × 1.35 kg (3 lb) chicken
2 carrots, cut into 2.5 cm (1 in) pieces
1 yellow onion, roughly chopped
2 celery ribs (stalks), cut into 2.5 cm
   (1 in) pieces
1.9 liters (64 fl oz/8 cups) water or
   Chicken Stock (page 237)
1 tablespoon salt

Dumplings
140 g (5 oz/1 cup) all-purpose (plain) flour
1 teaspoon salt
½ teaspoon freshly ground black pepper
2 tablespoons rendered chicken fat or butter
1 egg

Soup
2 tablespoons rendered chicken fat or butter
1 carrot, cut into 5 mm (¼ in) cubes
1 yellow onion, cut into 1 cm (½ in) cubes
1 celery rib (stalk), cut into 1 cm
   (½ in) cubes
1 tablespoon chopped parsley

Moldovan dumpling soup, similar to that of its Romanian neighbor, is made with all-purpose (plain) flour, rather than semolina. This recipe produces a more tender dumpling with less density, the result of the finer flour. Cooking dumplings in soup broth will make the soup cloudy, so if you prefer a cleaner broth, I recommend cooking the dumplings in a separate pot of salted simmering water.

Place the chicken, carrots, onion and celery in a pot. The chicken should fit in the pot snugly with the vegetables. Add the water or stock and the salt and bring to the boil. Immediately reduce the heat to low–medium and simmer very gently. Place a few small plates on top of the chicken to keep it submerged, then cook, uncovered, for 20–30 minutes until a thermometer registers 74°C (165°F) when inserted into the thickest part of the thigh and breast, and the juices run clear.

Meanwhile, make the dumpling dough. Sift the flour, salt and pepper into a bowl. Add the chicken fat and, using a fork, gently work it into the flour until it is broken up and looks like the beginning of pie dough (pastry). Stir in the egg with the fork, then add 60 ml (2 fl oz/¼ cup) of the broth from the pot and stir until a thick dough forms. It should be the consistency of thick biscuit (scone) dough, soft and sticky. Set aside in the refrigerator.

When the chicken is cooked, strain the liquid to remove any solids and reserve the broth. Leave the chicken until cool enough to handle, then remove the chicken skin and discard. Using your hands, shred all the meat from the carcass and discard the bones. Set the meat aside.

Rinse and dry the pot, then place over a medium–high heat and add the chicken fat. When the fat has melted, add the carrot, onion and celery and cook, stirring frequently for 3–4 minutes until the vegetables begin to soften. Add the broth and bring to a gentle simmer.

Using two teaspoons, scoop and drop small spoonfuls of the dough into the simmering broth, stirring to prevent the dumplings from sticking to the bottom, then simmer gently, uncovered, for 5–7 minutes until the dumplings are tender. Add the reserved chicken, season with salt and freshly ground black pepper and stir in the parsley.

Bureachiță

Serves 4 (about 10 pelmeni in each serving)

1 × 1.35 kg (3 lb) chicken, quartered
1.9 liters (64 fl oz/8 cups) water or
    Chicken Stock (page 237)
1 tablespoon salt
60 g (2 oz) butter
1 carrot, cut into 5 mm (¼ in) cubes
1 parsley root, cut into 5 mm (¼ in) cubes
1 yellow onion, cut into 5 mm (¼ in) cubes
3 garlic cloves, very finely chopped
675 g (1½ lb/3 cups) canned
    crushed tomatoes
40 Pelmeni (see opposite)
1 tablespoon chopped parsley, to garnish
120 ml (4 fl oz/½ cup) sour cream, to garnish

This soup can be made as just a tomato soup and is wonderful on its own, but the little time and effort to make pelmeni and add them to the dish are absolutely worth it. Traditionally Russian dumplings, pelmeni can be filled with meat, cheese, potato and fruit. Here, the addition is chicken, similar to the Eastern European kreplach. Raw or cooked chicken can be used to fill the pelmeni, and both versions are equally delicious. Whatever your preference, don't skimp on the garnishes – sour cream is a necessary condiment.

Place the chicken, water or stock and the salt in a pot. Weigh down the chicken under a few small plates to keep it submerged and simmer gently over a medium heat until the chicken pieces are cooked through, about 7–10 minutes for the breasts and 15–18 minutes for the legs and thighs. The meat should separate from the end of the leg bone when cooked, a thermometer will read 74°C (165°F) when inserted into the thickest part of the thigh or breast and the juices of the chicken will run clear.

When the chicken is cooked, remove from the pot and leave until cool enough to handle, then remove the chicken skin and discard. Using your hands, shred all the meat and discard the bones. Set a portion of the meat aside to make the pelmeni (see opposite). Strain the broth and reserve.

Wipe out the pot, then add the butter and melt over a medium heat. Add the carrot, parsley root, onion and garlic and sauté for 3–5 minutes until the vegetables are tender, but not browned. Add the tomatoes and broth, stir and cook for 3–4 minutes. Season with salt and freshly ground black pepper.

Add the pelmeni to the soup and cook gently for 3–4 minutes until the dumplings are cooked (make sure the pelmeni are cooked through if using raw chicken for the filling). Add the remaining shredded chicken meat halfway through cooking the dumplings. Serve garnished with parsley and sour cream and seasoned with salt and freshly ground black pepper.

Serves 4 (makes about 40 pelmeni using a pelmenitsa, or form as directed for handmade pelmeni, see page 133)

Dough
210 g (7½ oz/1½ cups) all-purpose (plain) flour, plus extra for dusting
½ teaspoon salt
1 large egg
60 ml (2 fl oz/¼ cup) water, plus extra as required

Filling
2 tablespoons vegetable oil
¼ yellow onion, very finely chopped
280 g (10 oz) ground (minced) or chopped raw chicken or 280 g (10 oz) chicken off cooked carcass from making broth, finely chopped

Pelmeni

Mix the flour and salt together in a bowl. Using a fork, stir in the egg and water. Once the dough starts to form, knead in the bowl or on a work surface until the dough is a cohesive ball. If required, add an additional teaspoon of water at a time until the dough is soft, but not sticky. Wrap the dough in plastic wrap and refrigerate for 45 minutes.

Melt the oil in a small pan over a medium heat. Add the onion and cook for 3–4 minutes until translucent, then remove from the heat and leave to cool.

Place the ground (minced) raw chicken or finely chopped reserved chicken in a bowl. Add the cooled onions, then generously season with salt and freshly ground black pepper and mix together until well combined.

Using a pelmenitsa, or cutting by hand (page 133), form and fill the pelmeni and place on a floured baking tray. Refrigerate until ready to cook.

Hunsekjuttsuppe

Serves 4–6

1 × 1.35 kg (3 lb) chicken, quartered
1.9 liters (64 fl oz/8 cups) water or
    Chicken Stock (page 237)
2 tablespoons salt
60 g (2 oz) butter
2 leeks, white parts only, thinly sliced
2 carrots, cut into 5 mm (¼ in) cubes
2 parsnips, cut into 5 mm (¼ in) cubes
4 tart apples, such as granny smith,
    peeled, cored and cut into 1 cm
    (½ in) cubes
45 g (1½ oz) all-purpose (plain) flour

Chicken, apples and parsnips are great friends, and when teamed in a silky soup, the cold winter and bare garden will seem all the more bearable. Norwegians know this well.

Place the chicken and water or stock in a large pot with the salt. Weigh down the chicken under a few small plates to keep it submerged and simmer gently over a medium heat until the chicken pieces are cooked through, about 7–10 minutes for the breasts and 15–18 minutes for the legs and thighs. The meat should separate from the end of the leg bone when cooked, a thermometer will read 74°C (165°F) when inserted into the thickest part of the thigh or breast and the juices of the chicken will run clear.

When the chicken is cooked, remove from the pot and leave until cool enough to handle, then remove the chicken skin and discard. Using your hands, shred all the meat and discard the bones. Set the meat aside. Reserve the broth.

Wipe out the pot, then add the butter and melt over a medium heat. Add the leeks, carrots, parsnips and apples and cook slowly, stirring for 6 minutes, or until the vegetables are soft. Add the flour and cook for another 2–3 minutes. Add the reserved broth, then, stirring constantly, bring to a gentle simmer for 10 minutes, or until the broth thickens. Stir in the reserved chicken and season with salt and freshly ground black pepper.

Supa de Pui cu Galuste de Gris

Serves 4–6

1 × 1.35 kg (3 lb) chicken, quartered
2.4 liters (81 fl oz/10 cups) water or
    Chicken Stock (page 237)
1 celeriac, quartered
2 small parsley roots, quartered or
    2 celery ribs (stalks), quartered
2 carrots, quartered
2 tablespoons salt
2 large eggs
1 tablespoon olive oil
7–8 tablespoons semolina flour
2 tablespoons chopped parsley

This is the closest thing to matzo ball soup I have eaten; in fact, the texture is perhaps even more delicate and satisfying – and they cook faster than the matzo ball soup I grew up with. This recipe is semolina based; however, some Romanian-born Americans use cream of wheat, farina or ground wheat. Whisking the egg whites before adding back the yolks creates an ethereal texture for the dumplings, and a gentle poach is essential for their incredible tenderness. Some cooks will garnish the soup with cooked carrot, but the dumplings are very much the star.

Place the chicken, water or stock, celeriac, parsley roots and carrots in a large pot with the salt. Weigh down the chicken under a few small plates to keep it submerged and simmer gently over a medium heat until the chicken pieces are cooked through, about 7–10 minutes for the breasts and 15–18 minutes for the legs and thighs. The meat should separate from the end of the leg bone when cooked, a thermometer will read 74°C (165°F) when inserted into the thickest part of the thigh or breast and the juices of the chicken will run clear.

When the chicken is cooked, remove from the pot and leave until cool enough to handle, then remove the chicken skin and discard. Using your hands, shred all the meat and discard the bones. Reserve the chicken meat for another use. Strain the broth and set aside.

Bring a large pot of salted water to a simmer over a medium heat.

Separate the eggs and whisk the whites to firm peaks in a stand mixer. Combine the egg yolks, oil and a good pinch of salt, then gently add to the whites. Stir in the semolina, 1 tablespoon at a time, until the consistency is thicker than pancake batter and not as thick as bread dough.

Dip a teaspoon into the simmering water for a few seconds to moisten it and make it hot, then take a spoonful of the dumpling mixture and lower it into the hot water – it will slide off. Repeat until you have used up all the dumpling mixture. Cover the pot with a lid and leave over a low heat for 10 minutes, or until the dumplings are cooked through and have expanded to twice their original size. Don't boil or the dumplings may break apart. When all the dumplings are cooked, cover with a lid and leave to rest for 5 minutes before serving.

Wipe out the pot used to cook the chicken, then pour the reserved broth into the pot and bring to a gentle simmer. Season with salt, add the cooked dumplings, season again with salt, if needed, and stir in the parsley.

Kneidlach

Mock Matzah Balls

Serves 4–6

175 g (6 oz) potatoes, such as yukon
    gold, peeled
1 tablespoon salt
450 g (1 lb) ground (minced) boneless,
    skinless chicken breasts
2 large eggs
½ yellow onion, finely diced
½ teaspoon baking powder
1.9 liters (64 fl oz/8 cups) Chicken
    Stock (page 237)
2 tablespoons chopped parsley or dill,
    or a combination, to garnish

Kneidlach, the Yiddish word for matzah (or matzo) balls, can be used for this mock recipe. Matzah balls are traditional Central and Eastern European Ashkenazi Jewish food. Due to migration, it is difficult to be certain, but their origins are believed to be in Romania. Traditional kneidlach (see page 167) are made from crushed matzah, eggs and fat (usually rendered chicken fat); however, this recipe uses chicken breast. Potato and egg keep the dumplings moist and tender, but be careful to cook the dumplings gently and slowly so that the lean meat does not dry out.

Cook the potatoes in a large pan of simmering water for 8–15 minutes until very tender. Drain and mash through a ricer or put back into the pot and use a potato masher to mash until very smooth. Leave to cool completely.

Place the potato, salt, and all the remaining ingredients, except the stock and parsley, together in a large bowl and very gently mix to combine. Cover with plastic wrap and refrigerate for 1 hour.

Bring the stock to a gentle simmer in a pot and season with salt. Using a tablespoon, make small balls of the chicken mixture, just smaller than a ping-pong ball, and drop them into the simmering stock. The chicken mixture will be soft, so form it gently into balls without compacting the meat too much. Cook the kneidlach at a very gentle simmer for 3–4 minutes until cooked through. Simmering too hard or boiling the kneidlach will make them tough or make them fall apart. Adjust the seasoning of the stock and stir in the parsley.

Temnyy Kuryachyy Sup

Ukraine

Serves 4–6

Broth

1 × 1.35 kg (3 lb) chicken, quartered
1 yellow onion, quartered
2 carrots, cut into 1 cm (½ in) cubes
2 celery ribs (stalks), cut into 2.5 cm
    (1 in) half-moons
3 garlic cloves, smashed
1 teaspoon black peppercorns
2 bay leaves
7 parsley sprigs
2 thyme sprigs
1.9 liters (64 fl oz/8 cups) water or
    Chicken Stock (page 237)
1 tablespoon salt

Soup

2 tablespoons rendered chicken fat
    or vegetable oil
1 small green cabbage, about 670 g (1½ lb),
    cored and cut into 5 cm (2 in) cubes
2 red beets (beetroot), peeled and cut
    into 1 cm (½ in) cubes
225 g (8 oz/1½ cups) dill pickles
    (gherkins), sliced
2 tablespoons sweet paprika
210 g (7½ oz/1 cup) puréed whole peeled
    tomatoes or Tomato Sauce (page 239)
240–350 ml (8–12 fl oz/1–1½ cups)
    pickle juice or caper juice
10–15 g (¼–½ oz/1–1¼ cups) chopped dill

To garnish

240 ml (8 fl oz/1 cup) sour cream
5 g (¼ oz/½ cup) dill, roughly chopped

This is borscht. Traditional variations exist throughout Eastern Europe. Beets (beetroot) overwinter well and are a good choice during the long, cold months when nothing grows in the garden. Dill pickles (gherkins) and pickle juice, or caper juice, add a welcome tang and balance out the earthiness of beets and cabbage. Garnish with plenty of chopped dill and sour cream. Rye bread is a good accompaniment, too.

Place all the broth ingredients in a large pot, place over a medium–high heat and bring to the boil. Immediately turn to a very low simmer. Remove the chicken breasts when cooked through, about 8–10 minutes, and the leg/thigh pieces when the meat separates from the bone around the end of the leg, a further 15 minutes. When the chicken is cooked through, a thermometer will read 74°C (165°F) when inserted into the thickest part of the thigh or breast and the juices of the chicken will run clear.

When the chicken is cooked, remove from the pot and leave until cool enough to handle, then remove the chicken skin and discard. Using your hands, shred all the meat and discard the bones. Set the meat aside. Strain the broth, discarding all the solids, then reserve.

For the soup, rinse and dry the pot, then add the chicken fat and melt over a medium–high heat. Add the cabbage, beets and pickles and sauté for 3 minutes, or until the cabbage begins to wilt. Stir in the paprika, then the tomato and cook for 1 minute, or until the sauce is thickened. Add the broth and gently simmer until the beets are tender, about 20 minutes. Stir in the pickle or caper juice, then the dill and reserved chicken. Season with salt and freshly ground black pepper. Ladle the soup into bowls and garnish with sour cream and dill.

Zelenyy Borshch

Serves 4–6

1 × 1.35 kg (3 lb) chicken, quartered
1.9 liters (64 fl oz/8 cups) water or
    Chicken Stock (page 237)
2 tablespoons salt
3 tablespoons rendered chicken fat
    or vegetable oil
1 yellow onion, cut into 1 cm (½ in) cubes
3 carrots, cut into 1 cm (½ in) rounds
30 spring (green) onions, cut into 2.5 cm
    (1 in) lengths
4 yellow potatoes, such as yukon gold,
    peeled and cut into 2.5 cm (1 in) cubes
50 g (1¾ oz/¼ cup) white long-grain rice
85 g (3 oz) spinach, roughly chopped
55 g (2 oz) sorrel, roughly chopped
30 g (1 oz) dill, roughly chopped
80 g (2¾ oz) parsley, roughly chopped
1 lemon

To garnish
6 large Hard-boiled Eggs (page 33),
    peeled and chopped
240 ml (8 fl oz/1 cup) sour cream

Springtime brings lettuces and herbs – and a welcome liveliness to heartier dishes that sustain us through winter. This Ukrainian and Russian version of green borscht is a celebration of the early spring garden. Sorrel delivers a distinctive brightness and a squeeze of lemon adds extra zing. Some versions include chopped hard-boiled egg, while others drizzle egg into the soup similar to Stracciatella alla Romana (page 227).

Place the chicken and water or stock in a large pot with the salt. Weigh down the chicken under a few small plates to keep it submerged and simmer gently over a medium heat until the chicken pieces are cooked through, about 7–10 minutes for the breasts and 15–18 minutes for the legs and thighs. The meat should separate from the end of the leg bone when cooked, a thermometer will read 74°C (165°F) when inserted into the thickest part of the thigh or breast and the juices of the chicken will run clear.

When the chicken is cooked, remove from the pot and leave until cool enough to handle, then remove the chicken skin and discard. Using your hands, shred all the meat and discard the bones. Set the meat aside and reserve the broth.

Wipe out the pot, then warm the chicken fat or oil over a medium heat. Add the onion, carrots and spring onions and cook slowly, stirring for 3–4 minutes until the vegetables are soft. Add the reserved broth, the potatoes and rice and bring to a gentle simmer. Season with salt and freshly ground black pepper. When the potatoes are tender, add the chicken meat to warm through and add the spinach, sorrel, dill and parsley. Stir to wilt the greens. Squeeze in the lemon juice, adding as much tangy flavor as possible without it becoming sour, then check the seasoning. Garnish each serving with chopped eggs and a dollop of sour cream.

SOUTHERN +
WESTERN EUROPE

Albania, Belgium, France, Germany, Greece,
Ireland, Italy, Malta, The Netherlands, Portugal, Spain

Southern European cuisine differs from that of northern and eastern Europeans mainly due to the influences of other regions and countries. Olive trees were first cultivated in the eastern Mediterranean around 7000 years ago; now Spain is the world's largest producer of olives. Fish stew made its way from Greece to influence now-iconic dishes in France (bouillabaisse) and in Italy (zuppa di pesce alla marinara).

Muslim culture also influenced food traditions of southern Europe by introducing spices, nuts, oranges, lemons, rice and sugar cane to the area. The Spanish cuisine reflects this Muslim tradition in its saffron-spiced rice and the use of nuts in sauces and desserts. Italians often use marzipan (sweetened almond paste) in their desserts and add saffron to rice to create dishes such as risotto alla Milanese, popular in northern Italy.

Western European food shares many ingredients with its neighbors to the north and east, including root vegetables and herbs. Soups often use cream and other dairy, creating filling and rich dishes, and potatoes are a common ingredient in the region.

Many soups across the south and west of Europe include rice, pasta or eggs. Albanian Supë Me Domate (page 204) is a simple and satisfying tomato soup. Few ingredients are needed and the soup is made quickly. Belgian Waterzooi (page 208) is both simple and so elegant, Dutch Koninginnesoep (page 230) is made with a roux before pieces of chicken are puréed into the broth. It is then fortified by adding an egg bound with cream, creating a rich, delicious dish. Malta's Tiġieġ u Ħaxix Brodu (page 229) is reminiscent of an Italian minestrone, reflecting the historically close relationships between the two nations. Overall, however, the countries of Southern and Western Europe are varied with distinctive culinary foods and traditions. A good rule of thumb: the colder the country, the heartier the soup.

Supë Me Domate

Serves 4–6

2 tablespoons rendered chicken fat
  or vegetable oil
1 onion, cut into 5 mm (¼ in) cubes
3 garlic cloves, thinly sliced
150 g (5½ oz/¾ cup) white long-grain rice
1450 ml (49 fl oz/6 cups) water or
  Chicken Stock (page 237)
840 g (1 lb 14 oz/4 cups) whole
  canned tomatoes, puréed, or diced
  fresh tomatoes
1 tablespoon salt
670 g (1½ lb) chicken breast or tenders,
  cut into bite-sized pieces

This simple chicken, tomato and rice soup is a quick and satisfying meal. Versions of the dish add cream. Using white meat, chicken breast or tenders cuts the cooking time, but be sure to cook the chicken gently and slowly to retain a tender texture.

Heat the chicken fat or oil in a large pot over a medium–high heat. Add the onions and garlic and cook for 3–4 minutes until the onions begin to become translucent. Add the rice and stir to coat in the fat. Stir in the water or stock and tomatoes and season with the salt. Bring to a low simmer and cook for 10–12 minutes until the rice is tender. Increase the heat to low–medium, stir in the chicken and cook for 3–4 minutes until cooked through. The low heat will keep the chicken tender. Adjust the seasoning to taste.

Supë Pulë me Rosnica

Serves 4

120 ml (4 fl oz/½ cup) olive oil,
    plus 3 tablespoons extra
1 × 1.35 kg (3 lb) chicken, quartered
2 tablespoons salt
2.9 liters (97½ fl oz/12 cups) water
    or Chicken Stock (page 237)
280 g (10 oz/2 cups) all-purpose (plain) flour
2 large eggs
115 g (4 oz/½ cup) butter, plus
    1 tablespoon extra

Few ingredients are needed for this simple, rustic soup, making it a standard in the kitchens of Myzeqe, southwestern–central Albania. Everyone in the region has stories of their grandmother making this soup, with variations from home to home. Almost similar to Italian frascarelli (pasta), the dough is made from just flour and a liquid, in this case eggs. After being toasted in butter and olive oil, like a roux, it is added to the simmering chicken soup and cooked until the broth thickens. Variations include herbs, fresh peppers, eggplant (aubergine) and onions.

Heat a large heavy-bottomed pot over a medium–high heat with 3 tablespoons of the olive oil. When the oil is hot, season the chicken with salt, add to the pot and brown on all sides. Add the water or stock with the salt. Weigh down the chicken under a few small plates to keep it submerged and simmer gently over a medium heat until the chicken pieces are cooked through, about 7–10 minutes for the breasts and 15–18 minutes for the legs and thighs. The meat should separate from the end of the leg bone when cooked, a thermometer will read 74°C (165°F) when inserted into the thickest part of the thigh or breast and the juices of the chicken will run clear.

Meanwhile, place the flour in a mound on a work surface. Make a well in the center of the flour and add the eggs to the well. Using your hands, work the eggs into the flour until the all-white flour dust has turned into crumbly yellow pieces, or has lost its whiteness. If white flour remains, add a ½ teaspoon water at a time until all the flour is soft yellow flaky pieces. This mixture should be dry and crumbly and not doughy and wet.

Heat the remaining olive oil in a large cast-iron pan over a medium heat. Add the flaky flour pieces and cook, stirring constantly, until very golden and toasty. Don't burn the flour.

When the chicken is cooked, add the toasted flour pieces to the soup and bring to a simmer. Cook for 20 minutes, stirring occasionally to make sure the flour does not burn on the bottom of the pan, or until the soup thickens. Stir in the butter and adjust the seasoning.

Supë Pulë me Veze e Limon

Albania

Serves 6

3 tablespoons olive oil
1 yellow onion, cut into 5 mm (¼ in) cubes
4 celery ribs (stalks), cut into 5 mm
  (¼ in) half-moons
3 carrots, cut into 2.5 cm (1 in) lengths
4 garlic cloves, very finely chopped
2 bay leaves
1 × 1.35 kg (3 lb) chicken, quartered
1 tablespoon salt
1.9 liters (64 fl oz/8 cups) water or
  Chicken Stock (page 237)
3 yellow potatoes, such as yukon gold,
  peeled and quartered
2 large eggs
juice of 2 lemons, making about 120 ml
  (4 fl oz/½ cup) lemon juice

This soup is similar to Avgolemono from neighboring Greece (page 216). Some versions include rice instead of potatoes and add a handful of parsley to finish, while others thicken it with a roux or add a dollop of tomato paste to the vegetables when they are tender. The lemony flavor brightens this popular soup, and the dish is filling but not heavy.

Heat the oil in a large pot over a medium–high heat. Add the onion, celery, carrots, garlic, and bay leaves and cook for 3–4 minutes until the vegetables are tender. Add the chicken, season with the salt and add the water or stock. Simmer gently over a medium heat until the chicken pieces are cooked, about 7–10 minutes for the breasts and 15–18 minutes for the legs and thighs. The meat should separate from the end of the leg bone when cooked, a thermometer will read 74°C (165°F) when inserted into the thickest part of the thigh or breast and the juices of the chicken will run clear. Add the potatoes during the last 8 minutes of cooking.

When the chicken is cooked, remove from the pot and leave until cool enough to handle, then remove the chicken skin and discard. Using your hands, shred all the meat and discard the bones. Set the meat aside.

Whisk the eggs and lemon juice together in a small bowl. Add 1 tablespoon of the hot broth at a time to the egg mixture until it is the same temperature as the soup. Over a low heat, slowly add the egg mixture to the soup, stirring constantly. Add the reserved chicken to the soup and season with salt and freshly ground black pepper.

Waterzooi

Serves 4–6

1 × 1.35 kg (3 lb) chicken, quartered
1.9 liters (64 fl oz/8 cups) water or
　Chicken Stock (page 237)
2 bay leaves
2 tablespoons salt
30 g (1 oz) butter
2 leeks, whites parts only, cut into thin
　half-moons
2 large carrots, cut into 5 mm (¼ in) cubes
2 celery ribs (stalks), cut into 5 mm
　(¼ in) cubes
1 yellow onion, cut into 5 mm (¼ in) cubes
240 ml (8 fl oz/1 cup) heavy (double) cream
2 tablespoons cornstarch (cornflour)
2 large egg yolks
40 g (1½ oz) parsley, finely chopped

This gorgeous soup originally was made with fish, but the chicken version is now equally popular. Whether using fish or chicken, the base remains the same: an egg and cream–thickened broth. Traditional vegetables include leeks, carrots, onions, potatoes and celeriac, and herbs might include sage, parsley, bay and thyme.

Place the chicken, water or stock and bay leaves in a large pot with the salt. Weigh down the chicken under a few small plates to keep it submerged and simmer gently over a medium heat until the chicken pieces are cooked, about 7–10 minutes for the breasts and 15–18 minutes for the legs and thighs. The meat should separate from the end of the leg bone when cooked, a thermometer will read 74°C (165°F) when inserted into the thickest part of the thigh or breast and the juices of the chicken will run clear.

　When the chicken is cooked, remove the chicken and bay leaves from the pot and leave until cool enough to handle, then remove the chicken skin and discard. Using your hands, shred all the meat and discard the bones. Set the meat aside and reserve the broth.

　Wipe out the pot, then add the butter and melt over a medium heat. Add the leeks, carrots, celery and onion and cook slowly, stirring constantly, for 6–8 minutes until the vegetables are soft. Add the reserved broth and bring to a gentle simmer.

　Place the cream, cornstarch (cornflour) and egg yolks in a bowl and whisk until very well combined. Add a spoonful of the hot broth to the yolk mixture and stir until combined. Repeat with more hot broth until the yolks have heated up. This will help the yolks to incorporate into the soup smoothly. When the yolks have enough broth to warm up, turn off the heat and add the yolk mixture to the soup, stirring constantly. Add the reserved chicken to the soup and stir to combine. Season with salt and freshly ground black pepper, then add the chopped parsley or serve on the side.

Poule au Pot

Serves 4

1 × 1.35 kg (3 lb) chicken
2 fresh bay leaves, or 3 dried
4 big thyme sprigs
5 cloves garlic, halved
20 black peppercorns
4 carrots, cut into 5 cm (2 in) lengths
4 ribs celery, cut into 5 cm (2 in) lengths
2 turnips, quartered
2 leeks, white parts only, cut into 5 cm
    (2 in) lengths
1 fennel bulb, cut into 1 cm (½ in) slices
240 ml (8 fl oz/1 cup) dry white wine
1200 ml (39 fl oz/5 cups) water or
    Chicken Stock (page 237)
1 tablespoon salt
200 g (7 oz/1 cup) white long-grain rice
chervil or tarragon, to garnish

King Henry IV of France (1553–1610) had such great pride in his country that he insisted that no French person should be too poor to enjoy poule au pot – which translates as chicken in the pot – for Sunday supper. Alas, French peasants in the countryside had a diet based mainly on bread, vegetables and soup; they rarely could afford or had the opportunity to eat meat. People living closer to towns would often buy inexpensive pieces of meat, which needed long cooking. Sometimes the dish included stuffing the bird or adding seasonal vegetables, such as spring peas, asparagus and zucchini (courgette). Serve with baguette, dijon mustard and cornichons.

Place the chicken, herbs, garlic, peppercorns, and vegetables in a pot. The chicken should fit in the pot snugly with the vegetables. Add the wine, water or stock and the salt and bring to the boil. Immediately reduce the heat to a very gentle simmer. Simmer, uncovered, for 20–30 minutes until the vegetables are tender and the chicken is cooked through – a thermometer will read 74°C (165°F) when inserted into the thickest part of the thigh or breast and the juices of the chicken will run clear.

Remove the chicken and vegetables from the pot and lay on a plate. Cover the chicken with foil. Add the rice to the broth and simmer very gently for 10 minutes.

Drain the rice through a colander into a large bowl to collect the broth. Season the broth with salt and freshly ground black pepper if necessary.

Cut the chicken into serving pieces, then serve in hot bowls with equal amounts of vegetables and rice in each bowl. Ladle the hot broth over the chicken and vegetables and garnish with chervil or tarragon.

Crème de Volaille

Serves 4

1 × 1.35 kg (3 lb) chicken, quartered
1.7 liters (57 fl oz/7 cups) water or
    Chicken Stock (page 237)
2 tablespoons salt
125 g (4½ oz/½ cup) unsalted butter
1 yellow onion, cut into 5 mm (¼ in) cubes
2 celery ribs (stalks), cut into 5 mm
    (¼ in) cubes
3 carrots, cut into 5 mm (¼ in) cubes
3 thyme sprigs
1 bay leaf
75 g (2¾ oz/½ cup) all-purpose (plain) flour
120 ml (4 fl oz/½ cup) heavy (double) cream
2½ teaspoons dry sherry
2 tablespoons chopped parsley, to garnish

As classic as it gets, cream of chicken soup is a fundamental French mother sauce, velouté, with the addition of small garnishes of chicken and mirepoix (onion, celery and carrot). The result is silky and special. In the 1950s, the Indianapolis, Indiana (USA), L.S. Ayers Tearoom made a version of this soup and named it velvet chicken soup. It earned a cult following, and even home cooks added it to their repertoire. The soup was canned and sold in supermarkets in the US in the 1960s and '70s, making assembling casseroles quick and easy. But don't be fooled: making this soup from scratch is King and Queen to any pauper of a counterfeit.

Place the chicken and water or stock in a large pot with the salt. Weigh down the chicken under a few small plates to keep it submerged and simmer gently over a medium heat until the chicken pieces are cooked through, about 7–10 minutes for the breasts and 15–18 minutes for the legs and thighs. The meat should separate from the end of the leg bone when cooked, a thermometer will read 74°C (165°F) when inserted into the thickest part of the thigh or breast and the juices of the chicken will run clear.

    When the chicken is cooked, remove from the pot and leave until cool enough to handle, then remove the chicken skin and discard. Remove all the meat from the bones in large pieces, then chop into small pieces, just a little larger than the vegetables. Strain the broth and reserve.

    Wipe out the pot, then add the butter and melt over a medium heat. Add the onion, celery, carrots, thyme and bay leaf and sauté for 2–4 minutes until the vegetables are tender, but not browned. Add the flour, stir to combine and cook for 1 minute. Add the reserved stock and whisk to combine. Bring to a gentle simmer and cook for 8–10 minutes until bubbly and thickened. Remove from the heat, remove and discard the thyme sprigs and bay leaf and stir in the cream and sherry. Add the reserved chicken and chopped parsley and cook for another minute just to warm the chicken. Season with salt and freshly ground black pepper and garnish with parsley.

Kreplach Chicken Soup

Serves 4

1.9 liters (64 fl oz/8 cups) Chicken
    Stock (page 237)
2 tablespoons chopped parsley or dill,
    or a combination

Dough
280 g (10 oz/2 cups) all-purpose (plain)
    flour, plus extra for dusting
1 teaspoon salt
3 large eggs
2–4 tablespoons water

Filling
2 tablespoons rendered chicken fat
1 yellow onion, cut into very small cubes
225 g (8 oz) chicken livers, sinew and
    fat trimmed
1½ teaspoons salt
½ teaspoon freshly ground black pepper
1 teaspoon ground caraway

Think of this as Jewish wonton soup. Stuffed pasta is thought to have migrated to Germany from Venice, Italy – a significant home for Italian Jews – during the fourteenth century. Kreplach are dumplings that can be made with chicken, beef, cheese or potato. This recipe encases chicken livers, which were originally an inexpensive cut of chicken and add richness, creaminess and elegance to this simple dumpling. When kreplach are made with potato or cheese, they are traditionally dressed in melted butter and served with sour cream and caramelized onions.

For the dough, place the flour and salt in a large bowl and make a well in the center. Add the eggs to the well and begin to knead into a dough. Add 1 tablespoon water at a time to the dough until it is smooth, cohesive and soft, but not sticky. Roll the dough into a ball, wrap in plastic wrap and refrigerate for 30 minutes.

For the filling, melt the chicken fat in a large sauté or frying pan over a high heat. Add the onions and cook, stirring frequently, for 3–5 minutes until the onions are golden and caramelized. Add the livers and cook for 3 minutes, or until golden on the first side, then flip and cook for a further 2–3 minutes until not quite cooked through in the middle. Remove the pan from the heat and place all the pan contents in a food processor. Pulse until a choppy and rough paste is formed, scraping the sides of the bowl down a few times during pulsing. Place the liver purée into a small bowl, season with the salt, pepper and caraway and set aside.

On a well-floured board, or using a pasta roller, roll the dough out as close as possible to paper-thinness, then cut into 5 cm (2 in) squares. Fill a small bowl with cool water.

Place a scant teaspoon of the filling in the center of the square and, using your index finger, moisten two adjacent sides of the pasta square with water. Fold the square into a triangle, squeezing out any air pockets. Moisten one of the long ends with water, then bring the two long ends together, similar to a tortellini. Place the kreplach on a lightly floured baking tray and repeat until all the filling is used up. The filling should make about 40 dumplings.

Bring a large pot of water to a vigorous boil, season with salt, drop in the kreplach and cook for 3 minutes.

Warm the chicken stock in a pot over a medium heat until hot, season with salt and add the cooked kreplach to the broth. Stir in the parsley and serve.

Hühnersuppe mit Knödeln

Germany

Serves 4–6

2 tablespoons rendered chicken fat
   or vegetable oil
2 large yellow onions, cut into 1 cm
   (½ in) cubes
2 tablespoons all-purpose (plain) flour
1 tablespoon paprika
1.9 liters (64 fl oz/8 cups) water or
   Chicken Stock (page 237)
1 × 1.35 kg (3 lb) chicken, quartered
1 tablespoon salt

Dumplings
3 large eggs
1 teaspoon salt
140 g (5 oz/1 cup) all-purpose (plain) flour

The German dish of chicken and dumplings is thought to have its origins in Jewish chicken soup. Cologne was the first German city populated by the Jewish community during Roman times. This simple soup, nourishing a family with few inexpensive ingredients, was a popular addition to their new country. The egg dough will slightly thicken the soup, giving it a satisfying, stew-like texture. Variations include the addition of root vegetables, and Kölsch, beer from Cologne, as part of the broth.

For the dumplings, mix the eggs, salt and flour together in a bowl to make a sticky dough. Set aside at room temperature.

Heat the chicken fat or oil in a large pot over a medium heat. Add the onions and cook for 3–4 minutes until the onions become translucent. Add the flour and paprika and stir to combine. Stir in the water or stock, the chicken pieces and salt and bring to the boil. Immediately reduce the heat to a very gentle simmer and simmer, uncovered, until the chicken is cooked through, a thermometer reads 74°C (165°F) when inserted into the thickest part of the meat and the juices run clear. The chicken breasts will take 10–15 minutes while the legs and thighs will take 20–30 minutes.

When the chicken breasts are cooked, remove from the soup and continue cooking the thighs and legs until the meat separates from the end of the leg bone. Just after removing the breasts, add the dumplings to the soup. Using two tablespoons, scoop tablespoon-sized portions of the dough with one spoon and scrape them into the soup with the other spoon. Repeat until all the dough is used. Partially cover the pot with a lid and cook at a gentle simmer for 15 minutes, or until the thighs and legs are cooked and the dumplings are tender.

When the chicken thighs are cooked, remove them from the soup and leave all the chicken until cool enough to handle, then remove the chicken skin and discard. Using your hands, shred all the meat, discarding the bones and add the meat back to the soup.

Season the soup with salt and freshly ground black pepper and serve in a bowl with the dumplings.

EUROPE

Avgolemono

Serves 4

1 × 1.35 kg (3 lb) chicken, quartered
1.9 liters (64 fl oz/8 cups) water or
   Chicken Stock (page 237)
1 tablespoon salt
1 yellow onion, cut into 1 cm (½ in) cubes
2 bay leaves
100 g (3½ oz/½ cup) white long-grain rice
3 large eggs
75 ml (2½ fl oz) lemon juice, plus extra
   to taste
dill, to garnish

I learned the recipe for this soup from a woman who immigrated to the US from Greece when she was nine. She taught me that whether I chose to shred the cooked chicken in the soup, or serve it on the side, either would be correct. She used skinless chicken or chicken with skin, but would discard the skin after cooking. Her family would use either orzo, rice or pastina, and variations were welcomed. The soup consistency was always the same, though. She was adamant that the soup should not simmer too hard or have too much liquid because the richness and silkiness would be lost. Traditionally, this recipe was used as a sauce to drape over cooked chicken, instead of being served as a standalone soup. Take gentle care when reheating, as too high a heat will cook the egg in the soup and the silky texture will be lost. More chicken is used to make the broth than is needed for the soup, so save the remaining legs and thighs for another use or double the soup recipe to use all the meat. Traditional garnishes are dill and black pepper.

Place the chicken in a large pot and add the water or stock. Add the salt, the onion and bay leaves and bring to a very gentle simmer. Weigh down the chicken with a plate or two, making sure it is fully submerged and cook for 20–30 minutes until a thermometer inserted into thickest part of leg and thigh and thickest part of the breast reads 74°C (165°F). Using a fine-meshed sieve, separate the chicken, onion and bay leaves from the broth. Place the chicken on a baking tray or plate and leave to cool at room temperature and discard the onion and bay leaves.

Bring the strained broth to a simmer, add the rice and cook for 7–9 minutes until just tender.

Meanwhile, use an immersion blender or blender to mix the eggs and lemon together until completely combined, then set aside. Using your hands, shred two chicken breasts into small pieces; this should yield about 350 g (12½ oz/2 cups) shredded chicken. Set aside.

When the rice is tender, ladle a few spoonfuls of the hot broth into the egg mixture. Add more broth, a spoonful at a time, until the egg mixture is warm. Adding too much hot liquid to the eggs will curdle them, so do this step slowly.

When the egg mixture is warm, you should have around two cups of liquid. Turn off the heat and drizzle the egg mixture into the hot broth, stirring constantly with a whisk. The soup should thicken and become silky. Add the reserved chicken and season with salt. Add lemon juice to taste and garnish with dill to serve.

Kotosoupa

Serves 4–6

1 × 1.35 kg (3 lb) chicken, quartered
1.9 liters (64 fl oz/8 cups) water or
  Chicken Stock (page 237)
2 tablespoons salt
2 tablespoons olive oil
2 yellow onions, cut into 1 cm (½ in) cubes
2 carrots, cut into 5 mm (¼ in) cubes
2 celery ribs (stalks), cut into 5 mm
  (¼ in) cubes
1 large potato, peeled and cut into
  1 cm (½ in) cubes
2 bay leaves
300 g (10½ oz/1½ cups) fresh or canned
  diced tomatoes
1 zucchini (courgette), cut into 1 cm
  (½ in) cubes
50 g (1¾ oz/½ cup) orzo pasta

Kotosoupa is the lighter and brighter version of its better-known cousin, Avgolemono (page 216). A clean and flavorful broth with vegetables, pasta and chicken, kotosoupa is a hearty meal without being too heavy. Chicken can be left in portions or shredded – either is just fine. Some versions include dried or fresh chili to add heat, while others include a squeeze of lemon to serve.

Place the chicken and water or stock in a large pot with the salt. Weigh down the chicken under a few small plates to keep it submerged and simmer gently over a medium heat until the chicken pieces are cooked through, about 7–10 minutes for the breasts and 15–18 minutes for the legs and thighs. The meat should separate from the end of the leg bone when cooked, a thermometer will read 74°C (165°F) when inserted into the thickest part of the thigh or breast and the juices of the chicken will run clear.

When the chicken is cooked, remove from the pot and leave until cool enough to handle, then remove the chicken skin and discard. Using your hands, shred all the meat and discard the bones. Set the meat aside. Strain the broth and reserve.

Wipe out the pot, then add the olive oil and heat over a medium heat. Add the onion, carrot and celery and cook for 3–5 minutes until the vegetables are tender, but not browned. Add the potato, bay leaves, tomato, zucchini and orzo, stir and cook for 1 minute. Add the reserved broth, then bring to a gentle simmer and cook for 8–9 minutes until the soup has slightly thickened and the orzo is tender. Add the reserved chicken and season with salt and freshly ground black pepper.

Chicken and Dumplings

Serves 4–6

1 × 1.35 kg (3 lb) chicken, quartered
1.9 liters (64 fl oz/8 cups) water or
    Chicken Stock (page 237)
2 tablespoons salt, plus ½ teaspoon extra
60 g (2 oz) butter
1 yellow onion, cut into 1 cm (½ in) cubes
3 large celery ribs (stalks), cut into 5 mm
    (¼ in) half-moons
1 teaspoon fresh thyme
140 g (5 oz/1 cup) all-purpose (plain) flour,
    plus 3 tablespoons extra
2 bay leaves
135 g (5 oz/1 cup) frozen peas
1 teaspoon baking powder
40 g (1½ oz) cold butter, cut into
    small pieces
2 large eggs
2 tablespoons milk

Savory dumplings are part of Ireland's traditional cuisine. Original recipes for the dough were based on two parts self-raising flour to one part suet. Often these dumplings were added to soups or stews, or served as part of a casserole. The dumplings should be tender, the interior steamed and the exterior poached and moist. Through time, chicken and dumplings became part of Irish cuisine, not unlike incarnations in Canada and the Southern states of the US. Variations of this stew include carrots and potatoes, while a healthy dose of black pepper gives strength to the base of this soup.

Place the chicken and water or stock in a large pot with 2 tablespoons of the salt. Weigh down the chicken under a few small plates to keep it submerged and simmer gently over a medium heat until the chicken pieces are cooked through, about 7–10 minutes for the breasts and 15–18 minutes for the legs and thighs. The meat should separate from the end of the leg bone when cooked, a thermometer will read 74°C (165°F) when inserted into the thickest part of the thigh or breast and the juices of the chicken will run clear.

When the chicken is cooked, remove from the pot and leave until cool enough to handle, then remove the chicken skin and discard. Using your hands, shred all the meat and discard the bones. Set the meat aside. Reserve the broth.

Wipe out the pot, then add the butter and melt over a medium heat. Add the onion, celery and thyme and cook slowly, stirring for 3–4 minutes until the vegetables are soft. Stir in 3 tablespoons flour and season lightly with salt and freshly ground black pepper. Add the reserved broth, which should measure 1450 ml (49 fl oz/6 cups). Add extra water, if necessary, to make up the amount. Add the bay leaves and peas and cook very gently for 2–3 minutes.

Place the remaining flour with the baking powder, butter and the extra ½ teaspoon of salt in a small bowl and stir to combine, breaking down the butter into pea-sized pieces. Add the eggs and milk and mix until combined into a dough. The texture of the dough should be wetter than biscuit (scone) dough.

Add the chicken meat to the soup to warm through. Using two spoons, make small dumplings and add directly to the soup. Simmer gently for 2–3 minutes until the dumplings are cooked. Adjust the seasoning and serve.

Chicken Skink

Serves 4–6

1 × 1.35 kg (3 lb) chicken
1.9 liters (64 fl oz/8 cups) water or
    Chicken Stock (page 237)
2 tablespoons salt
60 g (2 oz) butter
2 celery ribs (stalks), cut into 1 cm
    (½ in) dice
3 carrots, cut into 1 cm (½ in) rounds
2 small leeks, white parts only, cut into
    thin half-moons
2 bay leaves
4 thyme sprigs
4 spring (green) onions, cut into 2.5 cm
    (1 in) lengths
70 g (2½ oz/½ cup) frozen peas
3 large egg yolks
240 ml (8 fl oz/1 cup) heavy (whipping)
    cream
4 butter lettuce leaves, or other tender
    lettuce leaves, shredded

Cullen is a small town in Moray on the north-east coast of Scotland, known for its smoked haddock skink. The term skink, another word for broth, is an old Irish term that evolved to refer to other broths, such as chicken – hence, chicken soup came to be referred to as chicken skink. This lovely soup is sweet from the leeks and carrots, and evokes springtime with its peas and lettuce. The cream and egg yolks bind the broth, making it an elegant and substantial soup. Serve with crusty bread to dip into the skink.

Place the chicken and water or stock in a large pot with the salt. Weigh down the chicken under a few small plates to keep it submerged and simmer gently over a medium heat until the chicken pieces are cooked through, about 7–10 minutes for the breasts and 15–18 minutes for the legs and thighs. The meat should separate from the end of the leg bone when cooked, a thermometer will read 74°C (165°F) when inserted into the thickest part of the thigh or breast and the juices of the chicken will run clear.

When the chicken is cooked, remove from the pot and leave until cool enough to handle, then remove the chicken skin and discard. Using your hands, shred all the meat and discard the bones. Set the meat aside and reserve the broth.

Wipe out the pot, then add the butter and melt over a medium heat. Add the celery, carrots, leeks, bay leaves, thyme and spring onions and cook slowly, stirring for 3–4 minutes until the vegetables are soft. Add the reserved broth, the peas and the chicken meat and bring to a gentle simmer.

Combine the egg yolks and cream in a small bowl. Add a few tablespoons of warm broth to the cream, stir and add more, a little at a time. Make sure not to cook the eggs. Reduce the heat to very low and drizzle the egg mixture into the soup, stirring constantly. Keep the heat low, otherwise the broth will separate. Season with salt and freshly ground black pepper and stir in the shredded lettuce.

Chicken and Potato Soup

Serves 4

60 g (2 oz) butter
2 leeks, white parts only, thinly sliced
2 fat thyme sprigs
2 garlic cloves, very finely chopped
2 tablespoons all-purpose (plain) flour
4 × boneless, skinless chicken thighs
   (approx. 280 g/10 oz)
1450 ml (49 fl oz/6 cups) water or
   Chicken Stock (page 237)
4 yellow potatoes, such as yukon gold,
   peeled and cut into 1 cm (½ in) cubes
2 tablespoons finely chopped parsley

Potatoes are synonymous with Irish cuisine, but they did not originate there. Potatoes made their way to Europe in the 1500s after the Spanish conquistadors discovered them in the Andes mountains. They became an important staple for Irish working-class families, and remain so today. Potatoes are an excellent source of vitamin C, a good source of potassium and vitamin B6, fat and sodium, and are also cholesterol free. Some variations of this soup purée the mixture with a touch of milk or cream, then add the chicken back to the silky soup.

Melt the butter in a large pot over a low–medium heat. Add the leeks, thyme and garlic and cook slowly, stirring for 3–5 minutes until the leeks are tender. Add the flour and stir, making sure there are no lumps, then add the chicken and water or stock, increase the heat to medium–high and bring to a simmer. Cook the chicken gently for about 15 minutes, adding the potato halfway through cooking. The juices of the chicken will run clear and the chicken will shred easily with 2 forks when it is cooked through.

When the chicken is cooked, remove from the pot and leave until cool enough to handle. Using 2 forks, or your hands, shred the meat, then add to the soup. Stir in the parsley and season with salt and freshly ground black pepper.

Brodo di Pollo con Pastina

Serves 4–6

1 × 1.35 kg (3 lb) chicken, quartered
2.4 liters (81 fl oz/10 cups) water or
    Chicken Stock (page 237)
2 tablespoons salt
3 tablespoons olive oil
2 garlic cloves, sliced
1 yellow onion, cut into 1 cm (½ in) cubes
2 carrots, cut into 1 cm (½ in) cubes
3 celery ribs (stalks), cut into thin
    half-moons
1 sweet red pepper (capsicum), seeded and
    cut into 1 cm (½ in) cubes
2 bay leaves
225 g (8 oz) small raw pasta, such as acini
    di pepe, tubettini, or orzo
250 g (9 oz/2 cups) canned crushed
    tomatoes
55 g (2 oz) piece Parmigiano Reggiano rind
200 g (7 oz/4 cups) chopped spinach
7 g (¼ oz/¼ cup) parsley, roughly chopped
7 g (¼ oz/¼ cup) fresh oregano,
    roughly chopped
grated Parmigiano Reggiano, to garnish
good olive oil, to garnish

This soup is easy to love. Tomatoes lend sweetness to the simple chicken broth, pasta thickens the soup and gives it a stewy texture, and the fresh herbs lighten and brighten the dish. Save rinds from Parmigiano Reggiano wedges and store them in the freezer, then add a small chunk during cooking for a lovely umami richness. Drizzle with olive oil and finish with a grating or two of parmesan.

Place the chicken and water or stock in a large pot with the salt. Weigh down the chicken under a few small plates to keep it submerged and simmer gently over a medium heat until the chicken pieces are cooked through, about 7–10 minutes for the breasts and 15–18 minutes for the legs and thighs. The meat should separate from the end of the leg bone when cooked, a thermometer will read 74°C (165°F) when inserted into the thickest part of the thigh or breast and the juices of the chicken will run clear.

When the chicken is cooked, remove from the pot and leave until cool enough to handle. Remove the chicken skin and discard. Using your hands, shred all the meat and discard the bones. Set the meat aside. Reserve the broth.

Wipe out the pot, then add the olive oil and heat over a medium heat. Add the garlic, onion, carrots, celery, red pepper and bay leaves and cook slowly, stirring for 3–4 minutes until the vegetables are soft.

Meanwhile, bring a small pot of water to the boil, add the pasta and cook for 7–10 minutes until al dente. Drain the pasta and reserve.

Add the reserved broth, the tomato and Parmigiano Reggiano rind to the pot with the vegetables and bring to a very gentle simmer. Add the reserved chicken and pasta to the soup and stir to combine. Season with salt and freshly ground black pepper and stir in the spinach and herbs. Serve garnished with a sprinkling of Parmigiano Reggiano and a drizzle of olive oil.

Zuppa di Pollo e Orzo

Serves 4

1 × 1.35 kg (3 lb) chicken
1.9 liters (64 fl oz/8 cups) Chicken Stock
  (page 237)
2 tablespoons salt
140 g (5 oz/¾ cup) pearl barley
2 tablespoons rendered chicken fat
  or olive oil
450 g (1 lb) carrots, cut into 1 cm
  (½ in) rounds
4 celery ribs (stalks), cut into 1 cm
  (½ in) slices
1 yellow onion, cut into 5 mm (¼ in) cubes
4 sage leaves
2 fresh bay leaves
7.5 cm (3 in) rosemary sprig, leaves only
20 g (¾ oz) flat-leaf parsley leaves,
  roughly chopped
extra-virgin olive oil, to garnish

Italy's countryside is known for dishes such as this: warm, comforting and nutritious. Typical of Tuscany, this peasant food is hearty, and the recipe can be adjusted to the season. Versions of this soup include potatoes, peas, green beans and broccoli. As with Brodo di Pollo con Pastina (see opposite), add a chunk of Parmigiano Reggiano rind at the beginning of cooking to enhance the soup's flavor and add an umami quality.

Place the chicken and water or stock in a large pot with the salt. Weigh down the chicken under a few small plates to keep it submerged and simmer gently over a medium heat until the chicken pieces are cooked through, about 7–10 minutes for the breasts and 15–18 minutes for the legs and thighs. The meat should separate from the end of the leg bone when cooked, a thermometer will read 74°C (165°F) when inserted into the thickest part of the thigh or breast and the juices of the chicken will run clear.

When the chicken is cooked, remove from the pot and leave until cool enough to handle, then remove the chicken skin and discard. Using your hands, shred all the meat and discard the bones. Set the meat aside. Strain the broth and reserve.

Meanwhile, bring a pot of water to a simmer. Season the water with salt and add the barley. Cook for 20 minutes, or until the barley is tender, then drain and reserve.

Wipe out the pot used to cook the chicken, then add the chicken fat or oil and heat over a medium heat. Add the carrots, celery, onion, sage, bay leaves and rosemary and cook slowly, stirring for 3–4 minutes until the vegetables are soft. Add the broth, then add the barley and stir to combine. Stir in the reserved chicken and the parsley, then season with salt and freshly ground black pepper and garnish with olive oil.

Stracciatella alla Romana *Italy*

Serves 4–6

1 × 1.35 kg (3 lb) chicken, quartered
2.4 liters (81 fl oz/10 cups) water or
    Chicken Stock (page 237)
2 tablespoons salt
4 large eggs
25 g (1 oz/4 tablespoons) dried
    breadcrumbs or semolina
30 g (1 oz/4 tablespoons) grated
    Parmigiano Reggiano cheese
2 parsley sprigs (including stems),
    finely chopped, plus extra to garnish
150 g (5½ oz/¾ cup) arborio rice or pastina,
    such as acini de pepe or orzo

Similar to Chinese egg drop soup, stracciatella alla romana consists of swirls of whisked egg suspended in a rich, flavorful broth. Stracciatella means long strands and it can be used to describe a string cheese, an ice cream with strands of chocolate or, in this case, the strands of egg in a soup. Chicken meat can be added back to the soup, or left out, and often seasonal vegetables are added. The soup must be eaten fresh as the egg will lose its texture if frozen.

Place the chicken and water or stock in a large pot with the salt. Weigh down the chicken under a few small plates to keep it submerged and simmer gently over a medium heat until the chicken pieces are cooked through, about 7–10 minutes for the breasts and 15–18 minutes for the legs and thighs. The meat should separate from the end of the leg bone when cooked, a thermometer will read 74°C (165°F) when inserted into the thickest part of the thigh or breast and the juices of the chicken will run clear.

When the chicken is cooked, remove from the pot and leave until cool enough to handle, then remove the chicken skin and discard. Using your hands, shred all the meat and discard the bones. Set the meat aside. Strain the broth and reserve.

Meanwhile, mix the eggs, breadcrumbs or semolina, cheese and parsley together in a bowl. Season lightly with salt and freshly ground black pepper, then cover with plastic wrap and refrigerate until ready to use.

Rinse the pot and pour in the strained broth. Add the rice or pastina and cook for 7–10 minutes until tender. This will cloud the broth. If a clear broth is preferred, cook the rice or pasta in a separate pot, then add to the soup when cooked. When the rice or pasta is tender, add the reserved chicken to the soup and season with salt and freshly ground black pepper.

Remove the pot from the heat and immediately and slowly pour the eggs into the soup. Make sure to pour around the pot, not in the same place. The residual heat will cook the eggs and the heat from the stove will create a very tender cooked egg.

Gently ladle the soup into bowls without damaging the soft curds of cooked egg. Season with freshly ground black pepper and garnish with chopped parsley.

Tiġieġ u Ħaxix Brodu

Malta

Serves 4–6

1 × 1.35 kg (3 lb) chicken, quartered
2.4 liters (81 fl oz/10 cups) water or
  Chicken Stock (page 237)
2 tablespoons salt
3 tablespoons rendered chicken fat
  or olive oil
1 large yellow onion, cut into 5 mm
  (¼ in) cubes
80 g (2¾ oz) cilantro (coriander)
3 garlic cloves, very finely chopped
2 carrots, cut into 5 mm (¼ in) cubes
2 yellow potatoes, such as yukon gold,
  peeled and cut into 1 cm (½ in) cubes
2 tablespoons tomato paste
¼ head green cabbage, julienned
2 bay leaves
50 g (1¾ oz/½ cup) orzo pasta
4 basil sprigs, leaves roughly chopped
  and stems finely chopped
4 mint sprigs, leaves roughly chopped
  and stems finely chopped
10 parsley sprigs, leaves roughly chopped
  and stems finely chopped
10 dill sprigs, leaves roughly chopped and
  stems finely chopped

Malta is an island between Sicily and Tunisia. Its cuisine and culture reflect that of its neighbors. This classic Maltese dish is similar to Italian minestrone, including the addition of orzo. The word brodu, meaning broth, comes from the Italian word brodo. This soup is light, lively and nourishing.

Place the chicken and water or stock in a large pot with the salt. Weigh down the chicken under a few small plates to keep it submerged and simmer gently over a medium heat until the chicken pieces are cooked through, about 7–10 minutes for the breasts and 15–18 minutes for the legs and thighs. The meat should separate from the end of the leg bone when cooked, a thermometer will read 74°C (165°F) when inserted into the thickest part of the thigh or breast and the juices of the chicken will run clear.

When the chicken is cooked, remove from the pot and leave until cool enough to handle, then remove the chicken skin and discard. Using your hands, shred all the meat and discard the bones. Set the meat aside and reserve the broth.

Wipe out the pot, then add the chicken fat or oil and heat over a medium heat. Add the onion, cilantro stems, garlic, carrots, potato, tomato paste, cabbage and bay leaves and cook slowly, stirring for 6–8 minutes until the vegetables are soft. Add the reserved broth and bring to a very gentle simmer. Add the orzo and cook for 7–10 minutes until tender. Add the reserved chicken and stir to combine. Stir in the chopped herbs and season with salt and freshly ground black pepper.

Koninginnesoep

Serves 4

1 × 1.35 kg (3 lb) chicken, quartered
2.4 liters (81 fl oz/10 cups) water or
   Chicken Stock (page 237)
60 ml (2 fl oz/¼ cup) oude genever
   or aromatic gin
2 tablespoons salt
2 large carrots, cut into 5 mm (¼ in) cubes
155 g (5½ oz/1 cup) peas, fresh or frozen
60 g (2 oz) butter
60 g (2 oz/½ cup minus 1 tablespoon)
   all-purpose (plain) flour
1 fresh bay leaf, or 2 dried
120 ml (4 fl oz/½ cup) heavy (double) cream
2 large egg yolks

This Dutch dish is intended for the queen – it is smooth, rich and special. The soup is thickened in three distinct ways: first by creating a roux, second by finely blending the meat into the broth and third by adding egg and cream, which binds everything together and makes the soup rich and silky. Once the cream and egg are added, keep the soup over a low heat, otherwise the silky texture will be lost.

Place the chicken, water or stock and genever in a large pot with the salt. Weigh down the chicken under a few small plates to keep it submerged and simmer gently over a medium heat until the chicken pieces are cooked, about 7–10 minutes for the breasts and 15–18 minutes for the legs and thighs. The meat should separate from the end of the leg bone when cooked, a thermometer will read 74°C (165°F) when inserted into the thickest part of the thigh or breast and the juices of the chicken will run clear.

Meanwhile, blanch the carrots and peas separately in a pot of simmering water for 2 minutes, or until tender. Drain and leave to cool, then reserve.

When the chicken is cooked, remove from the pot and leave until cool enough to handle, then remove the chicken skin and discard. Using your hands, shred all the meat and discard the bones. Set the meat aside. Strain and reserve the broth. Wipe out the pot.

Blend the dark meat and 240–475 ml (8–16 fl oz/1–2 cups) of the reserved broth in a blender until very fine, then add to the remaining broth to make up to 1450 ml (49 fl oz/6 cups).

Melt the butter in the cleaned pot over a medium heat. Add the flour and cook slowly, stirring constantly, for 2–3 minutes. Add the bay leaf and the broth and bring to a gentle simmer, whisking gently as the soup thickens.

Place the cream and egg yolks in a bowl and whisk until very well combined. Add a spoonful of the hot broth to the yolk mixture and stir until combined. Repeat with more hot broth until the yolks have heated up; this will help to incorporate the yolks into the soup. When the yolks have warmed up, turn off the heat and add the yolk mixture to the soup, stirring constantly. Do not simmer the soup at this point or the egg will curdle and the soup texture will no longer be smooth. Add the reserved chicken to the soup together with the carrots and peas. Season with salt and freshly ground black pepper and serve.

Canja de Galinha, Azores

Serves 4–6

4 bay leaves
12 whole allspice berries
4 garlic cloves, thinly sliced
1 yellow onion, finely diced
3 carrots, finely diced
1 × 1.35 kg (3 lb) chicken
1 tablespoon salt
2.9 liters (97½ fl oz/12 cups) water
  or Chicken Stock (page 237)
200 g (7 oz/1 cup) white long-grain rice
120 ml (4 fl oz/½ cup) lemon juice
4–6 poached eggs, to serve

Similar to canja de galinha from Lisbon and Brazil, this Azorean version includes a poached egg, which is omitted in its Brazilian incarnation. This rice-based soup, sometimes thickened with egg stirred into the broth, is brightened with lemon juice, as opposed to its Brazilian sibling. The dish is a good example of how colonization carried culinary traditions across continents.

Place the bay leaves, allspice, garlic, onion, carrots, chicken and the salt in a large pot with the water or stock. Weigh down the chicken under a few small plates to keep it submerged and bring to the boil. Immediately reduce the heat to a very low simmer and cook for 20–30 minutes until the chicken is cooked through, a thermometer reads 74°C (165°F) when inserted into the thickest part of the thigh or breast and the juices of the chicken run clear.

When the chicken is cooked, remove from the pot and leave until cool enough to handle.

Add the rice to the broth and cook at a very gentle simmer for 15 minutes until the rice is very tender.

Remove the chicken skin from the cooled chicken and discard. Using your hands, shred all the meat from the carcass and discard the bones. Add the chicken to the soup and season with lemon juice and salt. Serve with a poached egg on top.

Sopa de Picadillo

Serves 4–6

1 × 1.35 kg (3 lb) chicken, quartered
2.4 liters (81 fl oz/10 cups) water or
    Chicken Stock (page 237)
2 tablespoons salt
120 ml (4 fl oz/½ cup) olive oil, plus
    2 tablespoons extra
100 g (3½ oz) bread, cut into 1 cm
    (½ in) cubes
200 g (7 oz) jamón serrano, finely chopped
8 garlic cloves, thinly sliced
60 ml (2 fl oz/¼ cup) dry sherry
175 g (6 oz/¾ cup) white long-grain rice
8 mint sprigs, plus extra to garnish
6 Hard-boiled Eggs (page 33), chopped

A typical dish from Andalusia, the autonomous region in southern Spain, this soup's main ingredient can be rice or fideo cabellín, short pasta (the preparation remains the same, although the cooking time for the pasta is shorter than for rice). The soup is often served without the addition of chicken meat. Variations of this soup include chickpeas, carrots and a final squeeze of lemon. And, in some versions, the broth includes bones and meat of several types of animals (cow, pig) in addition to chicken. This thick and comforting soup is delicious, especially in winter.

Place the chicken and water or stock in a large pot with the salt. Weigh down the chicken under a few small plates to keep it submerged and simmer gently over a medium heat until the chicken pieces are cooked through, about 7–10 minutes for the breasts and 15–18 minutes for the legs and thighs. The meat should separate from the end of the leg bone when cooked, a thermometer will read 74°C (165°F) when inserted into the thickest part of the thigh or breast and the juices of the chicken will run clear.

When the chicken is cooked, remove from the pot and leave until cool enough to handle. Remove the chicken skin and discard. Using your hands, shred the meat and set aside if using for the soup, or save for another use. Strain the broth and reserve.

Meanwhile, warm 120 ml (4 fl oz/½ cup) olive oil in a small pan over a medium heat. When hot, add the bread cubes in batches and stir until golden and toasted. Remove and drain on a plate lined with paper towel and repeat with the remaining cubes. Set aside.

Wipe out the pot from cooking the chicken, add the remaining olive oil and warm over a medium heat. Add the jamón and garlic and gently cook for 2 minutes, or until tender. Add the sherry and cook for a further 3 minutes, or until the liquid evaporates. Add the rice, mint and reserved broth, about 1.9 liters (64 fl oz/8 cups) liquid, and cook gently for 8–12 minutes until the rice is tender and the soup is thick. Add the reserved chicken if using in the soup.

Remove and discard the mint sprigs from the soup, Season with salt and freshly ground black pepper, then ladle into bowls and garnish with chopped eggs, the fried bread cubes and fresh mint sprigs.

Sopa de Fideos

Serves 4

1 × 1.35 kg (3 lb) chicken, quartered
1.9 liters (64 fl oz/8 cups) water or
    Chicken Stock (page 237)
2 tablespoons salt
2 roma or plum tomatoes, quartered
2 garlic cloves, sliced
¼ white onion
60 ml (2 fl oz/¼ cup) vegetable oil
225 g (8 oz) fideo noodles
15 g (½ oz) parsley, chopped
1 lime, cut into wedges, to garnish
2 avocados, cut into cubes, to garnish
½ bunch cilantro (coriander),
    roughly chopped, to garnish

Originally from Spain, this light soup found its way to Mexico and the Philippines during times of Spanish colonization. The soup's uniqueness lies in the toasting of the pasta, creating a depth of flavor not achieved with simply cooked pasta. Use vermicelli or angel hair pasta broken into 2.5 cm (1 in) pieces if fideos are difficult to find. Corn is also a common addition.

Place the chicken and water or stock in a large pot with the salt. Weigh down the chicken under a few small plates to keep it submerged and simmer gently over a medium heat until the chicken pieces are cooked through, about 7–10 minutes for the breasts and 15–18 minutes for the legs and thighs. The meat should separate from the end of the leg bone when cooked, a thermometer will read 74°C (165°F) when inserted into the thickest part of the thigh or breast and the juices of the chicken will run clear.

When the chicken is cooked, remove from the pot and leave until cool enough to handle, then remove the chicken skin and discard. Using your hands, shred all the meat and discard the bones. Set the meat aside. Strain the broth and reserve.

Meanwhile, purée the tomato, garlic and onion in a blender until very smooth. Set aside.

Wipe out the pot and place over a medium heat. Add the oil and fideos and cook for 2–4 minutes until the noodles are browned. Some noodles will be darker than others, but make sure to get some good color without any blackening. Add the reserved tomato purée, stir, then add the reserved broth and bring to a gentle simmer. Cook very gently for 4–5 minutes, then add the reserved chicken and chopped parsley and cook for another minute just to warm the chicken. Season with salt and freshly ground black pepper and serve garnished with lime, avocado and cilantro.

Larder

Single Chicken Stock

Makes 1.7 liters (57 fl oz/7 cups)

2.25 kg (5 lb) chicken bones
about 3.8 liters (128 fl oz/4 quarts) water

Place the chicken bones in a 5.7 liter (6 quart) stockpot and fill with just enough water to cover the bones. Bring to a rapid simmer over a high heat, then immediately reduce the heat to medium and simmer slowly for 6–8 hours until the stock is rich, reduced and flavorful. If the stock simmers too briskly, the fat will emulsify into the stock, rendering it greasy. If the stock reduces too quickly, add some extra water. This should not be necessary. Ideally, the stock will reduce by one-third to one-half when cooking slowly. As the stock is simmering, use a spoon or ladle to skim off and discard any foamy, dark impurities that rise to the top.

Set a fine-mesh sieve over a large, heavy-duty plastic container. Pour the stock through the sieve into the container and discard the chicken bones and any debris. If your sieve is not finely meshed, line the sieve with dampened cheesecloth (muslin) to catch any fine debris. Transfer the stock to airtight containers and refrigerate until cool. When the stock is cold, remove the fat by carefully scooping it from the top with a spoon. Follow the recipe for rendered chicken fat (page 239). Use the stock as is, or gently warm to melt it and package in airtight containers for freezer storage. To store the stock, refrigerate for up to 1 week or freeze for up to 2 months.

— To make a rich double chicken stock

Make the single chicken stock recipe with chicken stock instead of water and follow the same procedures as single stock. This will yield a richer blond stock.

— To make a roasted rich brown chicken stock

Preheat the oven to 230°C (450°F). Line a baking tray with baking paper.

Lay the chicken bones on the prepared baking tray in a single layer and roast for 20 minutes, or until nicely browned. Use the roasted bones in the single chicken stock recipe to make a darker and richer stock.

— To make chicken stock in an Instant Pot or pressure cooker

Makes 2.8 liters (95 fl oz/3 quarts)

1.35 kg (3 lb) chicken bones

If a very clear stock is desired, place the chicken bones in the canister of the Instant Pot, cover with water and bring to a simmer. Cook at a gentle simmer for 4–5 minutes, then strain the water. Add 2.8 liters (95 fl oz/3 quarts) water to the canister and lock the lid in place. Set the timer for 2 hours on pressure cook with slow release. When the stock is done, strain through a fine-mesh sieve and store in airtight containers.

Chicken Brine

Makes 950 ml (32½ fl oz/4 cups), enough for 1 × 1.35 kg (3 lb) chicken or the equivalent in chicken pieces

2 tablespoons salt
1 tablespoon superfine (caster) sugar
1 bay leaf
5 black peppercorns
2 garlic cloves
about 950 ml (32½ fl oz/4 cups) water

Combine all the ingredients in a medium pot and bring to the boil. Turn off the heat and leave to cool to room temperature. To brine a chicken, place the chicken in a large non-reactive container, add the brine and enough water to just cover the chicken, then cover with a lid and leave in the refrigerator for 24 hours for whole chicken or 12 hours for boneless chicken. Remove the chicken from the brine, pat dry with paper towel and proceed with the recipe: soup, grilling, frying or roasting.

Chopped Chicken Liver

Makes 800 g (1 lb 12 oz)

4 tablespoons rendered chicken fat
1 onion, cut into 5 mm (¼ in) cubes
225 g (8 oz) chicken livers, sinew and fat trimmed
1½ teaspoons salt
½ teaspoon freshly ground black pepper
1 teaspoon ground caraway

Melt half the chicken fat in a large sauté or frying pan over a high heat. Add the onion and cook, stirring frequently for 3–5 minutes until golden and caramelized. Add the livers and remaining chicken fat to the pan and cook for 3 minutes until golden on the first side, then flip and cook for a further 2–3 minutes until not quite cooked through in the middle.

Remove from the heat and leave to cool until just warm. Place all the contents of the pan in a food processor with the salt, pepper and caraway and pulse until a choppy and rough paste is formed, scraping the sides of bowl a few times during pulsing. Store in an airtight container in the refrigerator for up to 1 week.

Chicken Skins, Chicken Skin Chips

Makes 10 skins

10 chicken skins
2 teaspoons olive oil
2 teaspoons rosemary leaves

Preheat the oven to 180°C (350°F).

Toss the skins in the olive oil and rosemary. On a flat, baking paper–lined baking tray, spread the individual skins out flat, taking care that there are no folds. If the leg skins are connected, cut the skin so it will lay flat. Place another piece of paper on top, followed by another flat baking tray. Weigh the trays down with bricks or something very heavy such as tomato cans. Cook in the oven for 30–45 minutes until the skins are completely crispy and golden brown. Place on a cool baking tray and leave until they come to room temperature. Store in an airtight container at room temperature for up to 1 week.

Gribenes (Chicken Cracklings)

Makes approx. 2 cups

450 g (1 lb) chicken skin and fat, diced
    (scissors are the best tool here)
1 teaspoon salt
1 tablespoon water
1 yellow onion, cut into 1 cm (½ in) cubes

In a large sauté pan over a medium heat, stir to combine the chicken skin and fat with the salt and the water and spread out in one layer. Cook for 15 minutes, or until the fat starts to render and the skin begins to turn golden at the edges. Add the onion and cook for a further 45–60 minutes, stirring occasionally, until the chicken skin and onion are crispy and richly browned, but not burned. Strain through a sieve and reserve the chicken fat.

Return the gribenes to the sauté pan and cook over a high heat until they are crispy and crunchy. Drain the gribenes on a plate lined with paper towel. They are best used fresh.

Chicken Liver Mousse with Brandy

Makes 1.4 liters (47 fl oz/1.5 quart) terrine

570 g (1 lb 4 oz) chicken livers, sinew and fat trimmed,
    at room temperature
8 large egg yolks, at room temperature
4 tablespoons brandy
1 tablespoon kosher or sea salt
pinch of ground nutmeg
340 g (12 oz) butter, softened to room temperature
475 ml (16 fl oz/2 cups) heavy (double) cream
crusty bread, to serve
cornichons, to serve

Preheat the oven to 140°C (275°F).

Purée the chicken livers, egg yolks, brandy, salt and
nutmeg in a food processor until smooth. While the motor is
running, add the soft butter, 1 tablespoon at a time, until all
the butter is incorporated. If the mixture looks curdled, wrap
a damp warm towel around the processor until the mixture is
smooth. This may take some time, but is essential. Strain the
liver mixture through a fine-mesh sieve into a large container.
When fully strained, mix the cream into the liver mixture,
then pour the mousse base into a 1.4 liter (47 fl oz/1.5 quart)
terrine mold. Place the terrine in a water bath (a large roasting
pan filled halfway with hot water) and bake in the oven for
1 hour and 10 minutes, or until the top is lightly browned and
the mousse is slightly jiggly. Remove from the water bath and
leave to cool at room temperature. When cool, cover with
plastic wrap and refrigerate overnight

Serve in the terrine, or to unmold, dip the bottom of the
terrine in a pan of hot water for 10 seconds. Run a paring knife
around the edge of the mold and invert onto a platter. Serve
with crusty bread and cornichons.

Rendered Chicken Fat

The golden liquid floating gently on top of chicken stock
(page 237) as it cooks is rendered chicken fat (schmaltz).
Do not dismiss this as something to discard. This is liquid gold.
Skim it as the stock cooks and strain it trough a fine mesh
sieve, or cheesecloth (muslin), to remove any debris. Then,
cook rendered fat over a medium–low heat until all of the
liquid has evaporated and it is pure golden schmaltz. When
cool, pour into an airtight jar and keep refrigerated for up to
6 months. Use to cook potatoes, sear steaks and start cooking
vegetables in every batch of chicken soup.

Tomato Sauce

Makes 1450 ml (49 fl oz/6 cups)

1.25 kg (2 lb 12 oz/6 cups) puréed and strained
    whole peeled tomatoes
3 bay leaves
¾ teaspoon dried red pepper flakes (chili flakes)
170 g (6 oz/¾ cup) unsalted butter
1 teaspoon kosher or sea salt

Combine all the ingredients in a saucepan and bring to a gentle
simmer over a medium heat. Cook for 30 minutes until the
sauce thickens slightly and bits of melted butter rise to the top
of the sauce. Remove and discard the bay leaves and serve, or
leave to cool and store in the refrigerator for up to 1 week.

Index

About the Author

Jenn Louis has enjoyed a career in food spanning more than two decades. She grew up believing that a creative path was in her future, and found her calling early in the kitchen. She has owned three acclaimed Portland restaurants as well as a catering company. Jenn has competed on Bravo's Top Chef Masters and was named one of Food & Wine's Best New Chefs in 2012. Her simple, sophisticated cooking style, championing seasonal Pacific Northwest US ingredients, has earned her two nominations for the James Beard Foundation Award of Best Chef: Northwest. Her debut cookbook, *Pasta By Hand*, was nominated for an IACP from the International Association of Culinary Professionals in the single subject category; it was followed by *The Book Of Greens*, which won an IACP award in 2017 and was nominated for a James Beard Award. Jenn is involved with nonprofits including Alex's Lemonade and Portland Homeless Family Solutions. She lives in Portland, Oregon, with her three cats, Wasco, Silverado Silverstein and Tov, and loves to garden, read, and cook for her friends. *The Chicken Soup Manifesto* is her third book.

Find her on Instagram and twitter: @jennlouis

Acknowledgements

To Ed Anderson and George Dolese for being such amazing friends and a fantastic photography team. We are three books strong!

To Jane Willson, Anna Collett, Kathy Steer, Lucy Sykes-Thompson and the amazing team at Hardie Grant, you have been supportive, creative and so wonderful to work with.

To Larry Reichman, for all of your copy-editing expertise.

To my pop, Jeff.

To my brother and sister-in-law, David and Eleanor.

To my sister, Stacy.

To my nieces and nephews, Noah, Aliza, Maleah and Aaron.

In memory of my mother, Isabel.

Published in 2020 by Hardie Grant Books,
an imprint of Hardie Grant Publishing

Hardie Grant Books (Melbourne)
Building 1, 658 Church Street
Richmond, Victoria 3121

Hardie Grant Books (London)
5th & 6th Floors
52–54 Southwark Street
London SE1 1UN

hardiegrantbooks.com

 A catalogue record for this
book is available from the
National Library of Australia

The Chicken Soup Manifesto

ISBN 978 1 74379 568 2

10 9 8 7 6 5 4 3 2 1

Publishing Director: Jane Willson
Project Editor: Anna Collett
Editor: Kathy Steer
Design Manager: Jessica Lowe
Designer: Lucy Sykes-Thompson
Photographer: Ed Anderson
Stylist: George Dolese
Production Manager: Todd Rechner
Production Coordinator: Mietta Yans

Colour reproduction by Splitting Image Colour Studio
Printed in China by Leo Paper Products LTD.